# LOOK AT THE LAW

# LOOK AT THE LAW

*The Law is What the Layman Makes It*

By

PERCIVAL E. JACKSON

Counsel United States Senate Committee for the Investigation
of the Administration of Justice in the United States Courts,
1936; Member New York City, New York State, and
American Bar Associations

FOREWORD BY ARTHUR GARFIELD HAYS

NEW YORK · E. P. DUTTON & COMPANY, INC. · 1940

*Copyright, 1938
By Macfadden Publications, Inc.
Copyright, 1940
By E. P. Dutton and Company, Inc.
All Rights Reserved
Printed in the U.S.A.*

*First Edition*

*A portion of the material in this book
appeared serially under the title:*

*"Mistrial! The Uncensored Facts about
Judges, Technicalities, and Justice"*

# FOREWORD

# LOOK AT THE LAW

## *FOREWORD*

GEORGE KIRCHWEY addressed a group of young lawyers: "I was once Dean of Columbia Law School, later Warden of Sing Sing Prison. I meet many men on the streets whose faces are familiar but whose names I have forgotten. I never know whether to say 'When did you graduate?' or 'When did you get out?'"

One reading this book, particularly the chapter "Lawyers are Dishonest," might misinterpret Dean Kirchwey's statement, might not give due regard to the author's oft-repeated statement that lawyers as a class are not far different from other men, either in background, motivation, outlook or practice. But no one can quarrel with the author's thesis that lawyers should be different; that the law is a profession; that material reward should be secondary, that the lawyer has obligations to society which are sometimes inconsistent with what most men regard as obligations to themselves. The usual lay attitude is skeptical of the integrity of lawyers, yet there are few people who do not know some one lawyer whom they are inclined to trust above all other men.

Sometimes the practices of a lawyer, often due to his zeal as an advocate, are disapproved by laymen who feel that all lawyers, except their own, should take a judicial attitude and not that of an advocate. For instance, Mr. Jackson suggests that in the desire to win a case, lawyers are often inclined to take advantage of technicalities, to seek loopholes in the law. Far be it from me to deny this. I should, however, doubt the integrity of a lawyer who would fail to take advantage of all technical and legal rights that his clients had.

# LOOK AT THE LAW

That is not the lawyer's right. He should determine whether or not to handle a case. But when he has taken it, he should realize that his client has hired not a judge but an advocate. If this requires action of which he disapproves, he should retire from the case.

Someone once said that the Russian experiment in 1917 was based upon two theological fallacies: one, the immaculate conception of the revolution; the other, the infallibility of the proletariat. With great glee my radical friends would remark that at least Russia had accomplished one thing — it had rid the community of the nuisance of lawyers, who at worst were crooks and at best were parasites. My radical friends seemed to forget that in a complicated society there must be some men trained in the rules of the social game. Obviously, everybody cannot be familiar with all the rules, and as a matter of fact, lawyers, even after years of study, become familiar only with a limited number of them. It is to be noted that as time has gone on, lawyers have again taken their place in Russian society. It is true that the issues there are not so much between individuals as they are between government trusts. Where individuals are concerned, the recent Russian state trials have shown shocking results. Any complicated social system requires men who devote their lives to studying the rules. Often apparently technical rules, some of which we call constitutional guarantees, are necessary in order to protect the individual.

Mr. Jackson does state, however, that lawyers are not any worse, or at any rate, not much worse, than other groups in the community. For instance, one of his chapters refers to witnesses as liars. Judge Leventritt, formerly of the Supreme Court of the State of New York, once pointed out that his experience on the bench had persuaded him that truth would crop out even in sworn testimony. Mr. Jackson, whose career at the Bar has been notable, would perhaps agree with

# LOOK AT THE LAW

me that in most cases, witnesses color their stories rather than commit perjury. This is a human failing which is difficult to avoid. No two persons see anything alike; no one can tell the effect of the power of suggestion. It is easy to distinguish red from green, but as the colors merge, the distinction becomes increasingly difficult. The best one can do is to reconstruct what has happened in the past, as is indicated by Mr. Jackson's reference to the testimony of Max Steuer in the Hines trial. An interested party, however honest he may be, is bound to reconstruct the story in the color of his own predispositions, he is bound to be influenced by his predilections. My own experience in law has led me to believe that most law suits arise through honest differences of opinion where people see things from a different point of view. Many of the so-called technicalities of the law have been found necessary to protect people from rumor, hearsay and the kind of evidence which affects men's emotions instead of their judgment.

Let me illustrate one of the common technicalities of the law. Witnesses are not allowed to tell their stories in their own way. For instance, A and B have a dispute. A feels that there was a contract between himself and B. B denies it. A takes the stand and would like to testify that he and B agreed upon certain terms. B takes the stand and would like to testify that they disagreed. The law insists that both men reconstruct the conversations that occurred at the time, so that a judge or jury can determine whether those conversations constituted an agreement or not. Men are constrained to talk in a forced, instead of in a direct, language. Everybody knows they do not remember the words that were used. Yet the substance of the conversation is the necessary basis for any determination by a third party as to whether or not there was an agreement. I feel that, talking largely to laymen, Mr. Jackson should have pointed out the reason

# LOOK AT THE LAW

for technical rules like the above, instead of leaving it to the non-analytical public to damn the law as a maze of technicalities.

Many of us, after years at the Bar, feel that in the main most cases are decided about as fairly as human frailties warrant or permit. Under an ideal system the law would always work out justice, if anyone knows what justice is. It has been said that the purpose of law is to work out "justice in the long run," even though in individual instances hardship may result. Hard cases make bad law. It may well be better for society to have the law fixed, the rules of the game of life settled, than to have each individual case depend upon the constitution, attitude, viewpoint, humor, or state of health of the particular judge. Decisions ought not to depend upon the gout in the chancellor's foot.

I remember a story told of a case in the Russian courts where two girls had once occupied for a home a certain number of cubic feet of space, which was the allotted quantity. One of the girls moved out. The city housing committee moved in a young man. After the child was born, the man was haled before the court to determine how much he should pay toward the support of the child. His answer was that he felt no responsibility, that he had not chosen the girl, he had not even chosen his abode, that the housing committee that had moved him into the lodgings might well have known what the result would be. The so-called judges, encumbered neither by precedent nor training, concluded — and it seems to me quite properly — that the cost of supporting the child should be imposed upon the housing committee of the city of Moscow. In the individual case this was no doubt a just decision; in fact, it was poetically just. I am inclined to believe, however, that the principle underlying the decision would not be a sound guide for social action.

# LOOK AT THE LAW

In Latin countries the decision is not determined by precedent: they do not have vast and complicated tomes in which are buried decisions for hundreds of years, digests, encyclopedias, corpus jurises, ruling case law, dictionaries of definitions, indexes, sub-indexes, explanations of sub-indexes and so on. Often with us, the job of searching replaces that of thinking. Yet in those countries not ridden by precedent, lawyers have notebooks. Often these notes are published so that the courts may have former rulings as a guide. Control by precedent often means injustice, but unless precedents are pushed too far, such a system does give some basis for determination in advance. The *stare decisis* doctrine, so effectively ridiculed by Mr. Jackson, does have a reason for support.

On the other hand, I am always appalled, when hearing arguments in the appellate courts, at the comparatively rare reference made to justice. On one occasion I started with what seemed to me an eloquent argument on the justice of my cause. The presiding judge interrupted, "What's the law?" I answered that if I could persuade the court that my client was right, I was confident it would find plenty of law to support my position. Darrow once was charged with trying to prejudice the jury. "Surely, I am," he responded. "That's what I'm here for." The theory is that if both sides of any issue are fully presented, an impartial judge (or jury) is likely to reach a just decision. Hearings and trials before boards of review and commissions in Washington are conducted with little regard for technical rules. Indignant criticism by those involved indicates that the methods are not markedly satisfactory.

It is to be borne in mind that one of the purposes of the law is to get things behind people, so that they will live for the future instead of for the past. Mr. Jackson properly points out that it takes far too long to get things behind

# LOOK AT THE LAW

people under our present system. There is too much law, the law is too uncertain, the law is too rigid, the law is too technical, the law is hypocritical, the law is slow, and the law is expensive. These complaints have been repeated time and again for hundreds of years. In a struggling way both laymen and lawyers attempt to do something about it.

You have questions of system. It is hard to tell what system to adopt or whether to have any general system at all. Consider the expense. There is no game as fascinating as a law suit if one can afford the luxury. In England, for instance, fees are fixed so that theoretically one may know what litigation or legal advice may cost. Yet, while the system does not bring undue riches to any but the most successful lawyers, the expense of the individual litigant is very high. In large cases English fees, according to our standards, are extremely low; in small cases they are almost prohibitive. With us there are no fixed charges, which means that ordinarily lawyers charge all that the traffic will bear. The client often complains but rarely does he have recourse to the court which has summary power to deal with issues between lawyer and clients. Contingent fees are from some points of view objectionable, yet they are helpful in that a poor litigant at least has an opportunity for legal representation. No system or method can avoid expense and burden, sometimes apparently disproportionate to the money or issue involved.

In an English case, a defendant was convicted of bigamy. The defendant explained that his wife had been a drunkard, that he had not seen her for years, and that wanting a home, he had married again. The judge remarked that the defendant's desire was no doubt laudable, but that the next time he found himself in such a predicament he should first get a divorce from his wife. To which the defendant answered that he could not afford the expense of a divorce. Whereupon his lordship said, "All you have to do is to get

# LOOK AT THE LAW

a solicitor, the solicitor gets a barrister, they present your case to court and a divorce is granted. This can be done for as little as £10." "But," said the defendant, "I never saw so much money." Responded the judge, "Do you think in this free country of England there is one law for the rich and one for the poor?"

Legal aid societies, public defenders, simplification of procedure in small cases, arbitration societies, family and children's courts, show that we are trying to bring to the masses of people the advantages or disadvantages of litigation.

To make a law case or create a dispute requires perhaps only one incident, perhaps a few minutes of life, and only two individuals. Sometimes only one individual is necessary, for, while it takes two to make peace, it requires only one to make a quarrel. To settle an issue with understanding may require inquiry of hundreds of people and a vast amount of research. A serious and inherent difficulty is due to language. The interpretation of texts, whether of law, literature, the Bible or the Koran, always leads to endless controversy. Oral statements, based on the memories of witnesses, add to the confusion by leaving the text uncertain. The interpretation of acts leads us into further difficulty. Judging one's fellow man is a serious and complicated matter.

As with all other institutions, reform — perhaps vital reform — is required in the law. Lawyers are rarely as frank and illuminating as Mr. Jackson. But one must avoid losing a sense of proportion. Training, experience and knowledge are required to understand any social structure with due regard to the vast, historical and confusing background. The mental temptation is to destroy the structure and start all over again. It would take courageous and audacious men to do that, and in the course of time what they resurrect would probably greatly resemble what they had destroyed. The real trouble is that all systems — be they political, economic,

# LOOK AT THE LAW

religious or legal — are run by human beings and reflect the vices and virtues, merits and demerits of the civilization they serve.

ARTHUR GARFIELD HAYS

*November, 1939*

# CONTENTS

## *Introductory:*

| CHAP. | | PAGE |
|---|---|---|
| I. | THERE'S SOMETHING WRONG WITH THE LAW | 17 |

## *The Layman Says:*

| | | |
|---|---|---|
| II. | THERE IS TOO MUCH LAW | 25 |
| III. | THE LAW IS UNCERTAIN | 48 |
| IV. | THE LAW IS TOO RIGID | 82 |
| V. | THE LAW IS TOO TECHNICAL | 105 |
| VI. | THE LAW IS HYPOCRITICAL | 152 |
| VII. | THE LAW IS TOO SLOW | 198 |
| VIII. | THE LAW IS TOO EXPENSIVE | 225 |
| IX. | LAWYERS ARE DISHONEST | 254 |
| X. | JUDGES ARE CORRUPT | 289 |
| XI. | WITNESSES ARE LIARS | 303 |

## *Remedy:*

| | | |
|---|---|---|
| XII. | THE IMPORTANCE OF IT | 335 |
| XIII. | HOW TO GO ABOUT IT | 348 |
| XIV. | WHAT TO DO ABOUT IT | 364 |

*Look at the Law*

# CHAPTER I

## *INTRODUCTORY*

## THERE'S SOMETHING WRONG WITH THE LAW

*1.*

IN NEW YORK CITY recently, James J. Hines, a Tammany Hall district leader, was indicted for furnishing protection from the police and the District Attorney to a policy racket operated by a notorious gang headed by one "Dutch Schultz." After the usual preliminary legal moves by the defense, the case went to trial. Thomas E. Dewey, District Attorney of New York County, who had won nation-wide acclaim as a "racket-buster," was the prosecutor, and Ferdinand Pecora, who had had similar recognition as an exposer of crooked Wall Street practices, was the judge. The jury was selected from a blue-ribbon panel.

At the trial, the prosecutor offered the testimony of some fifty witnesses, including leading members of the Dutch Schultz mob who had pleaded guilty and had turned State's evidence. Among the early defense witnesses was a former Assistant District Attorney, who testified to occurrences before a Grand Jury that had previously investigated rackets in New York City. Cross-examining the witness, Prosecutor Dewey asked if the defendant had not been mentioned before this Grand Jury as having had some connection with another racket, the so-called poultry racket. Thereupon, the defendant's counsel claimed that the jury had been prejudiced by the question and moved for a mistrial. The judge adjourned court in order to study the question and arrive at a decision.

# LOOK AT THE LAW

The prosecution of Hines had become, by now, a cause célèbre. It involved a number of dramatic crosscurrents of personalities, politics and events. It had laid bare oft-charged but theretofore unproved links between politics and crime in New York City. John F. Curry, former Chief of Tammany Hall, had admitted Tammany's control of the New York City Police Department. Members of the Dutch Schultz mob had testified that they had contributed racket money to elect a New York District Attorney, from whose efforts they were assured protection; to have New York City magistrates "fixed" so that they would dismiss policy prosecutions; and to have members of the New York City Police Department who prosecuted them, "broken."

The testimony had revealed, in the argot of the gangsters and mobsters, the inside stories of the policy racket, theretofore only suspected; the picaresque personalities of the Dutch Schultz mob, theretofore only legendary; the methods, murders, intimidations, "rides," protections and other whimsies of the gangsters, theretofore only movie-ized.

When, therefore, after more than four weeks of such a build-up, defense counsel moved for a mistrial upon the merest technicality, his application came with dramatic intensity. And when the judge adjourned court to give consideration to the matter, a period of unbelievable public interest began. Over an ensuing week-end, during which the court took briefs from counsel and the newspapers issued periodic reports, bulletins, conjectures, surmises and opinions, even to printing the briefs and arguments of counsel, the suspense heightened to a point where crowds gathered about the courthouse, movie audiences alternately cheered and hissed pictures of principals, and casual streetcar and subway riders discussed the issues with unusual New York friendliness.

After a week-end of deliberation, the judge announced

that he was not yet prepared to give his decision. At a long-delayed afternoon session, he kept a packed courtroom and a milling street and corridor crowd waiting his arrival. And when, behind locked doors through which even reporters were not permitted to leave, he finally read a two-hour opinion that declared a mistrial, one might have thought him a movie director striving for effect. And he got it.

A blast of public condemnation of the law and its works followed the decision. Technicalities. Waste. Delay. Injustice. Inefficiency. Stupidity. Crookedness. Politics. Fixing. From every side came these characterizations; from the lay press, from the lay public. In news reports and editorials, in feature articles and cartoons, in letters from readers, the technicalities, the uncertainties, the hypocrisies, the wastes and the delays of the law were decried.

"Hines Trial May Hasten Reform: Bar Association Already at Work on New Rules," headlined the New York *Times*.

The judge had declared a mistrial because he feared the jury might be prejudiced against the defendant by the prosecutor's question. But he had not consulted the jury before he rendered his decision, so he could not have known how many jurors had heard the question, how many had understood it, and what, if anything, it had meant to those who had heard and understood it.

He had found the jury's usefulness impaired by the question, and feared that if he did not declare a mistrial, an appellate court would reverse his decision. Yet a long line of appellate decisions attested the rule that it is for the trial judge to use his own discretion in correcting such situations by instructing the jurors to disregard an improper question.

Out of the furor, three facts emerged: first, that the Hines trial, aside from its topical and civic interest of mat-

# LOOK AT THE LAW

ter and men, was a shocking revelation of legal deficiencies of which litigants have long been aware; second, that it had served to bring these deficiencies to the attention of a lay public which previously had had no knowledge of, or at least no interest in, them; and finally, that there is a large body of dormant lay opinion which believes the law and its administrators to be inefficient.

### 2.

The unanimity of public comment concerning the waste and delay of legal processes in the Hines case induces consideration of the ever-present and ever-increasing tide of complaints about the law and its personnel. The question "Is there something wrong with the law?" finds unanimity of answer.

Pick up your evening paper. Its headlines shriek the inefficiencies of the law and the laxity of its administrators; its columns bear testimony to the law's broken promises, its futilities, its infelicities, its disrepute. "President Flays Lawyers"; "Strikers Defy Court Order"; "Conference Demands Impeachment of Judges"; these are typical of headlines on every page of every daily newspaper. From Washington to Manila, the voice of the press challenges the intelligence and vision of judges and the honesty and integrity of lawyers.

Public officials are unsparing in their condemnation. "Today," Attorney General Murphy says, "a former feeling of reverence for the courts has given way in some quarters to an attitude of cynicism and disrespect. It is a bitter but undeniable fact that our courts do not enjoy the unquestioned respect that they did a generation ago."

And on the radio: "Mister, we represent the Popular Opinion Company. We are asking the man on the street if

# LOOK AT THE LAW

he thinks there is anything wrong with the law. What is your opinion?"

"There certainly is."

"What do you consider the main thing wrong with it?"

"Too many laws interfering with matters of business."

"May we have your name and occupation, please?"

"Samuel Scroggins, banker."

"Thank you, Mr. Scroggins . . . . Just a moment, Mister, what is your name, please?"

"Herman Blatz."

"Do you believe there is something wrong with the law?"

"I sure do."

"What do you consider its gravest fault?"

"They won't let us make a right turn on a red light."

"Who won't?"

"The cops."

"What do you do for a living?"

"I drive a taxi."

"How about you, sir? Do you think there is anything wrong with the law?"

"*Is* there? See this wooden leg? A jury gave me five thousand for my own leg, but I just about managed to buy a wooden one with what I had left after the lawyers got paid."

Whether he wins or loses, the litigant's plaint is resounding. But he is not the only critic of the law. Every layman joins in the resentment, for be he ever so humble, there is no one that the law does not reach. The law is something we are born with and something we die by. Even that is understatement, for the law has been at us before our births, and death brings no surcease.

Before we are conceived, the law determines our future existence and our physical well-being by prescribing or by failing to prescribe the conditions under which our parents

# LOOK AT THE LAW

may wed. After our deaths, the law upholds or thwarts our will respecting the transfer of the possessions for which we have spent a lifetime of effort. In between, the law sends us to school, regulates our business and social habits and prescribes our standards of conduct and living.

If, as children, we play hookey from school, the law sends truant officers after us; if, as men, we are too successful at our business, the law sends trust-busters after us. If we are inefficient and too scrupulous, we find ourselves in the meshes of the bankruptcy law; if we are efficient and too unscrupulous, we find ourselves in the clutches of the criminal law.

We can't go out for a peaceful Sunday outing without being under the eye of the motorcycle cop; we can't stay in for an honest day's work without expecting the sanitary inspector or the tax collector.

Nor does it matter whether the law be efficient or inefficient. Its directions and restraints, however needful, irk the man they affect. The street peddler, with no overhead, is angered by the law which keeps him from competing with the storekeeper who pays rent. The taxi driver is impatient with the regulations that slow him down in order to let the pedestrian pass.

The consequence is a crescendo of condemnation, justified or unjustified, reasoned or emotional, of the law and its works.

### 3.

In his criticism of the law, the layman is not discriminating. Neither is he analytical nor rational.

He criticizes the law, the legislators, the judges and the lawyers, largely without qualification or restriction. He does not separate the delinquencies of the legislator from

# LOOK AT THE LAW

the deficiencies of the judge. He makes no attempt to assess his own faults or to measure their contribution to the ills of which he complains.

He knows little of these refinements of discrimination, and cares less. He merely knows there's something wrong and he wants it remedied.

Within limits, this is as it should be. It is not for the layman, but for those trained in the law, to separate and segregate its faults and to devise and suggest the remedies.

Therefore, if and where the legal system does not work, it is for the lawman to show the layman why. It is enough that the layman is dissatisfied, for the law cannot function efficiently without his respect and his confidence. No lawyer's "plea in abatement," that old technical plea by which a lawyer gets rid of a case without going into its merits, will suffice, for that is one of the very grounds of the layman's complaint. The lawman must go beyond that. He must first "plead in confession" before he may dare "plead in avoidance," that other ancient plea by which the defendant confesses that what the plaintiff claims is true, but avoids its consequences by some hook or crook.

Nor may the lawyer say to the layman, "There's no such thing as 'the law' as a separate and independent thing apart, which you can accuse." The lawyer has been insisting, far too long, that there *is* such a thing. And it is not enough for the lawyer to tax his accuser with his own delinquencies, and to rest with that. It is too late now for the lawyer to say, "The law is just you, Mr. Layman; it is what you say and what you want; so if you have any kick about it, look to yourself."

The layman has the right to consider the law as a thing apart, to view and treat it as an entity. He has a right to be its accuser, to bring his complaints against the law and its manipulators, to step up to the Bar and to state his charges.

# LOOK AT THE LAW

And it is for the legal profession to present its defenses—not technical ones, but defenses that go to the merits, so that it may be determined what the reasons are for the ever-present criticism of the law, to what extent they are justified, to what extent they are remediable and, where remediable, to what extent remedies are available.

That having been done, it is for the layman, armed with knowledge, to choose his remedy, and to insist upon its application.

For those purposes, the layman's complaints are considered in the following pages.

# CHAPTER II

## *The Layman Says:*
# THERE IS TOO MUCH LAW

### *1.*

"It wasn't my fault," you say; "the other fellow was on the wrong side of the white line. He came straight at me. He was going much too fast, too; well over forty . . ."

"That should make him liable, that is, if the witnesses will bear you out," says the lawyer. "Let's see, he's guilty of violating subdivision (a) of Section 7 of the Code of Ordinances—here's what the statute says: 'Any one who shall drive at a rate exceeding forty miles per hour'—and here's subdivision (d): 'any one who shall fail to keep to the right of a white line in the middle of a highway, shall be presumed to be guilty of negligence.'"

"Well, that's that," you say. "He certainly was on the wrong side of the line and coming too fast. Why, I saw him a block away."

"You did?" says the lawyer. "And what did you do?"

"Just kept going," you answer.

"Well," says the lawyer, "that does make a difference. You can't recover, for you were guilty of contributory negligence."

"Where does it say that in the book?" you ask.

"Oh, that's not in this book," says the lawyer. "This book contains only the statutes and ordinances. The contributory negligence rule is common law, not statutory law."

"What's common law?" you ask.

"That's the law the judges make," says the lawyer. "You don't find that in the statutes; you find that in the decisions of the judges."

# LOOK AT THE LAW

That's a new one on you—you thought the legislatures made the law, while the judges enforced it. But you were wrong; our judges not only enunciate the law but they make a large portion of it.

When we find John Q. Public voicing the most prevalent public criticism of the law, "There's too much law," we are listening to a popular plaint of laymen who do not really know how much law there actually is. They have some vague notion that there are criminal laws and civil laws; they know that Congress and the State legislatures meet periodically and pass laws. But what, beyond this, do they know about our body of law?

Did our complaining citizenry desire precise information, we might take them on a tour of one of our larger law libraries. There are seventeen of these in this country, each of which has more than 100,000 volumes. The Harvard Law Library leads, with over half a million volumes, all bearing on some phase, direct or indirect, of the law.

Suppose we try the New York City Bar Association library, where, in an irregular, lofty room perhaps 100 by 100 feet, are contained 220,000 volumes, all oversize by ordinary standards, resting in over half a mile of running feet of bookshelf space, ranging from incunabula and reprints of the old Roman Institutes of Justinian to the most recently received volume of Corpus Juris Secondum, a voluminous, current digest of the law, as yet unfinished.

But let our guide speak:

"Here is Blackstone's *Commentaries*, the original four volumes as written by the great English jurist and law professor, between 1759 and 1769. Here is all the law an ambitious law student in this country needed to read for many years in order to hang out his shingle. But now the tyro must go beyond that.

"First he must be familiar with the Federal Constitution.

# LOOK AT THE LAW

Here it is. It consists of seven Articles and twenty-one Amendments. These, with explanatory notes, and including signatures, cover seventeen pages of printed text."

"What's in the rest of the book?" you ask.

"That follows the Constitution, the way trade follows the flag," is the answer. "It's called 'Constitutional Construction and Interpretation,' and is a digest of decisions explaining just what the contents of the first seventeen pages mean. The explanations are just in summary form and in fine print, but they come to — let's see — 2,220 additional pages, contained in three volumes.

"But, of course, the Constitution, though important, is only the basis of our law. Since its adoption, Congress has been engaged in passing new laws. To find these, we must go to the Code of Laws of the United States, which is the official restatement of the general and permanent laws of the United States in force in 1925, which were theretofore scattered in twenty-five volumes. It took twenty-eight years of effort to complete this codification, which up to 1925, including the perennial 'Construction and Interpretation,' digested and finely printed, came to fifty titles filling sixty volumes, each averaging 500 pages,—a total of 30,000 pages.

"New legislation since 1925 has furnished an average of 100 pages of addenda to each volume, making another 6,000 pages for the already overburdened law and lay novitiates.

"The Federal Code has 2,000 pages of index, and 275 pages devoted to a table of titles alone.

"These are only the unrepealed Federal statutes which have been enacted by Congress since 1789. And one must not think that that early date is used merely for effect, for we are still operating under 500 or more statutes passed by Congress between June 1, 1789, and January 6, 1800.

"But we cannot spend too much time on these Federal

# LOOK AT THE LAW

statutes. There are such things as States' rights, and forty-eight States and their political subdivisions are clamoring for representation in the survey.

"In 1909 the New York Legislature collected the New York statutory law and, together with amendments and decisions construing it, it is to be found in some eighty volumes, ranging from twenty-five pages of Arbitration Law to 1,500 pages of Education Law. An index of some 800 pages gives a fair idea of the complexity of the content.

"But these are not all of New York's general laws. There are general independent statutes, local laws and practice acts. There is a Civil Practice Act which regulates civil procedure, and a Code which regulates criminal procedure. For the courts, there is a Children's Court Act of the State of New York, a Court of Claims Act, a Surrogates Court Act, a Justices Court Act. For the resident of New York City, there is a New York City Charter and Code of Ordinances, a New York City Court Act, a New York City Municipal Court Act, an Inferior Criminal Courts Act, a Domestic Relations Court Act.

"Here on one shelf are to be found a statutory index—just an index to statutes, New York statutes—in four volumes of 3,000 pages; a book entitled *The Criminal Codes of New York*, containing over 2,000 pages; a Building Code of the City of New York, running to 1,200 pages; while lurking in the corner are two volumes—not too thin—one entitled *Manual of Procedure*, and the other, *Rules and Regulations of the Police Department of the City of New York*. No wonder someone has said that if a New York policeman read, rapidly and steadily, eight hours a day, all the laws with which he is required to be familiar, it would take him over seven weeks to read them."

But these statistics are like fleeting mileposts, for as quickly as we estimate, our figures are left behind by the

# LOOK AT THE LAW

legislative mills, relentlessly grinding out more fodder for a law-fed populace.

The 75th Congress culled from 17,092 bills about 10 per cent, and enacted them after the lawmakers had formulated, and presumably had studied, the greater number. The 74th Congress similarly passed 1,722 new laws. This makes an average of four or five a day, all year round, including vacations. And some of these laws constitute no small volume.

In 1937, forty-three States passed 17,483 new laws in regular sessions, while 1,000 laws were passed in special sessions, a total of 18,483. Of these, New York enacted 1,248, an average of over three a day, and Pennsylvania passed 756, an average of over two a day.

In one State, in one year, so many bills were passed and sent to the governor for consideration that he had to consider an average of forty a day for more than a month to finish the job within the statutory time, in consequence of which many of the bills which required careful and detailed consideration received but cursory attention.

From 1900 to 1908, there were 87,193 new State laws adopted, according to figures compiled by the New York State Library Index of Legislation. From 1917 to 1924 there were enacted by State legislatures 71,125 new laws, according to records kept by Raymond Manning of the Legislative Reference Service of the Library of Congress. Conservative computation, on a basis of these figures, justifies an estimate of 375,000 new State laws placed on our State statute books since the turn of the century.

In addition, in each of the States, we have minor legislative and administrative bodies, city, county, town and village boards, all dedicated to and constantly working at the principle of law and more law. Taking the year 1924 as an example, in this one year fifteen typical American cities

# LOOK AT THE LAW

added 4,833 new laws to their books. On that basis there is passed, on the average, a new law every day in every city in the United States.

However, that is not the sum total of our law, as we have heretofore indicated. The law student who confessed to the bar examiners that all the law he knew was that to be found in the statute books, was told he'd better study some more so the legislature couldn't meet some day and repeal all the law he knew.

The fact of the matter is that the bulk of our law is not to be found in legislative statute books, but in the records of the opinions rendered by judges. Just as our written Federal Constitution of seventeen pages is bloated by hundreds of thousands of pages of judicial opinions which have been written concerning it, so the smaller mass of statute law enacted by our legislatures is swelled and supplemented by millions of pages of judicial opinions delivered by judges in the Federal and State courts of the United States. Many of these judicial opinions merely apply accepted rules of the law to the facts before the judge; many of them, however, formulate new rules and modify existing rules of law. For every rule of law found in a statute book, there are hundreds of subsidiary rules of law which can be found only in the recorded opinions of the judges.

The practice of recording judicial opinions may be said to date back to Moses. The 27th chapter of the Book of Numbers records "the law of inheritance as set forth by the Lord" in the suit brought by the daughters of Zelophehed.

Our modern system goes back to 1218, when an English lawyer named Bracton started to record opinions of English judges. Ultimately, these written opinions of judges were given the force of law and became the most substantial part of what is known as the common law of England. After

## LOOK AT THE LAW

the separation of the American Colonies, our various States (excluding only Louisiana, which came from the French and followed the French civil law) adopted as their own the common law of England and, except as modified by later judicial decision or legislative statutes, this remains as the prevailing law of our States today.

The bulk of our judge-made law is impressive. At its base are the judicial opinions which have been accumulating in England since the early days of the thirteenth century. Its structure comprises innumerable opinions of innumerable judges of innumerable superior and inferior courts which have been accumulating in a varying number of States and territories since 1789. A recent survey estimates that there are now more than 1,800,000 reported judicial decisions.

The opinions of our Federal courts are at present to be found in some 800 volumes which contain some 800,000 pages. Each State has its own collection of judicial opinions; in New York State alone some 700 volumes containing over a half million pages are required to record the conclusions of the State judiciary.

And it need not be thought that a litigant or a lawyer may take refuge behind the bulwarks of the decisions of his own State Court. Good judges are not insular; with catholic taste, they dip freely into their neighbors' brews. So, for example, in seven volumes reporting the decisions of the New York Court of Appeals between January, 1919, and October, 1921, the court cited 207 English cases, 238 Massachusetts cases, 73 Illinois cases and miscellaneous smaller numbers of decisions from various other States.

The bulk of judicial opinion may be gauged by the legal digests to which lawyers go when they seek a judicial opinion on a particular subject. These digests succinctly state the gist of decisions, indexing them under the particular subjects to which they refer.

# LOOK AT THE LAW

One digest, completed in 1896, contained judicial opinions reported in the American, State and Federal reports up to that time. This compendium of a half-million or more opinions required fifty volumes of about 2,500 pages each; twenty-four additional volumes appeared in 1916; twenty-nine more in 1926.

Another standard legal digest is known as Corpus Juris. Up to 1935, this consisted of seventy-two volumes with an average of 1,300 pages per volume, a total of almost 100,000 pages, carrying an index of 3,700 pages. Annual supplements issued each year produced a volume of 2,125,000 words over a four-year period. Four hundred and fifty classifications of topics are to be found, with sub-divisions running into five figures.

And do not think there is but one case to a topic. Perish the thought that a judge would fear to plagiarize! One opinion is merely incentive for another.

For example, in the law of agency, the rule that makes the principal liable for the acts of his agent is enunciated 270 times under the single topic head, and these are the patrician cases—the digest does not deign to notice many of those of the inferior courts. To give another example, the rule of Section 347 of the New York Civil Practice Act has been explained, interpreted and analyzed no less than 1,000 times, by 1,000 judges.

Nor are the summaries in these digests any token of the plenitude of words that lie behind them. A principle of law may be briefly digested, but it may mask an overpowering judicial, verbal profligacy. For example, a New York judge, in a case determining that a woman and her deceased paramour were common law husband and wife, devoted to his exposition no less than 267 pages of text containing 120,000 words—approximately the wordage of three much more entertaining murder mystery novels.

# LOOK AT THE LAW

And executive law administrators, who are not part of the judicial branch of the government, are contributing more and more to the wealth of written laws.

Arthur T. Vanderbilt, former President of the American Bar Association, said in a recent speech that while, in 1937, "in the Federal Courts, there were somewhat over 200,000 cases disposed of, . . . in one department alone of the administrative branch of the Federal Government, there were 600,000 cases decided." He added that "in volume as well as in importance of controversies, the administrative tribunals overshadowed our traditional courts, both in the Federal Government and in the several States."

So we find ourselves subject to additional Federal and State legislation, variously called rules, rulings, regulations, instructions, orders, circulars, bulletins, notices, memoranda and the like, issued by Federal administrative departments, including the Executive, Treasury, Agriculture, Immigration, Commerce, Labor and Post Office Departments, and a host of major and minor alphabetical administrative agencies, including the A.A.A. and F.C.C., the F.T.C., the I.C.C., the N.L.R.B., the S.E.C., etc., etc., as well as by numerous State agencies, including Public Service Commissions, Labor Departments, Compensation Bureaus and other similar bodies.

And the verbosity of administrative bodies matches that of the judiciary. A recent report of the National Labor Board in a case concerning the Republic Steel Company ran to 100,000 words.

The increasing volume of the outpourings of the administrative branches of the law is shown by an Associated Press report from Washington, which says, "Five Government attorneys are working on a set of books by which they hope to let Government agencies know what their neighbors are doing. The first issue will contain five volumes of

3,000 pages each. These will serve as nucleus for a code of Federal regulations patterned after the code of Federal laws. The need for a reference book, officials said, developed with the increase in Federal agencies during the last five years."

Though not strictly law material, in the sense that statutes, judicial decisions and administrative rulings are law, there is a constantly growing mass of legal and semilegal literature that is to be found in textbooks, in law reviews issued by some fifty-odd law schools, in Bar Association journals, in reports of Bar Association committees and their sections, and in reports of local proctors, judicial councils, and other legal and quasi-legal bodies. These are also entitled to be added to what may be called the literature of the law.

*2.*

While there can be no doubt that we are afflicted with much law, the real question is: Do we suffer from too much law?

Under existing conditions, we have much of everything. Our population has grown and, with it, everything else has developed. We have more money, more business, more unemployment and more complications than we have ever had before.

In this process the law has been no laggard. The lawyer who rode circuit in the earlier days of our republic carrying all the law he needed in a volume of Blackstone in his saddlebag would be helpless today without a law library in a trailer.

But whether the law has merely kept pace with our other institutions or whether it has grown unnecessarily bulky is another question.

Much law in a civilization such as ours is inevitable. The

# LOOK AT THE LAW

need for law is fundamental—and the need is neither new nor novel. The earliest savages lived by the rule of law—by much the same rules of natural, physical law that still govern us, however civilized we may think we are. These are the rules that Nature imposes upon us: the instinctive laws of life, the desire for food and shelter, the instinct to propagate. Even outlaws and philosophic anarchists have their rules of conduct.

Social habit is itself an instinctive law. Man tends to group with man, as animals tend to herd and fish to school. Even as a herd of animals acts as a unit for the protection of its members, so man, living in a simple tribe or clan, acts collectively. And instinctive acts, upon repetition, become so habitual that it becomes difficult to distinguish between instinct and habit.

The law grows as man develops. While he lives alone, man's habits are his own concern. Once he herds, the tribe, however savage, exacts conformity by each member to certain standards of habit or conduct. A lone savage may worship his ancestors or not, as he pleases. But when the tribe concludes that the neglected ancestor will haunt not only his immediate descendant but the whole tribe, then what might have been a self-imposed and individual habit becomes a tribal custom.

While a big savage may steal a little savage's wife, his dog, his horse or his weapon, once they join a common tribe the need for mutual safety and protection results in a tribal custom that denies the stronger the right to ravish the nuptial bed of the weaker, or to ravage his other property. Even the savage has his customary rules for the protection of his property rights, to say nothing of a wealth of taboos for the protection, fancied or real, of his person and property.

The moment people begin to feel that a violation of cus-

# LOOK AT THE LAW

tomary rules—of good taste or of good manners—harms the community, they begin to say "there ought to be a law."

A man may stuff himself with food and drink, he may contract diabetes or Bright's disease, and his miseries will be considered nobody's business but his own. But let him have two highballs on an empty stomach and climb into the driver's seat of an automobile, and whether he can hold his liquor becomes everybody's affair.

While a man is violating natural laws, the community stands aside and lets nature take its course. When his violations begin to step upon the toes of his neighbors, those injured begin to clamor for restraints and punishments. Here begins the domain of our positive law.

Positive laws are the rules that some of us make, at least presumably, for the rest of us. Few people advocate a law punishing theft to keep themselves from stealing, yet everybody recognizes the necessity of such a law for others.

The transition from customary rules of good manners to positive rules of law is readily illustrated by the automobile. Men, women and children walk and ride up and down a village lane; each gives way to the other and thus avoids collision and controversy. Then some village swain acquires a horse and buggy and rudely begins to ride down leisurely strolling pedestrians. The pedestrians get together and adopt an ordinance limiting the speed at which these intrepid buggy-riders may drive, requiring them to keep to the right and otherwise curbing their activities. From now on, a breach of what once were rules of good manners, enforced by the force of social opinion, becomes a violation of ordinance enforced by penalties of fine and imprisonment.

Later comes the age of the automobile. Now the buggy-drivers clamor for protection for themselves and their horses. They join with the pedestrian in changing the laws which once sufficed to protect the stroller in the horse-and-buggy

# LOOK AT THE LAW

age, to make them adequate against the new and more dangerous vehicle. The simple regulations that sufficed to hold the buggy-driver down to five miles an hour have become inadequate for a dangerous mechanism that can do wholesale manslaughter. Now there must be a thousand and one major and minor regulations, provisions for liability insurance, drivers' licenses, periodic brake examinations, etc.

Ultimately, the motor-car drivers become a majority; they impose their will on the pedestrians and require them to keep to the sidewalks, except at periodic and fleeting intervals when the Juggernauts stand throbbing and impatient. The walker is now placed under restraint; those who stroll when and where they will now become the nuisances, the jay-walkers and the law-breakers.

So, though a Hindu may sit motionless by his river bank, letting his hair and beard grow tangled and matted while he himself becomes diseased and vermin-infested, a cook or waiter in a crowded community is required by law to wash his hands after functional exercise. A Gandhi may confine his wardrobe to a loincloth, resorting to a blanket for formal occasions, but a woman wearing a pair of shorts on the virginal streets of Yonkers, New York, or the more sophisticated byways of Reno, Nevada, may be called to account for shocking the so-called public sense of decency. Similarly, what one could once do with impunity outside the farmhouse bedroom window on a cold night becomes catalogued in the penal code of large cities as an indecent exposure.

The more progress man makes in material and physical matters, the greater becomes his need of law. Living with a multitude begets a multitude of positive rules, so that the least restrained may be forced to conform to the standards of the more disciplined.

The result of the process of progress and law is an endless

## LOOK AT THE LAW

one. Progress and community living require laws, and then, outmoding them, require new laws. Every scientific discovery invites laws and more laws. The pioneering of Morse and Marconi ultimately results in the appointment of a nation-wide Federal Communications Commission, supplemented by a host of local Public Service Commissions and Commissioners, each with a staff of assistants and a multitude of regulatory statutes, voluminous but periodically found insufficient. The Wright Brothers leaving the ground at Kitty Hawk were trespassing upon the domain of the land owner whose ownership extended from the center of the earth to the topmost aerial part of the firmament, and were thereby laying the groundwork for a Code of Aerial Law to meet the new conditions they were creating.

For each new custom, habit or need, for each new mode or thought or action that we discover or create, we find need for new and different rules and regulations.

As the tribe increases, the opportunities to satisfy the animal wants of its members grow in progressive proportion. Greed breeds competition, and competition breeds selfishness. The more one has, the more one wants and the less he is willing to leave for anyone else. No one is safe, woman or child, the poor or the crippled. All are fair game for gain. Ultimately, everyone needs protection from everyone else. Like the never-ending race between battleship armor and big guns, so as every new chicanery and fraud displays an unprotected chink in the law, a new law is needed to close the gap. As initiative is spurred, our legal needs are increased; as our law increases, initiative is curbed. Community life breeds law, until life and law become interchangeable and interdependent.

This, then, is the penalty of living in a community. At the one extreme of civilization is the individual savage, making his own rules of conduct and obeying only the instinc-

## LOOK AT THE LAW

tive and habitual natural laws. At the other are found the city cliff dwellers, living in such close proximity that their leases, so finely printed as to be unreadable, include a mass of mutual rules that concern the inmost intimacies of their daily lives: the hours they may play their radios, the time they must get up to dispose of their garbage, and take in their milk and bread; whether or not, and when, they may have dogs or visitors. In between, we find the tribe, the clan and the gang, all necessarily bearing a burden of law—natural, customary or positive—in varying degrees.

We have so much law that we cannot keep abreast of it. Citizens break laws they never knew existed. Even judges and lawyers cannot keep up with changing laws.

When next you read the "Wanted" notices in your local post office, you may find alongside the notice,

"WANTED FOR MURDER!
LUKE McDUKE,"

another poster enjoining you to

"GET A STAMP BEFORE YOU SHOOT."

At first glance you may wonder if, when the Government catches Luke, they're apt to follow the Al Capone theory of prosecution and charge Luke with failure to buy a stamp before he let his victim have it. Not until you make inquiry do you learn that since the Government found that even ex-Justice Van Devanter, of the United States Supreme Court, did not know he had to have a stamp on his hunting permit from the Department of Agriculture when he went out to shoot wild ducks, the authorities decided they had better instruct common citizens in this little-known addition to our abundance of laws.

In a case in the Federal courts, the Government was

# LOOK AT THE LAW

engaged in prosecuting defendants for a violation of a provision in an N. R. A. Code. The case had started in 1932; it had been heard by the two lower Federal courts and finally, by 1935, it found its way into the United States Supreme Court. Then, for the first time, the prosecuting authorities, the Court and the defendants discovered that for two years, that is, since 1933, the defendants had been charged with violation of a section of the law which had been withdrawn by an Executive order and was no longer in effect.

The bulk of our law is such that not even our legislators can keep track of it. The 75th Congress, according to the Associated Press, amended the Employees' Compensation Act of 1916 to include osteopaths among the medical men mentioned in the law, although such an amendment had already been adopted in 1926. The same body passed a bill on June 2, 1937, amending another Act which itself was not passed until fourteen days later.

Lawyers spend their lives resolving that they will read regularly the "advance sheets" of new decisions and legislation which are issued periodically, but the majority of lawyers die with most of them unread. Meanwhile, their existences are constantly haunted by the fear of the last unheard of judicial and legislative word.

### 3.

But though it is inevitable that we should have much law, this does not wholly account for its bulk. That results principally from its over-fecundity.

As things are, we take on new statutory law so rapidly that we lack time for weighing adequately the need, or for ascertaining and fitting the remedy. Our legislators write so fast that they lack opportunity to select their words

# LOOK AT THE LAW

judiciously. Over 1,000 new bills clogged the hopper of the 76th Congress on the first day of the session. Bids for publicity and votes are often the main objectives when legislators introduce bills.

When Wisconsin legislators enact a statute which provides that every restaurant proprietor must serve cheese with every meal or pay a penalty, one more unworkable law is being added to the already overloaded total of statutory law because the Wisconsin solons want to establish themselves in the hearts of their cheese-making constituents. When the Connecticut lawmakers put into the criminal class anyone who carries a watch showing other than standard time, someone is trying to get votes in the next election from the harried farmer who objects to having his daily habits interrupted by city slickers' law. Similarly, when the State of Washington regulates the length of hotel bedsheets by law, or when communities in California do legal Red or Japanese baiting, one may be sure that the mass of the law is being enlarged by vote-seeking politicians who believe their constituents are prepared to trade votes for votes.

Some States adopt laws in competition with other States, in an effort to bid for corporation and industrial business, to attract tourists, or to solicit transients seeking easy divorce or hoping to avoid State taxes.

But it is not only the legislator who is at fault in these respects. Many others contribute to the law-making process. Majorities try to enforce their wills on minorities by laws. Minorities seek to perpetuate their power or their profits in the same way. Preachers seek to convert Biblical texts into legal injunctions. Reformers try to breathe mandatory life into academic injunctions. Solecists try to define and determine right and wrong by statutory pronouncements. Natural laws, habitual laws and economic laws are taken from

## LOOK AT THE LAW

their proper niches and are needlessly and sometimes harmfully made positive laws. Rules of physics and economics, concepts of ethics, dictates of manners, are imported into our statutes and are added to an already intolerable burden.

Whether the legislator is seeking publicity by pandering to what he conceives to be the public taste in legislation, or whether he is answering a demand for legislation by clamoring minorities, the need for election and frequent reelection finds him ready to climb aboard transitory, emotional, legislative specials, to aid Divine Providence, to right wrongs, to set aside natural laws, to substitute politics for science, by the adoption of legislation.

Public whims, passing waves of emotion, fear or hatred that sweep the country, result in torrents of hasty and ill-considered legislation. Disasters spawn unenforceable statutes, which are heavily publicized. Abuses of morals or good taste that find their way into print result in the cry "there ought to be a law"; agitated emotional desires to inflict punishment lead legislators to define new crimes. A catastrophe, such as a theater fire or a boat-sinking, a notorious crime, such as the Lindbergh kidnaping, a publicized scandal, any prejudice, natural or subsidized, may result in laws hastily drawn, unneeded, and ultimately unheeded.

As we shall see in discussing faults of the law in later chapters, this excess of law, like any other human excess, takes its toll. The American system of quantity production, with great mechanical efficiency, turns out at little cost a highly standardized but effective industrial product. But there is no assembly line for the output of our political institutions. Haste without coordination rules. Production is in the hands of unskilled and untrained workers. Policies are dictated by emotions, and quality is sacrificed to quantity.

# LOOK AT THE LAW

Every attempt to regulate industry or labor or agriculture justifies excuse for further encroachments; every new lane through which legislation is channeled invites further experiment by regulation. We seek to remedy in a day the abuses of years. We tolerate no halfway measures; we go whole hog, and then find it necessary to expend endless legislative activity in additional tinkering, repair and redress.

Not only pitfall statutes but verbose and uncraftsmanlike judicial decisions conceal snares that trap unwary suitors, provide fodder for distinguishing lawyers in later litigation and invite more judicial discussion to cure uncertainties, to repair ambiguities or to set at rest falsities. Unneeded words offer opportunities for carelessness, disclose ignorance, reveal bad reasons for good results and furnish untenable precedents that later call for more judicial explanation and evasion. We shall have examples of these in later chapters.

By the time much of our unneeded legislation becomes law, it is no longer even wanted, yet it remains on the books, for it is rarely, if ever, repealed. There are some examples (but so rare as to be of interest only to the collector) of laws passed for a specific term of one or more years. Practically all of our laws are perpetual; they remain, regardless of change of time and circumstance. The older they get, the more veneration and respect they seem to be accorded; they take on a vintage that does not reckon with bouquet; they become a part of habit and cling like custom.

We still have laws adding bulk to our statute books which were passed to protect communities from marauding Indians. Statutes are still effective to regulate dueling. Ancient traffic laws regulating the speed of vehicles according to the horse-and-buggy era still survive in many communities, and decree that a speed of five miles per hour may not

# LOOK AT THE LAW

be exceeded on bridges or in turning corners. Ordinances still protect horses unaccustomed to horseless vehicles.

New England communities still have blue laws prohibiting work or play on Sundays, which, in spite of continued and open violation, persist without repeal. There is so much of this legislation that Bruce Barton, Congressman from New York, made "repeal a law a day" the loudest plank in his platform, and it gained him much publicity, if it didn't actually help to elect him. Incidentally, once he was elected, his repeal plank went the way of most political platforms.

The legislature has the privilege of changing judge-made law by statute, as the judges have assumed the ungranted privilege of changing legislative law by judicial construction. Judges may in effect "repeal" their own law by later decisions overruling earlier ones. Both methods are too rarely employed; in consequence, we still tread paths marked out for us by the outmoded footsteps of the dead, increasing the tortuous mileage of the living.

### 4.

It should not be necessary to make one's choice with Montaigne when he says it would be better to have no laws at all than to have them "in so prodigious numbers as we have," for the bulk of our law should be susceptible of reduction.

Later we discuss the basic problems of regulation and restriction underlying our law. Here we are concerned with ministerial problems.

As to our statutory law, if our legislatures met less frequently, if they limited the time for introduction of bills and provided a sufficient period for consideration, improvement along these lines might be expected. This could be

## LOOK AT THE LAW

done by having bills introduced in one year, and having deliberation and adoption or rejection in the next. Such a procedure might result in the rejection of a good many bills which are introduced and passed impulsively.

Periodic revision of existing laws should be helpful. It might be well to have legislative statutes classified into permanent and limited classes, and to require the latter to be reenacted at the end of stated periods; or there might be a periodic session exclusively for codification, reenactment and repeal.

Federal and also State law revision commissions such as already exist in New York State should prove most helpful in these tasks, as the New York Commission is proving.

Other suggestions made in the following chapters should tend to clear up the morass of legislative law which encumbers our statute books and burdens and confuses our lives.

In between the legislature and the judiciary lies an ever-increasing field of administrative, semi-judicial and delegated legislative functions exercised by municipal, State, and Federal bodies having jurisdiction over trade and security practices, labor laws and other quasi-public services. Each of these bodies, by rule and decision, is exercising law-making functions, in an independent and most uncoordinated manner. They add to the bulk and to the confusion of the law.

A special committee of the Government reported that individuals and business concerns in the United States made about 97,500,000 reports and returns to questionnaires sent out by administrative agencies of the Federal Government in 1938. In addition, individuals and businesses had to prepare 38,000,000 nonadministrative returns and reports, characterized by the committee as a "substantial amount of unnecessary duplication."

Ultimately the plethora of discordant, uncollected and

## LOOK AT THE LAW

unrelated legislative, semijudicial and administrative material being turned out by these bodies will make the present mass of our law a mere microcosm of the future. It is imperative that it be related and collated before it becomes overwhelming.

If the recent suggestion of the American Bar Association to require all of the 130 administrative agencies of the Federal Government to promulgate rules and regulations, so as to promote certainty, were followed, that would still leave a terrifying bulk of unrelated and perhaps even conflicting statutes. Why not a general body of rule emanating from Congress, applicable to all bureaus and supplemented by special regulations only when needed? Solicitor General Robert H. Jackson has already conceded the necessity for greater uniformity of procedure before the various Federal bureaus.

The task of codifying our law should not be neglected as so many of our States have neglected it. In some of the States it is still impossible to determine what laws are still in force and what laws have been repealed. Codification of statutes has, in many cases, been left in unofficial hands. But while many States have assumed the burden of codifying their statutes, none assumes the task of digesting and collating its judicial law. This is left to private industry, though it might well be a task assumed by the State in an effort to curtail the present output of judicial opinions.

If opinions were published "per curiam," their volume would decrease amazingly. An opinion bureau could be established in courts in large communities, similar to legislative bill-drafting bureaus. The judge who decided a case could then turn over to the bureau the statement of facts and law upon which he based his decision. Trained opinion writers could then determine whether any new principle of law or any novel set of facts was involved in the case; if

# LOOK AT THE LAW

not, a brief statement of facts and reasons for the decision could be issued.

Adherence to such practice would soon reduce the quantity of judicial law to elements which lend themselves not only to understanding but to ready inclusion in a structure of cohesive law. This would ultimately produce an almost automatic restatement of the substantive law—a task upon which the American Law Institute has been engaged for some years, with varying conclusions of result—and would cut much of the fat from the bones of the judicial frame. There is little excuse for its present hoglike size. A strenuous regime of diet and exercise is required, if for no other reason than to reduce its uncertainty.

# CHAPTER III

## *The Layman Says:*
## THE LAW IS UNCERTAIN

*1.*

IT is inconceivable that the Court of Appeals, the highest court of the State of New York, should order Mary Hartung set at liberty, when she had killed her husband and had been duly convicted of the crime. But it did, though it found that she had been properly tried and legally convicted. Between the date of Mrs. Hartung's conviction and the date of the hearing of her appeal, a careless legislature had repealed the existing law which imposed the death penalty for murder, and had passed a new statute. But it had forgotten to include in the new statute the usual provision that murders previously committed should be punished under the old law.

In consequence, Mrs. Hartung's lawyer argued that she could not be hung under the old statute since it was no longer in force, and that she could not be punished under the new one since it had not been in effect when she had committed the crime. In addition to this unanswerable argument, he pointed out that the legislature had also neglected, in the new statute, to prescribe a method of execution. In consequence, he argued, there was no way of executing his client legally. The Court of Appeals confessed that it found itself unable to determine how the legislature wanted convicted murderers executed, whether by the old method of hanging, or, as the Court said, by the "method prevailing in France, or Russia or Constantinople." As a result, after

# LOOK AT THE LAW

hemming and hawing about the matter for almost five years, the judges turned the woman out of the death house and let her go scot-free.

We have no available record from which to ascertain the cause of this unquestioned uncertainty in the law. It is a fair assumption that a carousing legislature passed this emasculated measure in the hectic turmoil that marks the closing hours of every legislative session. The committee system prevalent in our legislatures promotes this method of legislation without comprehension. Bills are introduced and referred to committees in the first few days of the session. There they languish until the early hours of the dawn of adjournment day, when they are reported out and voted upon in such profusion and amid such scenes of confusion that needed measures are forgotten while joker bills are slipped through.

A Texas judge humorously said: "The ancient Germans, from whom the Anglo-Saxon race sprang, used to propose their laws in their legislature while drunk and considered their passage while sober. And it is suspected by some that their descendants propose laws in legislatures of the present day while in the same condition, though their enactment may not be considered while sober, as by their ancestors."

The minority leader of the New York Assembly told the New York Constitutional Convention that the practice of having the governor send twelfth-hour emergency measures to the Assembly required legislators to act on bills which had not even been printed, bills which the legislators had not seen and bills of which they knew nothing. He did not, however, refer to the greater evil of the prevailing committee system which results in reporting out practically all of the important bills in the closing days of the legislative session.

Nor did he refer to the recent sessions of Congress when

## LOOK AT THE LAW

executive demands for hasty passage of legislation were such that only two or three copies of bills were available for the consideration of the entire House, and in one case "not ten of 435 members had had a chance to glance" at the bill, according to a *Saturday Evening Post* article. The same article said that on one occasion the Administration leader in the Senate had "introduced a folded newspaper as a substitute for a 'must' bill that hadn't yet come up from the public printer." A Washington dispatch to the New York *Times* said that of the fifty Senators listed as sponsors of a measure designed to tax war profits (and which it was demonstrated would have levied a total in Federal and State taxes of more than 100 per cent in the upper brackets), only six, other than the authors of the bill, would say that they had actually read it through.

A large number of ill-considered laws thus find their way into the statute books. A New Jersey legislature passed a "Fair Trade Act" of which one paragraph, containing only thirty-five words, was such a jumble that a New Jersey Vice-Chancellor confessed his utter inability to construe the statute. A Delaware legislature was reconvened in special session in 1936 because, in the riotous closing hours, it forgot to enact appropriation measures necessary for the continued operation of the school system.

A New York judge said that the administrative code of the City of New York was "impossible, most inconvenient and hard to understand and a cumbersome jig-saw puzzle which costs the city about $150,000 a year." He recommended that it be rewritten.

However, it is not only the weaknesses of our legislative system that result in laws of doubtful meaning. The legislators themselves are often none too clear about what they are trying to do.

Obviously, our legislators cannot be masters of all the

# LOOK AT THE LAW

varied social and economic problems that our broadened conceptions of governmental functions currently include. It is an unusual legislator who is capable of understanding many of the technical and intricate questions cast into his lap, for the necessary qualifications, first and last, of a legislator are political. He may have other qualifications of education and of character, but they are subsidiary, if at times they are not actually disqualifications unfitting him for the rough and tumble of the political arena. Consequently, many of our legislators justify Blackstone's statement that of all the trades and professions, it is only that of the lawmaker for which no education or training is needed.

We do little to spur our legislators to pursuit of learning. Generally, we distinguish only between party emblems in electing our lawmakers. Our theory of democracy requires frequent elections, so that our legislators are hardly through being elected before they must begin to work on political fences in order to obtain renomination and reelection. This requires them to fetch and carry for individual constituents, and they spend a good part of their time and effort in doing such political chores. Ex-Senator Moore of New Jersey recently expressed himself strongly on the peonage of the legislator.

At the same time, we give our legislators such meager salaries that they can do no more than pay their political and legislative expenses, with the result that unless they graft they must spend most of their waking time in earning a living for themselves and their families.

The consequence is that the average legislator views his job as a political one, and handles it accordingly. He introduces bills that are handed to him by his political sponsors, by his fellow legislators or by other persons or groups whom he wants to put under obligation or to whom he owes favors. He makes no effort to study bills up for passage; instead, he

# LOOK AT THE LAW

votes as he is instructed to, or as political expediency dictates. As Gilbert and Sullivan wrote:

> "When in that house M. P.'s divide,
> If they've a brain and cerebellum too,
> They've got to leave that brain outside
> And vote just as their leaders tell 'em to."

Unless the legislator happens to study a bill as a committee member, he can know little or nothing of it. He frequently is unfamiliar with bills he himself introduces or sponsors, as the Congressional example heretofore given demonstrates. Even committee members, it was testified in a recent bribery trial of the chairman of a New York legislative taxicab committee, did not read the report and accompanying bill which was submitted by the committee to the legislature.

Nor is legislative debate any source of real knowledge; it is limited in time and information. Most of the reported Congressional "debate" is never heard on the floor; it is merely printed in the *Congressional Record* for vote-getting consumption.

Mayor La Guardia of New York recently said that his fourteen years in the House had convinced him that 100 of its 435 members "never do anything."

The fact of the matter is that major legislation rarely springs from the legislative mind. It is a practical impossibility to expect a legislature or a Congress to receive and frame independently the technical legislation our present complicated system demands.

Even conceding a legislator adequate time, education and experience, the intricate problems of our civilization make demands beyond the powers of the average person. When, as Tourtoulon says, "very little observation is sufficient to establish the fact that . . . in spite of his utmost care and

# LOOK AT THE LAW

greatest efforts, the most vigorous thinker will not deal with even a comparatively simple subject without showing evidence somewhere of insufficiency, contradiction and incoherence," when the best of us suffer from "diseases of thought," arising from "ignorance, lack of reflection, limitation in means of testing, language and historical myths, fashions in doctrine and practice," what may we expect of the collective thought of legislative assemblies?

The legislature must either let the Executive Department formulate and recommend legislation, or it must go for help to outside sources, to political, scientific, social or economic groups, public or private, virtuous or wicked. But even this gives no assurance of certainty of purpose or expression in legislation, even though the legislation is suggested and formulated by representative public groups. For it is difficult for us to make up our own minds.

Our law needs to be molded to our social system, to its changing needs and concepts and to our understanding of them. Yet we have no clear comprehension of these matters. Our emotions cloud our mental processes and prevent recognition of unpalatable truths. We reject biologic verities for narcotic fallacies. Our lives are governed by such chance and disordered circumstances, our thoughts are so deadened by habit, we are so credulous though fearful, we are so ignorant though egotistic, that it is impossible for us to think and to act logically. Besides, we are surrounded by tugging, selfish propagandists and misguided altruists, by pseudo-scientists and "practical" seers, who pull us to the left and to the right. In between, we find ourselves bewildered by their conflicting claims and conclusions.

Shall we tolerate particular abuses, or run the risk of stifling private initiative by overregulation? Shall we have a planned economy, or is it the road to Fascism? Shall we maintain freedom of speech, though it be abused by the

## LOOK AT THE LAW

lunatic fringe within and the alien enemy without our gates? Which is the greater evil, the abuse or the suggested remedy?

Though we recognize abuses, we cannot always ascertain the remedy.

In creating a commission to study and propose anti-crime and corruption legislation, the 1939 New York State Legislature said that "though there is an overwhelming public hostility to crime and corruption in public office, there is, at present, no trustworthy crystallization of public sentiment as to what changes should be made in existing laws and agencies."

Even when we agree upon an abuse and its solution, we are often unprepared to adopt known remedies. We all agree that poverty is an evil, unemployment wasteful and economic slavery degrading. But are we willing to pay the price to alleviate them?

Are we willing to pay in taxes the added cost of social measures designed to minimize crime, or do we prefer to pay as we go, in prisons and asylums, the cost of poverty and its consequences?

Do we want chain stores and monopoly with greater efficiency and lower costs and their consequent concentration of power, or do we prefer individual initiative and inefficiency with a more democratic structure?

And even when we do know what we want, our legislators may be unable to ascertain our collective will, for the legislator's divining rod is none too scientific or accurate. The legislator reads his newspaper and his mail, and figuratively keeps his ear to the ground. But his newspaper editor may be influenced by advertisers and his mail may be flooded by subsidized or otherwise improperly stimulated communications.

Even when the legislator turns to experts for aid, he can-

# LOOK AT THE LAW

not always achieve certainty. No matter how much expert help is sought, new legislation devised to regulate virgin fields is necessarily ambiguous when its sponsors are uncertain of the causes of the condition they are trying to adjust, or of its remedy. Only trial and error can ultimately clarify such laws.

According to a special dispatch to the New York *Times*, President Roosevelt volunteered the information that he had discussed the subject of clarification of the National Labor Relations Act. The objective of clarity of language was common to the drafting of all statutes creating new government agencies, the President observed, although human draftsmanship had not reached the point where the objective was always obtained. That, he said, was as true of the Labor Act as of other laws.

For example, we have had, since the Sherman anti-trust law of 1890, laws prohibiting monopolies in restraint of trade in this country. Just what these laws are intended to prevent has never been made clear. In 1901, with the Sherman Act on the books, J. P. Morgan, Judge Elbert Gary and others conceived and organized the huge steel combine known as the United States Steel Corporation. Judge Gary is reported to have said that if the Government let them alone for ten years, they would not be convicted of a violation of the monopoly laws; if it interfered before that time, they would be. He apparently was right, for by 1913 the Supreme Court imported a "rule of reason" into the statute (which had not been written into it by Congress) that enabled the Steel Trust to win the anti-monopoly suit the Government had brought against it.

Nevertheless, uncertainty in the anti-trust field still reigns. Twenty-five years later, with a long list of intermediate successful anti-trust prosecutions by the Government, including suits against the Standard Oil Company, the Reading Com-

## LOOK AT THE LAW

pany, and the Aluminum Company of America, the following article by Isabel Patterson appeared in the New York *Herald Tribune:*

"The most ingenious cross-word puzzle ever devised has been printed piecemeal in the news columns of 1938.

"It began with the conviction of the oil operators in Wisconsin some months ago. They had been urged by the Federal Administration to combine and fix prices. They did so. They were subsequently prosecuted by the same Administration, under the anti-trust laws, for doing as they were bid.

"Next the leading motor manufacturers were indicted, under the same anti-trust laws.

"Next, Mr. Elliott Roosevelt expressed sympathy for the convicted oil operators. But that didn't reverse their sentences.

"Next Professor Thurman Arnold, Assistant Attorney General, objected to any attempt to clarify the anti-trust laws, affirmed that 'all violations' of those laws will be 'vigorously prosecuted,' and explained that 'the application of the principle . . . necessarily requires the exercise of the judgment . . . (of) the Department of Justice.' He admits the law is ambiguous, and says it must remain so. Nobody is to know what constitutes breach of it until or unless an indictment is sought. Now the only extant definition of the 'principle' of the law is that it forbids monopoly or restraint of trade. Yet at the same time Professor Arnold added that 'if an industry has gone so far on the path of monopoly control that competition can never be restored, government regulation is necessary.' Thus it appears that if the principle is clearly applicable, it must not be applied, because it would be of no use. More than that, in such case, that is, if monopoly can be clearly shown to exist, it must be confirmed and maintained by political authority. A very odd principle, and an even more peculiar practice, by which the only hope of escaping prosecution would consist of being guilty. Conversely, it would seem that if anyone were to be prosecuted, it could only be innocent parties."

# LOOK AT THE LAW

The obvious conclusion to be drawn from Miss Patterson's puzzle is that executive officers are prepared to substitute their conceptions of public policy for legislative fiat, to legislate by a process of criminal indictments and civil consent decrees, to substitute complete uncertainty for what should be written law.

This policy finds expression in the attempt by the Department of Justice similarly to solve the difficult questions of "group medicine." Clearly this is a milieu for the legislative and not for the executive plow and harrow. Yet, here, too, the Government has sought to legislate by indictment.

In both these situations, the courts have rebuked the prosecution's approach. In the oil cases the Circuit Court reversed, holding, as Miss Patterson suggested, that the defendants had only done what the Government, through the N. R. A., had urged them to do. In the social medicine case, the court dismissed the indictments on the technical ground that the anti-trust laws have no application to a profession.

Obviously such an extra-legal method cannot be justified under a democratic system. It compounds felonies; it constitutes intimidation and extortion. It abrogates the functions of the judge and makes him a puppet of the prosecutor. It not only makes the prosecutor judge and jury, but substitutes him for the legislator. In short, it destroys our tripartite theory of government and combines all three parts in the *procureur du roi;* only lettre de cachet powers are lacking.

At this late date a far-reaching monopoly investigation by the Federal Government is being conducted, while under-Secretary of the Treasury Berle attacks the premises upon which much of our anti-monopoly anathema has been based.

Clearly this is one of the many matters of which we know little or nothing. Our reasoning has been political; our reactions emotional. Yet we have been legislating con-

# LOOK AT THE LAW

cerning it, by statute and judicial decision, for almost half a century.

## 2.

At the bottom of the uncertainty in much of our legislation is not only the failure to know what we want, but the inability to say what we mean. This disability is a natural one. One may read the confessionals of trained workers, who testify to the labor pains of self-expression after a lifetime devoted to its art. What can one expect of a legislator or a judge in whose training the pen is but an incident? Legal synonymic phraseology—"the defendant did thereupon assault, attack, assail, batter, strike, set upon, poke, thrust at, deal blows to, kick, slap, etc., said John Doe . . ." is a clumsy legal device designed to overcome the uncertainties of language and definition.

At best, the meaning of words is variable, as our dictionaries attest. But beyond that, as Stuart Chase points out in his *Tyranny of Words*, we even fall into error when we reconcile words with accepted and unchallenged meanings. How much worse when, with our limitations of language, we use words of doubtful shades of meaning, unskillfully and vaguely!

When words are strung into phrases, phrases into clauses, clauses into sentences and sentences into paragraphs, to the risks of language are added the chances of illogical placement and arrangement, the oddities of punctuation and the confusion of content. Then the complexities of expression mount by geometrical progression and one finds no brew for amateurs.

Bad grammar or improper punctuation in other fields may mean rebuke, even ridicule; in the terrain of statute-making, the improper insertion or lack of a comma or a semicolon may free a criminal or imprison an innocent man.

# LOOK AT THE LAW

In the law, accepted meanings are often held meaningless. Word myths and dictionary definitions are frequently discarded. Judges lend to words a flexibility that would confound a cross-word puzzle expert. An entire classified branch of the law called "Statutory Construction" is devoted to the judicial art of gainsaying Noah Webster.

So "intoxication," to quote Corpus Juris, a standard compilation of legal definitions and decisions, becomes "a broad and comprehensive term, having a different meaning to different persons . . . and perhaps the courts are not in harmony in respect thereto. . . . According to some definitions, the word may be applied to any mental exhilaration, however slight, produced by alcohol, without regard to its effect on the judgment or reasoning processes . . . while elsewhere it is synonymous with drunkenness." By the same process, drunkenness in the law is merely a comparative term, ranging in meaning from the state of one who is dead drunk, through the stupid drunk, the staggering drunk, to the foolish drunk.

In defining words and phrases, judges resort not only to the language and arrangement of a statute but also to the intention of the legislature, the object to be attained, and such extrinsic matters as the circumstances attending its passage, the sense in which it was understood by contemporaries and its relations to other laws.

With such criteria, can a legislator guess what will move a court in defining the poor words he uses as tools to express his meaning? How can he use the simplest words with any measure of certainty that there will be concurrence between legislative foresight and judicial hindsight?

The New York *Times*, commenting on an admission by a judge that the wording of a law was unintelligible, said: "Such boldness on the part of a judge is unusual. The general practice is for him to retire to his study with the law in

# LOOK AT THE LAW

question, to read it over and over, to meditate upon its language and if necessary to pray for guidance, and finally to emerge triumphantly with a meaning."

How, for example, can the legislator use the simple word "person" in a statute without the risk that he will thereby relegate it to the purgatory of uncertain law? He may understand the word as meaning a "being having life, intelligence, will and separate individual existence, distinguished from an irrational brute, an inanimate thing," as Webster defines it. But having used it, did he intend to include a "dead person"? If not, how about a lunatic or a man sentenced to life imprisonment, since both are civilly dead? Does it mean an alien, an army officer, a bankrupt, a Chinese, a colored man, an Indian, a Filipino, a common informer, a corporation, a corporate officer, a corporate agent, a customs officer, a depository, a druggist, an employee, a farmer, a forwarding agent, an inhabitant, a resident, a slave, a witness, a restaurant proprietor, a woman, a widow, a child, a premature child, a stillborn child, an illegitimate child? These are not imaginary definitions; every term used represents an actual controversy in which the question was judicially raised and determined. And with varying results.

A North Carolina court held that the word does not mean simply the visible body, for then it would apply equally to a corpse, while a New Hampshire court held that "person" means the material person—the body in the flesh and not the spiritual soul. Georgia and Pennsylvania courts held the word included both sexes; Florida, Maine, Utah, Washington and Canadian courts held that the word as used in particular statutes meant "men only." Some courts, while including women, exclude married women, while others include widows. A Federal court excluded children too young to be charged with self-care.

When the word becomes part of a phrase, dubiety reigns.

# LOOK AT THE LAW

Persons "intending to procure a miscarriage," "acting under orders," "by whose order," "entitled to vote," "dealing with others," "offending," "so employed," are persons of even greater uncertainty. Or when an adjective is used: "fit," "insured," "negligent," "culpable," "no" or "any" persons; or a participle: person "charged," "accounting," "acting," "affected," "appointed," "claiming"—these and a thousand other dilemmas arising from the legislative use of the simple word "person" have engaged the attention of the courts in an effort to decipher the legislative mind.

And this difficulty is not uncommon. A so-called law dictionary is published in twenty-three volumes and contains in 24,588 pages approximately 60,000 judicial definitions which vary materially from Noah Webster's definitions, and from each other.

In short, as the esteemed Oliver Wendell Holmes said: "A word is not a crystal, transparent and unchanged, it is the skin of a bony thought and may vary greatly in color and content according to the circumstances and the time in which it is used."

That being so, how can legislative certainty be assured when one set of men makes the laws and another determines what they mean?

President Roosevelt recently took a novel course in signing the Hatch bill, which sought to dissociate politics and Federal office holding. He sent a message to Congress giving his understanding of the meaning and content of portions of the bill which might be misconstrued and thereby laid the ground for greater certainty in later lay, official and judicial construction.

A legislature cannot conceive every contingency which its legislation will encounter. It cannot fit its statutes to every strain to which they will be subjected. It cannot, for example, provide against the possibility of a legislating

# LOOK AT THE LAW

court. A naive Indiana legislature attempted to do this by passing a law requiring that words and phrases in statutes be taken in their plain, ordinary and usual sense, and requiring that technical words and phrases be understood according to their technical import. Whereupon an Indiana court construed the statute and said that it meant nothing more than what the courts had always said. And, it added, the legislature, by so saying, had not intended to prevent the court from applying other judicial rules of equal dignity and importance, such as those which reckon not with what the legislature says but those which determine what the court reckons it means!

Yet, to meet contingencies for which it has not provided, a legislature sometimes needs the aid of a legislating court.

For example, though a legislative statute provided unequivocally and without reservation that a "widower" should inherit the property of his deceased wife, a Missouri court refused to recognize as a "widower" a man who had killed his wife, the court saying that "widower," as used in the law, meant "one who has been reduced to that condition by the ordinary and usual vicissitudes of life, and not one who, by felonious act, has himself created that condition."

Determination of the legislative intent often turns upon some unrelated statutory ambiguity that has no real connection with the question at hand. Thus, the question of whether criminals indicted and convicted shall be turned out because their indictments were illegal rested upon the question of whether women could legally serve as grand jurors in three of the counties of New York City. In turn, this question depended on the judicial construction of a statute referring to exemption from jury service, which had been on the books before the New York legislature authorized women to serve as jurors. The resultant technicalities were so refined as to be "irritating to the layman, meat and

# LOOK AT THE LAW

drink to the specialist," according to the New York *Times*.

Any attempt by the most discerning legislature to visualize every situation that might arise would require such a volume of provision that it would defeat its own purpose in a welter of attempted overcertainty.

For example, Senator Wagner of New York sought to amend the New York State Constitution in such express terms that no reactionary court could in the future, as in the past, defeat enlightened legislation affecting human rights by saying it violated the clause in the Constitution that prohibits the taking of "property" without compensation and due process of law. He therefore proposed to add to the Constitution a provision that would expressly deny that legislation affecting "wages, hours of work, bargaining power, living conditions, prices, unemployment, sickness, disability, or waste of natural resources" could be deemed legislation taking "property." Then in an excess of caution and to take care of specific matters he had not provided for, he added to the exception any legislation promoting the "physical, social or economic welfare or security of the people."

Imagine the result. Having spent 150 years and tons of words in defining "property," how long would it take the courts to agree upon the meaning of the additional terms the Senator would have imported into the Constitution, to say nothing of definitions of what "promotes" the "physical, social or economic welfare or security" of the people?

Nor can a legislature, however astute, guard against pettifoggery.

It needs no documented thesis to demonstrate that no one, not even the great bard, has been able to express himself in language in which no pettifogger, sophist or hair-splitter can find ambiguities and contradictions.

No artifice will avail to defeat the art of the lawyer who

can "quote from criticism." It is impossible to select a phrase or a practice that a lawyer cannot confuse or confound, misconstrue or challenge. What legislative draftsman would have thought of providing for the forfeit of blood with the pound of flesh in Shylock's bond? And if a mere Portia can thus confound the law, what of the corporate defendant whose business brings its regularly retained counsel repeatedly into the courts? Commercial corporations such as those that insure against accident, sickness and death are skilled in employing evasions and ingenuities with little scruple and much skill, in an effort to avoid liability.

For example, an insurance company had insured a man against death caused by accidental means. The insured had been taking veronal under a doctor's prescription. By mistake he took an overdose and died. The insurance company refused to pay, saying that it had not insured him against accidental death, but against death by accidental means. It contended that while he had died accidentally he had not taken the veronal accidentally and that therefore the means were intentional and not accidental. This caused the court to say that few ordinary people could understand this logomachy; that insurance policies upon which the public rely for security in death, sickness, or accident should be plainly worded, in understandable English, free from fine distinctions which few can understand until pointed out by lawyers and judges. Incidentally, the insurance company lost, but not until after it had put the policy holder to the cost and delay of not less than three court hearings to collect all of $2,000.

Another insurance company, by similar means, sought to avoid liability on a policy which it had issued to a restaurant owner insuring him against any claim that should be made by a customer for any accident occurring on the premises. By some mischance, a piece of glass had worked its way

## LOOK AT THE LAW

into a tongue sandwich and the customer sued the restaurant, claiming he had cut his mouth while eating the sandwich. The insurance company refused to defend the suit, saying that it had guaranteed only against an accident occurring on the premises and that, though the customer had bought the sandwich in the restaurant, he had eaten it and cut his mouth outside. However, the judge held that the accident occurred when the glass worked its way into the sandwich and not when it was eaten, and since that occurred in the restaurant, the company was liable.

In another case, according to the New York *World-Telegram*, "by intervening in a lawsuit in which it had no interest, the Prudential Life Insurance Company so confused a Supreme Court Justice that he admitted improper evidence, excluded competent evidence and perhaps decided the case wrongly, the New York Appellate Division, Second Department, decided in an opinion criticizing the company's tactics."

The layman's opinion of the dishonesty of such practices is illustrated by a story concerning a farm paper, the *Rural New Yorker*, which guarantees its subscribers against loss from "trusting any deliberate swindler, irresponsible advertisers or misleading advertisements" in its columns.

A subscriber complained that her husband, having taken out a $1000 one-year-term insurance policy and having been killed during the term, the insurance company had made "various excuses and finally ended up by sending me 40 cents." The newspaper "went after" the insurance company and finally succeeded in compelling it to make full payment to the widow.

The subtleties of language are such that legislators may readily confuse their own enactments, when they are of a mind to do so. "Jokers" are standard in legislative practice; innocent-appearing statutes are found to conceal unsuspected barbs, while ferocious pronouncements are negatived by elusive prepositions or conjunctions, lurkingly but deliberately inserted by designing legislative draftsmen to confuse and confound later interpreters.

Mark Sullivan recently taxed the New Deal with "misleading art in the use of words" employed for political effect, in substituting, for example, "installment credit" for "installment debt." He threatened to "go into an etymology court and obtain a writ of replevin" to rescue the word "liberal."

Generally, when evasion of legislative enactments is sought, protection must be sought from the judges, though they themselves, it is true, are not always overprecise in their own choice of language, and judicial law is not always free from the uncertainties that beset our statutory law.

### 3.

A third and most striking phase of the uncertainty of the law is illustrated by the conflict in decisions of different courts, the conflict in decisions of the same court and, finally, by the conflict in opinions of different judges in the same case.

When the legislature in Nevada permits divorce after six weeks' residence in Nevada, while the New Jersey legislature requires two years as the period of residence, there should be neither legal conflict nor legal confusion. And there would be none if New Jersey residents stayed at home and patronized their own divorce industry. But when, in an impatience to substitute new yokes for old, a New Jersey resident transports herself to Reno for a quick Nevada divorce, the basis for legal conflict and legal confusion is laid. And when she remarries and returns to New Jersey, the reign of legal uncertainty begins.

# LOOK AT THE LAW

It is no longer the narrow question of whether the Nevada courts will hold that by using the term "residence" the Nevada legislature meant bona fide or permanent residence, or whether it contemplated a mere transient, divorce residence. It now becomes the more complicated question of what the New Jersey courts think the Nevada legislature meant or what the New Jersey courts think of the effect of what the Nevada legislature meant. If the Nevada legislature meant that one who goes to Nevada with intent to stay there permanently may get a divorce after six weeks, it did not intend to legitimatize a divorce by one who had no intention of staying on after the divorce was granted. And if that is what the New Jersey judges think the Nevada legislature meant, the divorce is invalid and the subsequent marriage bigamous. If, assuming a different attitude on the part of the Nevada legislature, the New Jersey court thinks it intended to establish a divorce mill, it still remains for the New Jersey court to decide whether one New Jersey resident may go to a neighboring State and there, after a transient six weeks' residence, validly divorce another New Jersey resident.

Here we find fertile ground for legal uncertainty and confusion, for conflict between the decisions of various courts, so fruitful that an entire branch of the law, called "Conflict of Laws," is devoted to it.

Each of our States has its own legislature, which makes its own statutory law. In spite of efforts to make these laws uniform, they differ mightily. Forty-seven out of our forty-eight States (South Carolina only excepted) permit divorce. In all, there are thirty-three grounds for divorce, ranging from adultery, which is common to all States, to matters like incompatibility, habitual bad temper, premarital unchastity of a wife, etc., which are peculiar to certain States. The residence requirements, preliminary to suing for di-

# LOOK AT THE LAW

vorce, also differ. The result is that one need but cross a State line after divorce to remarry, to create legal confusion, uncertainty and conflict of far-reaching consequences. Men and women lawfully married in one State become bigamists and adulterers in another. Children lawfully conceived in one State lose their status and rights of inheritance in another.

The results are sometimes even more remote and perplexing.

A husband from whom his wife had obtained a Nevada divorce was charged, with an accomplice, in a Bahama court, with kidnaping his own child. His former wife's testimony was essential to the prosecution. However, the judge refused to permit her to testify upon the ground that, under the law of the Bahamas, a Nevada divorce was not entitled to recognition; that in the Bahamas, the parties were still husband and wife (though the wife had since remarried and was then living in the Bahamas with her second husband); and that a wife could not testify against her husband. Both defendants were thereupon ordered acquitted.

The uncertainty of decision between the courts of different States is not confined to their interpretation of the effect of conflicting statutes. They differ in their reasoning and conclusions as to the effect of a law even when both States have similar statutes.

A number of States, including New York, Utah and Oregon, have a law which permits a person to bring an action to "declare" his rights in advance and thereby to avoid the delay of an actual controversy and the expense of suffering actual damages. This law is known as the declaratory judgment law and has been generally hailed as beneficent and remedial legislation.

Men who wanted to run race tracks in Utah and Oregon, when threatened with arrest by the police for permitting race-track betting, brought actions against the authorities

# LOOK AT THE LAW

under this declaratory judgment law to have the courts declare whether race-track betting was legal or illegal. Thereupon, the courts in Utah and Oregon ruled on the questions and gave judgments declaring the rights of both the operators and the authorities.

Later, in New York State, the police threatened to arrest the proprietor of a dog-racing track, charging him with maintaining an establishment for gambling. With the Utah and Oregon precedents before him, the dog-track proprietor's lawyer started a suit against the authorities so that the court might declare whether dog-track betting was legal or illegal. After a trial, the court found dog-track betting legal. The District Attorney appealed, whereupon the appellate courts dismissed the suit, saying they would not "take the responsibility of deciding a question of criminal law in a civil declaratory judgment suit." They told the police to arrest the dog-track operator and to try the issues all over again on the criminal side of the court. The result was one rule of law in Utah and Oregon and another in New York, both concerning the selfsame statute. Of course, if the question comes up hereafter in any of the other States which have a similar law, the result must be uncertain until the highest court has indicated the school of thought it will join.

Conflict in the law and its ensuing uncertainty is not confined to statutes. Nor can it be restricted to differences between the courts of the various States. It extends to judge-made law, which, though called common law, has rules which are by no means common in all the States. It also extends to differences between the State courts and the Federal courts, at times sitting in the very same State.

When, for example, a telegraph company has been negligent in transmitting telegrams respecting sickness and death, actions are sometimes started to recover damages from the

# LOOK AT THE LAW

telegraph company. In these cases, money loss resulting from the delay or failure of the company to deliver the telegram is unusual. The damage claimed results from worry or annoyance or similar "mental anguish." If the message goes from State to State, there can be no such recovery, according to the United States Supreme Court. If it is sent and delivered wholly in Alabama, however, such a recovery will be permitted; likewise, in Iowa, Kentucky, Louisiana, Nebraska, Nevada, North Carolina, Tennessee and Texas. But not in Georgia, Illinois, Kansas, Minnesota, Mississippi, Ohio, Washington and West Virginia. Any lawyer advising his client in such cases must look to the prior decisions of his State, if there are any. If there are none, he can only guess what caravan his judges will join. Even then he cannot be too certain, because the Indiana court first allowed a recovery and then, in a later case, went over to the other side; while in Arkansas, Oklahoma, South Carolina, Virginia and Wisconsin, the courts said "no," though the legislature said "yes."

Where there is a variance between the legislative or the judicial law in two States, grave uncertainty exists in determining which rule of law is applicable to a case that does not reckon with State boundaries. If, for example, a corporation is organized in Delaware and does business in Ohio, when does Delaware statutory law and when does Ohio substantive and statutory law apply to it? If a child is born out of wedlock in Arkansas, where his father was domiciled, though he was legitimatized by an Arkansas statute, may he, as a legitimate heir, take a share of his grandfather's estate in Maryland? A Maryland court said "no," while a Louisiana court said "yes." What lawyer or layman could predict what a Massachusetts court would say about the right of a Maine resident to sue a married woman domiciled in Massachusetts upon a contract made in Maine, when by

# LOOK AT THE LAW

the laws of Maine she was permitted to make such a contract, while by the laws of Massachusetts she could not? The Massachusetts court said she could be sued — and in Massachusetts.

The uncertainty that could only be partially resolved by determining whether a State or Federal judge sitting in the same State was going to decide a case is finally at an end. Jerome Frank, in his *Law and the Modern Mind*, tells of the vicissitudes of client and counsel in a case involving a contract made in Kentucky between Kentucky corporations which the Kentucky State courts held invalid but which the Federal Court, sitting in Kentucky, considered lawful. He points out how the problem was solved by having the plaintiff Kentucky corporation become a Tennessee corporation and then suing in the Federal Court in Kentucky instead of in the Kentucky State Court. He discloses the uncertainties of the situation which were emphasized by the final result in the United States Supreme Court, where six justices held one way and three another.

Frank did not, however, stress the ultimate uncertainty in the case, the question of whether the United States Supreme Court would continue to adhere to the rule that where there is a difference between the common law as construed by the State courts and the common law as construed by the Federal courts, the latter, though sitting in the very same State, must subscribe to the Federal and reject the State rule. It was hardly conceivable that that rule of conflict, adopted by the United States Supreme Court in 1842, should be abandoned after an adherence of almost one hundred years, although, in the very case of which Frank wrote, Justices Holmes, Brandeis and Stone pointed out to the majority of six the error of the ways the Court had been traveling for so many years; and although later, in February, 1938, Justice Black pointed out to the majority judges deciding an

# LOOK AT THE LAW

insurance case which arose in Montana that they were improperly following the Federal rule and ignoring the Montana law. Even then the majority held to the old rule. Yet less than three months later, they switched to hold that the hundred-year-old rule was extra-constitutional, and decreed that hereafter the Federal courts should follow the State decisions on matters of general law and thereby avoid the century-old conflict.

With that ground of confusion removed, some of the avoidable uncertainty in the law was obviated. But every clarifying decision brings its own complications and uncertainties. And this one was no exception. For now the Federal judge, in rejecting the Federal rule for the State rule, is called upon to decide what State rule he will apply. For example:

A resident of Pennsylvania brought an action in the Federal Court in New York to recover damages for the negligence of the defendant. The defendant pleaded that since the plaintiff had previously been convicted of murder in Florida, he was civilly dead and could not maintain a suit. The plaintiff's lawyer admitted that if the plaintiff had been convicted of murder in New York, he would be civilly dead; he also admitted that under Federal law and Pennsylvania law, he was civilly dead; but he claimed that he was not civilly dead under the Florida law and argued that since he was convicted in Florida, though he was a resident of Pennsylvania and had sued in New York, the court could not apply the New York, the Pennsylvania or the Federal law, but must let him sue under the Florida law. And the court held with him.

But there is uncertainty in the law, even where there is no conflict of law except in the minds of the judges who decide what the law is. It is incredible that at this late day, Federal judges would be unable to agree on whether a Fed-

# LOOK AT THE LAW

eral judge has the right to comment on the evidence in jury trials. Yet two of the three judges of the Seventh Federal Circuit Court of Appeals have lately held that a Federal judge who so commented violated the defendant's constitutional rights, even though he assured the jury that it was not bound to conform to his views. The dissenting judge held that the right of comment by the judge had been unquestioned in the Federal courts for seventy-five years, although it has been forbidden in the Illinois, New York and other State courts.

Changing social, economic or political conditions unsettle the force of existing precedents. The need for progress in the law necessarily and properly makes the law uncertain. No one will deride the Supreme Court for its honest confession that the hundred-year-old rule of Federal jurisdiction that it advocated was contrary to enlightened legal opinion.

No better illustration of this element of uncertainty can be found than in the course of the New Deal legislation with which the Supreme Court has dealt in the last seven years.

No one, in Congress or out, knew what fate awaited the volume of legislation enacted by Congress from 1933 to 1937. True, contradictory as it may seem, judicial bent or bias introduced some elements of certainty in the situation. It was known that opposition to liberal legislation could be anticipated from Justices McReynolds, Sutherland, Van Devanter and Butler, while support could be expected from Justices Brandeis, Cardozo, Stone, Reed, Black and Douglas. Where the Chief Justice and where Justice Roberts would go on a particular measure was anybody's guess. And some of the legislative guesses were bad. The entire Court, liberals as well as reactionaries, turned thumbs down on some of the New Deal measures; for an example, see the opinion written by Justice Brandeis for the entire Court, invalidating

## LOOK AT THE LAW

the Frazier-Lemke Act for extension of farm mortgages.

Not even the lower court Federal judges can make adequate guesses at what the Supreme Court will hold the law to be. The United Press reported that a survey by the Department of Justice revealed that all sixteen cases which were heard by the United States Supreme Court upon appeals from the Third Circuit Court of Appeals sitting in Philadelphia in the 1937 Session were reversed; that the Ninth Circuit, including California, Oregon, Washington, Nevada, Montana, Idaho, Arizona and the territories of Alaska and Hawaii, was reversed in fourteen and sustained in only three cases; that the Seventh Circuit—Indiana, Illinois and Wisconsin—had eleven reversals and three affirmances; that only one Circuit Court—the Second, covering New York—was sustained more often than it was reversed. (In all fairness, it must be remembered that the Supreme Court does not grant leave to appeal except in a small percentage of doubtful cases.)

The uncertainty of result apparently increases in proportion to the number of judges sitting on the bench. The late Justice Cardozo said that the availability of ten judges of the New York Court of Appeals, where only seven sit at a time, makes for such uncertainty that where the question is a close one a case decided one way one week might well be decided differently the following week. A change of judicial personnel often marks change in the law.

A Washington Scripps-Howard staff writer reported that the Federal Fifth Circuit Court of Appeals ruled twice on the same day concerning the question of whether good faith was an element under the Frazier-Lemke Bankruptcy Act. In one case, by a 2-to-1 vote it held it was not; in the other case, by a 2-to-1 vote it held it was. Each case was heard by three judges, but the membership varied; four judges in all were involved.

# LOOK AT THE LAW

The variances between judges' opinions in a single case demonstrates that the law is an inexact science, if, indeed, it is a science at all. Justice Cardozo pointed out a case where one Johnson had sued the Cadillac Motor Car Company to recover damages for injuries resulting from a defective automobile. The lower Federal Court judge found in Johnson's favor. The three judges of the Federal appellate court held in favor of the Cadillac Company and sent the case back for a new trial. On the second trial, the Federal trial judge dismissed the complaint in accordance with the opinion of the appellate judges, whereupon Johnson appealed.

Meanwhile, one McPherson had been suing the Buick Motor Company in the New York State Court upon a similar state of facts, involving the same question of law. McPherson won his suit, not only in the lower court, in the intermediate appellate court, but also in the highest State appellate court.

Fortunately for Johnson, the McPherson case was decided in his (McPherson's) favor, before Johnson's appeal was heard; whereupon the Federal appellate court, on Johnson's appeal, overruled its prior ruling, and, finally, allowed Johnson to recover.

Fortunately, too, for Johnson, he knew the law was uncertain and he lacked faith in the finality of the court's opinion. Had he relied on it and quit—as a sensible man would have—he would have lost his case, as other litigants have lost their cases and their money because they lacked his pertinacity and skepticism.

In a case brought by the executrix of one Evans to recover death benefits from the Royal Arcanum Lodge, of which Evans had been a member, the lodge refused to pay on the ground that Evans had forfeited his membership by failing to pay an assessment. Evan's widow pleaded that he did not pay the assessment because the New York Court of Appeals had held it to be void, and stated that Evans, in failing to pay, had relied on that decision of the highest court of the State of New York. In reply, the lodge pointed out that it had appealed from that decision to the United States Supreme Court, which had held the assessment valid.

The lower court judge held in Mrs. Evans' favor, as did three judges in the lower appellate court. Two judges of that court voted in favor of the lodge. When the case came to the Court of Appeals, the very court that had held the assessment void, four of its seven judges voted for the lodge, saying "The fact that this Court . . . had erroneously decided that the assessments . . . were invalid was not a legal excuse for non-payment. When he (Evans) refused to pay the assessments he took his chances that the decision of this Court, on appeal, would be sustained."

In consequence, Mrs. Evans lost, though, incidentally, she had offered to pay the assessment.

This recognition by judges of the fleeting character of their own decisions produced an awkward and expensive result in still another case. A landlord had dispossessed his store tenant. The tenant appealed from the order of the lower court but was unable to get a stay, so he had to vacate his store. The landlord then tore the building down and in its place erected a large new motion picture theater. Meanwhile, the tenant was going ahead with his appeal, and finally, to the consternation of the landlord, the appellate court reversed the lower court's decision and ordered the tenant reinstated in his store. The landlord then appealed to the court for relief, saying that the old building had been destroyed and a new one had been erected in its place. But the court was adamant. It said the tenant was entitled to be restored to the possession of his old store regardless of what the landlord had to do to accomplish that result; that when the landlord wrecked the old building and con-

# LOOK AT THE LAW

structed a new one, though in reliance upon the order of a court, he should have known that the decision might be reversed and that he should have governed himself accordingly.

The record does not disclose the subsequent proceedings, but it may not be doubted that the landlord paid through the nose for his faith in the certainty of judicial decisions.

Judicial decisions do not always promote certainty. As we have previously pointed out, unworkmanlike, unnecessary and unnecessarily redundant judicial decisions lay the ground for later confusion and controversy. The justices of the Supreme Court, in recently telling Mayor Hague that we were still operating under a constitutional form of government, found themselves obliged to write five separate opinions (and only seven judges sat). Justices Stone and Roberts wrote the prevailing opinions; Justices Butler and McReynolds the dissenting one. Justice Hughes concurred in the result with a statement of his own reasons.

The result was a statement the following day by the United States Attorney that the Government was going to find it difficult to determine a policy; that it was not clear which of the prevailing opinions stated the law as determined by the Court.

The otherwise excellent opinion by the Federal judge who decided this case in the District Court similarly had been marred by ambiguity to a point where neither plaintiff nor defendant was sure who had been the victor until the judge in a later statement, according to the New York *Times*, "incidentally made it clear that the plaintiffs were the victors."

As an example of juristic ambiguity, the New York *Times* once quoted what it ironically called a "simple penetrating sentence" which occurred in a summation delivered by an English judge: "Quite plainly in my view as a lawyer,

## LOOK AT THE LAW

I cannot find it very difficult to see how you can fail to find that this woman is not guilty of manslaughter."

Certainly, the English jury thus addressed might have returned any verdict and still have felt an accord with the judge.

*4.*

Years ago, when all the existing law could be found in less than fifty volumes, Lord Bacon said, "Certain it is that our laws, as they stand, are subject to great uncertainties and variety of opinion, delays and evasions." Today, with our laws in many thousands of volumes, the consequent abuses are magnified in direct proportion to their bulk.

Try as we will, we cannot make the law certain.

As we have seen, we find it difficult to understand our needs and to agree upon remedies. When remedies are devised, we hesitate to adopt them.

And however clear our intentions may be, we cannot always draft a statute that will automatically speak its piece. Nor do we always want to. The judicial art of "statutory construction" is not exercised in a mere effort to determine word definitions. Those can be found in the dictionary. The purpose of this judicial groping is to reconcile our legislative statutes with the needs of living men, to breathe life into them where they are lethargic, to quiet them when they become overviolent. In this fashion intelligent judges complement and ripen the necessarily poor efforts of the legislative branches of our government.

As Professor Thomas K. Finletter pointed out in discussing proposed legislation designed to bar private armies of Fascist organizations, "Where . . . the subject matter is not susceptible of exact definition, jurisprudence has always approved the use of general enactments which in effect are but declarations of policy accompanied by authorizations to the courts to complete the legislation."

At the same time, improvement in statute-making, a better understanding of the problems and greater preparation for remedy, less haste, less politics, less emotion, less self-advertising, less log-rolling, would produce more certain and less indefinite legislation.

Our approach to the subject of legislation should be scientific rather than political. Legislative service should be made a career. To insure better qualifications, legislators should be compelled to qualify by examinations. Service should be made attractive. Adequate compensation should be paid and terms lengthened. Generally, inducements should be offered to attract better men; the office should have greater dignity and honor, so that it may become an end and not, as at present, a means of obtaining further political advancement.

Legislators should be provided with adequate means for ascertaining public opinion. They should not be left to be influenced by private agencies, like the Gallup Institute of Public Opinion, however able and honest such agencies may appear to be. The government itself should set up agencies to poll public opinion and to make scientific surveys, as recently suggested at a conference of the National Municipal League. But this should be done in substitution of, not in addition to, existing government agencies, which in 1938 sent 135,000,000 questionnaires to be answered by American citizens.

There should be permanent governmental agencies for the investigation and control of propagandist and lobbying activities. We need a Pure Food and Drug Act for propaganda; and an effective one.

The Federal Government has already required the registration of foreign propagandists. Many states require lobby-

# LOOK AT THE LAW

ists to register. There should be registration and licensing requirements for domestic propagandists. A public relations counsel should report his activities, so that they may be confined to legitimate purposes. He should be licensed and held responsible for his undertakings and their logical consequences.

Radio broadcasting of legislative sessions might improve their tone; certainly wider popular education and enlightenment concerning the work of our legislatures might tend to awaken popular interest and make our legislators more susceptible to public interests and less amenable to private and political interests.

Special legislative investigating committees should be less political and less patronage-dispensing, less publicity-seeking and more fact-finding vehicles. In fact, the average special legislative fact-finding committee could be dispensed with entirely if the Legislative Council experiment adopted in Kansas in 1933, and since copied, according to *Current History,* in Illinois, Nebraska, Kentucky, Connecticut, Virginia and Michigan, became universal. The Kansas Legislative Council consists of legislators and research experts, who take and consider suggestions and needs for legislation, and report concerning their factual phases.

Improvement in legislative bill drafting is also essential. That task cannot be left to volunteers; special experience in such work is needed. Even trained lawyers are not necessarily good statutory draftsmen. Judge (formerly Dean) Clark said in a recent speech that throughout the twenty years that the American Bar Association was advocating reform in Federal Court procedure, the bill before Congress was a defective drafting job.

There should be liaison bodies to coordinate legislative, executive and judicial effort. Judicial councils and law revision commissions already are proving effective in co-

# LOOK AT THE LAW

ordinating and harmonizing statutes and judicial decisions, thereby avoiding conflict and uncertainty. The work of the New York Law Revision Committee should be duplicated in other States.

There should be greater popular support for these bodies, and there would be if there were greater public understanding of their functions.

If, by these methods, careless and ignorant legislation can be supplanted by studied statutes, and then coordinated with existing law, many of the uncertainties with which our judges must now deal will be eliminated. The need for substituting an intelligent judicial intent for a haphazard legislative one by forced judicial construction of language will be avoided. The necessity of twisting phrases to harmonize with previously existing statutory law will be obviated.

The precautions suggested in the preceding chapters will not only decrease judicial verbosity but should also rid our judicial law of the loose language that now breeds confusion. A more closely-knit structure will be built which will promote closer harmony and clearer thinking. These matters rest with our judges, and improvement in their personnel and character, as is later suggested, will promote certainty in the law they write into the books.

Unfortunately, when we have done these things, our law, like the glory of an April day, will still remain uncertain. But at that stage, uncertainty will be a virtue rather than a vice, for a measure of and ability to change is a mark of liability and progress. The law may not remain static. It must be freer to shake off the fetters of the past which, uncertain as the law is, still cling to its structure.

# CHAPTER IV

## *The Layman Says:*
## THE LAW IS TOO RIGID

*1.*

CONSIDER the seal. Not the aquatic, carnivorous mammal, but the legal seal.

Seals are of great antiquity. They date back to 2900 B.C. The seal was originally an impression made upon wax or wafer or some other tenacious substance capable of being impressed. The great lord of the manor may not have been able to write his name, but he had a distinctive heraldic device by which he was known. He impressed this as his signature upon the messages, the contracts, and the bonds which others wrote for him.

Without a writing and a seal, one could not sue upon a contract in the old English court. A written contract alone would not sustain an action. A mere signature was insufficient. A seal was the requisite mark.

However, as education undermined baronial ignorance and supremacy, judges came to recognize signatures as being of more importance than seals, and the rule that an unsealed written contract needed to be sealed to support an action was abrogated. Yet seals retained much of their importance in the common law of England, and the ancient practices were perpetuated by legal rules exalting sealed instruments.

So, for example, a contract under seal bound only those who signed and sealed it. A person who did not sign could not be sued on a contract under seal, as he could upon a

# LOOK AT THE LAW

contract not under seal, upon the theory that he was the undisclosed principal of the agent who signed it. A contract not under seal required a consideration to support it; a contract under seal required no consideration; the law said the seal imported a consideration and made proof of consideration unnecessary. Likewise, a sealed contract could not be modified or discharged by an unsealed agreement.

Through the years these rules persisted, though the seal itself degenerated from the impression of an individual mark or device upon wax to a round piece of red paper with some adhesive on its back, or a written, printed or typewritten scrawl consisting of brackets or parentheses, enclosing the word "Seal," or the mere letters "L. S.," meaning *locus sigilli*—the place of the seal.

The physical degeneration of the seal was accompanied by periodic expressions of judicial disdain. Our Chancellor Kent, in the early nineteenth century, recognized the fact that the seal was a mere survival of a ruder age, though, with the respect lawmen accord venerable institutions, he said the presence of the seal lent dignity to a document. Later a judge characterized this "dignity" as "factitious," and, of late years, it has become the common habit of American judges to deprecate the seal. "It has caused great inconvenience and injustice," said one judge. "It is arbitrary and unmeaning," said another. "It is a distinction made by technical law, unsustained by reason," said a third.

Yet our judges continued to apply the age-old rules and restrictions respecting seals to modern suitors until the late Justice Cardozo was moved to say: "The law will have cause for gratitude to the deliverer who will strike the fatal blow."

In one case a man denied liability on a contract, saying he had received nothing in exchange. The defendant said, "Oh, yes, you did get something. Look at the contract, it says: 'In consideration of the sum of One Dollar, lawful

# LOOK AT THE LAW

money of the United States, receipt whereof is hereby acknowledged.'"

The plaintiff: But I didn't get the dollar.
Judge Story (a famous United States Supreme Court Justice): Hush, hush, you can't say that.
Plaintiff: Why not?
Judge: Because there is a seal on the contract.
Plaintiff: What of it? I didn't get the dollar, or anything else, for that matter.
Judge: When there is a seal on the contract, consideration is conclusively presumed and you cannot be heard to deny it.
Plaintiff: What if there were no seal?
Judge: That would be different. Then you could be heard to deny that you received the dollar, and if you did not, as I believe you did not, I would set the contract aside.

Though Judge Story was dead and gone, the ancient precedent he had followed remained to plague suitors. And although in 1921 Judge Pound of the New York Court of Appeals had said that "the sealing of a contract is as often a mere circumstance as a deliberate solemn act and deed," as late as March, 1937, that Court still held that a man could revoke an option he had given if it was not under seal, but that if it was, he could not revoke it.

Thus the seal and its tenacious history illustrate the antithesis of uncertainty in the law—the judicial worship of certainty. By uncompromising adherence to precedents, the law is rendered immobile and rigid; and reactionary or unheeding judges permit it to break before they will let it bend.

Judicial adherence to precedents rests upon an effort to

# LOOK AT THE LAW

make the law certain and consistent—to combat its uncertainty by application of the rule of *stare decisis*, which requires judges to heed and follow prior judicial decisions where the facts are similar. The words, *stare decisis et non quieta movere*, translates into the rule and one of its reasons: "to adhere to precedents and not to unsettle things which are established." The canonization of this rule is found in the words of Sir James Mackintosh:

"There is not, in my opinion, in the whole compass of human affairs, so noble a spectacle, as that which is displayed in the progress of Jurisprudence; where we may contemplate the cautious and unwearied exertions of a succession of wise men through a long course of ages, withdrawing every case, as it arises, from the dangerous power of discretion, and subjecting it to inflexible rules; extending the dominion of justice and reason; and gradually contracting, within the narrowest possible limits, the domain of brutal force and of arbitrary will."

In a democratic system, we must have such a rule. The die is cast at the very outset. Shall we adopt the Greek system, where the king sat in judgment, transmitting the presumed judgment of the gods to the litigants before him, each case and each judgment standing by itself; or shall we adopt the English system of human judgment based on precedent? The basic conflict manifests itself in a variety of forms. What is the definition of the word "justice"? Is "justice" the equivalent of "right," or does it mean "equality"? Does "justice" require that the decision in every case be right, or does it merely require that it conform to the standard by which every man is treated? Is it satisfied if every man receives the same treatment as his neighbor; if, in thinking of his legal duty, as Stammler says, "he can still regard himself as his own neighbor"?

Are we to have a government of laws, or one of men? Are

## LOOK AT THE LAW

we to let ourselves be judged by caprice, however wise, or are we to depend upon rule, however fallible?

Do we want our law to be certain? Do we want to be able to pursue our courses knowing what the law is, or do we want to entrust our affairs to the chance or haphazard decision of a judge bound by no rule?

The answer to each query is obvious. And collectively they tally.

Of course we want the same treatment our neighbor receives; we would not be satisfied with less. Equality is one of the roots of a democratic system; conformity is the democratic definition of "right."

And we want to be ruled by laws, not by men. That, too, is one of the basic principles of our form of government.

And, manifestly, we want to know what the law is, for how else can we observe it? We want to know what we may and what we may not do. We want to know that we may freely pursue our inclinations in speech, in religious worship and in the pursuit of happiness, without hindrance through the whim of some official, however petty or exalted. We want no rule of bureaucracy, administrative or judicial.

For these are the indicia of rule by and for the people.

So we have no complaint when one judge, in announcing the law, follows the law as determined by his predecessor judges. Thus we obtain equality before the law—what we call justice: the same treatment our fellow citizens receive.

However, though the same treatment for one's case as for his neighbor's is a requisite of justice, it does not follow that, to attain justice, one must be dealt with as was his remote ancestor two hundred years ago.

Obviously, the rules that suited the decision of a lawsuit between men whose moldering bones have been dust for hundreds of years were more fitted to those times than to these. Yet astigmatic judges, with noses steeped in their yel-

# LOOK AT THE LAW

lowing precedents, apply an established judicial rule until it becomes a curse. They are like the musician who wrecked the harmony of the orchestra with a discordant note. When reproached by the conductor he pointed out the note on his score.

"Why, that's not a note," said the leader, "it's a dead fly."

"I knew it," replied the musician, "but it was there, so I played it."

The theory of certainty is overmaintained and produces a twin complaint, the complaint that the law is too rigid, too reactionary, too fixed, too unyielding. Why should we retain an unfair, an arbitrary, an anachronistic, indeed even a misleading or fraudulent rule, because somebody may have relied on it to mislead or defraud someone else? Knowing that Sir William Blackstone collated and construed the legal rules of human conduct of England for the benefit and advantage of the English landed gentry, and knowing that our early American judges, Marshall, Kent, Story and others, were enamored of these tenets of the reactionary English ruling classes, why should we let such outworn doctrines restrict the application of the revelations and reforms of later advanced legal and social philosophers?

The Associated Press quoted Supreme Court Justice Frankfurter as saying to his law school class, referring to the English legal custom against quoting from live authors: "That does not take into consideration that dead authors may be alive and live authors may be dead."

There need be nothing inherently objectionable in antiquity. Who of us does not benefit by a periodic taste of Plato and Aristotle? There is nothing amiss when a judge, in deciding in 1931 that an owner of land running to the high bank of the Missouri river was not the owner of land which was an accretion to the upland, relied upon the authority of one, the Roman Florentius, who wrote in the old Roman

# LOOK AT THE LAW

Law Digest, "In agris limitatis jus alludionis locum non habere constat; idque et Divius Pius constituit"—"In limited fields the right of accretion is certainly held to have no place; and the Divine [Emperor] Pius has so decreed."

There has been no change in modern conditions that renders this old rule objectionable, and it may still be applied.

But suppose, while driving your automobile, you collide with another car driven by Smith, and, as a result, Jones, a passenger in Smith's car, is hurt. Jones sues you for damages for the injuries he has sustained, but he doesn't sue Smith, the other driver, because Smith is a friend of his. Jones says the fault is yours; you say the fault is Smith's, or, in any event, that both you and Smith were at fault. Is there any good reason why you alone should be held liable because Jones sued you alone? Why, because in some remote day prior to the eighteenth century, the English courts laid down the technical rule that "one of several tort feasors has been held responsible for an injury, he has no right of contribution against the other tort feasors, although they were equally liable for the injury," should you have no right to make Smith pay his share of the damages? That rule might have sufficed in a day when unwitting accidents were few, and the law said that it would not interfere to help men who deliberately did others harm, even as between themselves. But it works obvious injustice in a day when unintended motor accidents furnish the greater part of our lawsuits.

Yet that harsh rule has been followed by our judges, even to the point of strictly interpreting liberalizing legislative statutes which have sought to avoid it.

We have mentioned the reluctance with which our modern and even our enlightened judges are abandoning the old technical rules that flowed from the inability of ancient knights to write their names and the consequent deification

# LOOK AT THE LAW

of their marks. Yet rules still survive that resulted from those ancient practices, though only legal research experts know that these archaic rules were born of the old seal practices.

For example, if a farmer, hurt by drought, cannot pay his feed bill, and the feed dealer says, "Bring that Holstein cow of yours around with her calf and I'll take them instead," and the farmer says, "O.K.," one would think that they had made a deal which the law would sustain. But no. The farmer delivers the cow and the feed merchant takes her. Then the farmer comes around with the calf and the feed dealer says: "I'm sorry, I've changed my mind. I won't go through with the deal. I want two cows and the calf."

The farmer says, "We made a deal, and I'll hold you to it."

The feed man says: "Pay your feed bill or I'll sue you for it."

The farmer goes to a lawyer, but the lawyer says that he can't do a thing to help him; that the feed dealer can sue and recover on his feed bill and the farmer can't stop him by pleading that he made a deal with him for payment and is perfectly willing to fulfill it.

"How come?" asks the farmer.

"Well," says the lawyer, "you agreed to settle your bill; that agreement is what the law calls an accord. But you didn't satisfy the bill. That's what the law calls a satisfaction. In this state an accord without a satisfaction is still not binding."

"But," says the farmer (if he knows enough), "I made a contract with him and a contract is binding. Suppose we'd put it in writing, would that have helped?"

"It wouldn't have made a bit of difference," answers the lawyer. "A contract for an accord is no defense to an action to recover the debt unless there has been satisfaction. That's

# LOOK AT THE LAW

one kind of contract that isn't binding unless you've gone through with it."

"Why not?" asks the farmer.

Maybe the lawyer knows. If he does, he is an exception. The exception will answer:

"Because during the time that contracts without a seal weren't recognized by the English courts, an English judge held such an arrangement as the farmer made was no defense to the creditor's suit. He did this because of the old seal rule. Later, in 1700, an English judge, not recognizing that the real reason for the decision was the absence of the seal, said it was the rule that 'an executory accord with a satisfaction is not a bar to an action.' Other English judges followed this statement as one of rule until, in 1797, another English judge looked into the matter and said he thought there was no basis for such a rule, but he hesitated, as he put it, to 'overthrow all the books.' So he passed the rule along and we still have it and apply it today, regardless of its lack of rhyme or reason."

There are many such apocryphal rules in the law; rules which grew, phrase by phrase, from obscure and fallacious beginnings. How futile it is to challenge such rules; reason has lain buried so long under a welter of repetition. Only now and then does a judge turn the penetrating ray of suspicion upon their parentage and reveal their bastard birth.

The United States Supreme Court did this when it recently reexamined the bases for the hundred-year-old rule that the Federal courts will hold to their own precedents and disregard State laws and, as a consequence, rejected the rule. A State Court judge traced to its sources the repeated judicial statement that a ten-year limitation applied to an action against directors of a corporation, and found that, logically, it should be limited to six years.

If Mr. Justice Black of the United States Supreme Court

## LOOK AT THE LAW

is not ultimately acclaimed a great judge, at least he should prove to be a much-needed, skeptical one. He has already refused to be awed by the refinements of judicial technique or by the bulwark of judicial agreement upon matters that admit of challenge. So, he pried away encumbering precedents to reveal that the judiciary and not its makers extended the protection of the 14th Amendment to corporations, that the existing rule originated in a mere oral dictum and had no sanctity except that of judicial iteration for half a century. Justice Black's attack upon the devices by which, with court approval, patentees have extended the life of patents beyond their statutory limits, his challenge of the fictions which the courts have substituted for the facts in rate-making, are also examples of a healthy juristic incredulity of accepted formulae, and now begin to find repetition in legislative and other quarters.

But, meanwhile, judicial recognition of these and other futile precedents goes on apace.

For example, within recent years the New York Court of Appeals, a liberal and enlightened court, stood on precedent to deny relief to a corporation which sued to recover the money it had paid for worthless mortgage certificates. The court's decision was placed upon the ground that the plaintiff had failed to send the certificates to the defendants when demanding its money back, before starting the action. It had, it is true, written the defendants offering to return the certificates if the defendants would return its money. But it had not actually and physically sent the certificates around to the defendants. There was no doubt that the defendants would have refused the certificates if they had been physically tendered; they never asked for them or offered to return the plaintiff's money; in fact, everybody conceded that the certificates were practically worthless, anyway. Nevertheless, the plaintiff was thrown out of court

91

# LOOK AT THE LAW

after a long, costly and delayed litigation because the defendants cited precedents that held that a plaintiff could not recover, in such a case, without having made a physical tender of the property purchased.

In another recent case, the receiver of one corporation sued the officers of another corporation on a note made by the latter and endorsed by them. The defendant endorsers claimed the receiver had failed to present the note for payment and to protest it for nonpayment. They conceded that they knew all about the note; they had signed it, not only as endorsers but as officers of the corporation; they knew it was outstanding and conceded that it would not have been paid by the corporation had it been presented for payment. Nevertheless, the judges said that, under the precedents, the defendants could not be held liable, because of the rule that lack of formal presentment and protest of the note prevents recovery from endorsers on a note.

The Court added that "if exceptions are made to fit particular circumstances, the purposeful rigidity of the law is frittered away."

*2.*

Blind adherence to outworn precedents comes from a variety of causes. Academically speaking, lower court judges have little option; it is for their superiors, the higher court judges, to change existing judicial law, if it is to be changed. So, a lower court judge said frankly that he was acting reluctantly in refusing a taxpayer a refund of $75,000 on his tax claim because he (the taxpayer) had signed the necessary form of protest only once and not twice, as the law required. The judge said he had no choice in the matter; that he was bound by a ruling made by the higher court a number of years before.

Practically, however, lower court judges often manage to

# LOOK AT THE LAW

reject precedents when they are so minded, by taking refuge behind the facts.

So, when Mrs. Jones sues her husband for support and maintenance and Jones' counsel comes into court behind a barricade of law books containing decisions holding that a husband need not support a wife who unreasonably refuses to share his bed, the judge need follow those precedents and deny Mrs. Jones alimony only if he finds that her refusal to inhabit the connubial couch was "unreasonable." If the judge doesn't want to follow the precedent, if he thinks the rule too harsh in the case of the pulchritudinous Mrs. Jones, all he needs to do is to find that her refusal to sleep with her spouse was not "unreasonable," that Jones' bed manners were bad, or worse. Once the judge has found that Mrs. Jones' refusal to cohabit with her husband was factually justified, the rule of legal precedents becomes nil in the case of Jones v. Jones.

A decision on the facts is an effectual barrier to a precedent in the law. The practice is common for judges to refer the issues of fact in a case to the jury or to decide the issue of fact for the defendant instead of dismissing the plaintiff's complaint on the law. Then if the jury finds for the defendant, or since the judge has found for the defendant on the facts, the judge need have no further concern with the legal precedents the defendant's counsel has set before him.

The principal reason that many lower court judges follow precedents more or less blindly and vaguely, may be found in the training of the judicial personnel.

Legal education in this country has been subjected to much proper criticism. Many of our law schools, and particularly those in large cities which offer only part-time instruction in afternoon and evening sessions, are unable to teach the law student anything more than what judges in the past have held the law to be. Why they held as they did; what they should have held; the manner of, and reasons for, the decisions; their historic, social and economic background; their relationship to existing customs and mores—all are untouched and unsung. Indeed, many of the students, by training, education and background, would be wholly unprepared for, and unreceptive to, any such homilies. They would not appreciate either their significance or their purport. They would consider such instruction a waste of time. They want to know what the law is in their States, not what it should be, as quickly and as cheaply as possible, so that they may use their knowledge to start making a living as quickly as they can. The law schools try to meet this demand by telling them what judges have done in the past in cases that have come before them. This glorifies the practical, the actual, which is what a practical lawyer needs to make money.

Faulty and insufficient legal education is also the consequence of poorly regulated law schools which, run for profit, train their students inadequately. It may also be ascribed to States that have low scholastic requirements for admission to law schools and which have insufficient scholastic and legal requirements for admission to the bar.

The necessary consequence of such instruction of the law student is a bar which believes the law to be an entity consisting largely of judicial precedents and of statutory dictates and restrictions. The lawyer looks for a case in point, and in the search, the copious footnotes culled from the social sciences with which Justice Brandeis interlarded his opinions seem so much trivia.

Lawyers with such background of scholastic and legal training, or lack of it, are the nucleus of our lower court judges. The selection of the latter is not generally based on examination in general or legal education or in legal ex-

# LOOK AT THE LAW

perience. Too frequently it is based only upon political availability. The result is that many of our lower court judges are taken from the more practical and less academically inclined of our lawyers; those who conceive the law as little else than a legal bricklayer's structure built of precedents, requiring only additions that will fit its chinks and cavities and will conform to its present structure.

But rigid adherence to precedent is not confined to these judges. There are others, men with no lack of general and legal education who either overstress the need for certainty or underestimate the need for change. These judges are reactionary in their concepts of law and life and have surrounded these concepts with veneers of crystallized definitions.

Word worship, Frank and other legal philosophers point out, precludes thought and restricts action. "New definitions of 'liberty' and 'property' coined by the Supreme Court in the nineties," writes Mason on Brandeis, "were . . . the means . . . of the judiciary's becoming substantially 'a perpetual censor upon all legislation of the States.'" Definitions of property, dictated by social and economic practices of the nineteenth century, unless discarded, make the law a straitjacket for social, economic and political progress. And judicial progress is unnecessarily slow when it encounters the need for a change of accepted judicial dogma.

The clash between physical, mental and moral safeguards of the citizen and feudal-born concepts of property and property rights illustrates the tortoiselike process of mutation in the social law. The judicial paths of minimum wage laws, workmen's compensation acts, bills limiting hours of labor for men, women and children, and child labor laws, have been unjustifiedly tortuous and weary.

In 1907, Judge Gray of New York was denying the right of the legislature "under the guise of a labor law, arbitrarily,

## LOOK AT THE LAW

as here, to prevent an adult female citizen from working any time of day that suits her." It took the court eight years before it confessed, in reversing its stand, that it had not known eight years before that "night work in factories is widely and substantially injurious to the health of women." Even after that, in 1917, former Justice Sutherland was saying, in rejecting liberal legislation on a basis of old precedents: "In the old days it was the liberty of person, the liberty of speech, the freedom of religious worship, which were principally threatened. Today it is the liberty to order the detail of one's daily life for oneself—the liberty to do honest and profitable business—the liberty to seek honest and remunerative investment that are in peril."

In 1938, a New Jersey Vice Chancellor, in denying the right to picket in a labor case, declared: "There are two classes of constitutional rights: (1) absolute rights, and (2) qualified rights, which latter are more in the nature of privileges. Absolute rights are the inherent rights of the citizen, sometimes referred to as natural or human rights. These rights preceded government, are inherent in the very nature of man himself, were not given, but declared, by the Constitution, and are inalienable."

After giving examples of what he considered natural rights, the Vice Chancellor concluded that "they are essentially property rights which it is the duty of government to protect."

Finally he defined qualified rights: "Qualified rights, or privileges, are those granted and created by the Constitution. They did not precede government and they are not inalienable, but are subject to forfeiture." And then he said: "Among these qualified constitutional rights, which are more in the nature of privileges than rights in the strict sense of the word, is the so-called right of free speech, a privilege often confused with absolute rights."

# LOOK AT THE LAW

To some extent, judicial progress must be slow and conservative. Even the most enlightened judge cannot cast the law loose from its moorings and embark it upon a sea of personal opinion, however desirable this may seem in a given case. Louis Stark, newspaperman, in a recent book tells the story of the attempt made to have the late Justice Holmes interfere to prevent the execution of Sacco and Vanzetti. Judge Holmes, according to Stark, frankly expressed his opinion that Sacco and Vanzetti had not had a fair trial. But that, said the Justice, was not enough to give a Federal judge jurisdiction.

"If I listened to you any more," said the Justice, "I would do it. I must not do it," he continued as he turned away.

Nevertheless, the law cannot be kept inflexible. It rests on shifting sands. As one legal philosopher put it, it is "common conviction." It is the expression of the popular demand, and the popular demand shifts with every changing tide, as the public conscience is illumined by rays of education, advanced thought or scientific discovery.

One day the law upholds the husband who beats his wife when she fails to obey him; the next day it condemns him. In one country it jails the bigamist; in the next it praises him. A man may be a criminal in one day; under the same circumstances, he would be esteemed a hero in another. In one era a man is authorized to kill another if he is attacked, else he may be branded a coward; in another, the law may require him to retreat under penalty of being considered a murderer. Early colonial statutes branded unwed mothers; fascistic governments subsidize them; and a recent American court decision recognized the mother's right to support by her illegitimate son. The precedents of one day will not long suffice for the next.

"*Stare decisis*," said Justice Brandeis, "is ordinarily a wise rule of action. But it is not a universal, inexorable command.

# LOOK AT THE LAW

The rule as announced must be deemed tentative. For the many and varying facts to which it will be applied cannot be foreseen."

There is, therefore, a growing tendency to relax the rigidities of rule.

Higher court judges to whom is entrusted the power to discard anachronistic judicial precedents are becoming more change-conscious. While they have been influenced to some extent by the researches and expositions of our legal philosophers, they probably have been moved, within recent years, far more strongly by the New Deal drives which has translated philosophical concepts into pulsating statutes.

The drive on the United States Supreme Court has not only been successful in changing personnel but it has changed the high judicial mores. Physical evidence of the first is found in the substitution of Justices Black and Reed for Justices Van Devanter and Sutherland; of the second, in the transition which their written opinions disclosed in Chief Justice Hughes and Justice Roberts. Executive and legislative pressure was justified by the charge, corroborated by the facts, that judicial realization of economic, social and political evolution was lagging and that its change was in too slow a tempo.

Today even lower court judges make gestures of liberality. County Judge Fitzgerald of Brooklyn, New York, in permitting a district attorney to inspect a grand jury's minutes, a practice charged to be contrary to precedent, said: "If precedents stand in the way of State and Federal agencies against the proper and effective pursuance of their duties, the precedents must be knocked down."

Nevertheless, a lower court judge must be discreet in thus evidencing no fear of the appellate courts, as one trial judge readily discovered. He had said: "A real judge with courage and intellect will set aside and hold for nothing decisions of an appellate court when they are wrong." Incidentally, he quoted from Shakespeare. This gave the appellate court the opportunity for a last word, and in reversing the judgment, said: "We have great admiration for the English bard, but feel constrained to hold that the maunderings of Falstaff cannot take the place of the Oklahoma judiciary and statutes. We feel the learned trial court is a better authority on *A Midsummer-Night's Dream* than he is on the laws and decisions of this State."

*3.*

In the quest for certainty in the law, a system has been evolved which results in a mead of inflexibility and a measure of reaction in adapting the stately processes of law to the scurrying wants of a changing civilization. And this is necessarily so, since there is need for delicate balance between these elements that no human being could adequately maintain at all times. If the law becomes too flexible, the opponents of change cry that it has become too uncertain; if it becomes too unyielding, the proponents of progress term it bourbonistic. Yet both sides must recognize that the judicial system is charged with the same germs of struggle between "justice" and "mercy" that manifest themselves elsewhere in our democratic system, and that neither the judge nor the law is primarily responsible for its symptoms.

The primary fault lies with the legislature. Under our system, the legislature is the direct voice of the people. It is periodically and frequently elected, in order that it may express current thought. It is supposed to act quickly in response to the public need, so quickly that, at one end, the Constitution and, at the other, the courts are provided to supply it with needed drags and anchors.

If the judges lag in changing outmoded judicial rules, the

# LOOK AT THE LAW

legislature can and should act promptly. Yet even after the courts call attention to the impropriety of established rules of law, the legislatures often do nothing about them for long periods of time. In New York, for example, Professor Walsh of New York University Law School pointed out a provision of law concerning title to real property that remained, though outmoded for a century, without legislative attention—the subject lacked emotional or popular appeal.

The hesitancy of the legislature to amend or repeal its own statutes makes legislative incursions into the fields of the social sciences dangerous, for when statutory enactments encroach upon natural laws, they tend to make them rigid and inflexible. When statutes interfere with the natural operation of such laws as those of supply and demand, there must be constant legislative vigilance if rigidity of positive law is not to produce economic catastrophe.

However, though the legislature must bear its share of responsibility, the judicial tug of war between the need for certainty and the need for change can never be settled by rule or regulation, for it is the rule which is the subject of the contest. The best that anyone can do is to effect a measure of temporary balance from time to time, and for this we can only look to the intelligence and good judgment of our judges. The task is a superhuman one, and the best of our judges find it difficult to determine when to stick to static rule and when to change.

Justice Cardozo, quoting Dean Pound, put the judicial problem thus: "Law must be stable and yet it cannot stand still. Here is the great antimony confronting us at every turn. Rest and motion, unrelieved and unchecked, are equally destructive. The law, like human kind, if life is to continue, must find some path of compromise. Two distinct tendencies, pulling in different directions, must be harnessed together and made to work in unison."

# LOOK AT THE LAW

The judge must be able to discern the changing conditions and to know the state of the public need. But a fertile public mind is also a primary requisite. A judge cannot anticipate, he cannot lead; he must follow. He cannot mold public opinion; he cannot educate it. Nor can he combat prevalent heresies. He must remain cloistered and unassuming. He may not be presumptuous or daring.

But there must also be judicial willingness for change. Legal and judicial training tend to deify certainty. Even capable judges tend to permit precedent and usage to weigh too heavily in the balance, while inert judges often lack the courage or the energy to take the needed forward step. They content themselves with the statement that it is for the legislature to change the law, and let it go at that, while they follow the beaten path.

It is an interesting comment in this connection that Chief Justice Crane, an enlightened and courageous jurist, participated in the decision of the New York Court of Appeals applying the outmoded rule of seals, referred to earlier in this chapter, although years before he had written an article in the *Columbia Law Review* deprecating such continued adherence. Yet, when the question came up in his own court, as he later confessed, he lacked "the nerve to follow up what I had written as a Supreme Court judge." He justified himself by saying that by that time members of the New York legislature must have read his article (a perhaps unwarranted assumption) and they could have changed the law had they wanted it changed. (Incidentally, they have since done so.)

Methodical judges tend to serve outworn precedents; they "sacrifice life to logic and become the slaves of their own abstractions." Class-conscious judges uphold property-right precedents with no regard to changing social mores (and because of the common-law heritage, precedents are

# LOOK AT THE LAW

strongest in those branches of the law which affect property rights). Reactionary judges void liberal legislative statutes by injection of their personal philosophies into a constitution termed written, but which, in fact, is largely judge-made and unwritten.

Some few remaining judges deny that judges make the law; they hold to the outworn alibi that judges merely enunciate the law. A multitude of reasons give a hollow ring to this evasion. The power to set aside legislative statutes as unconstitutional is judge-made law; it is not expressed in the Constitution but has been assumed by the courts under their own declarations of power. It is true that where there is a statute, change is for the legislature; theoretically the courts are powerless to interfere. Actually, judges outlegislate the legislatures under rules of statutory construction. But where the law is judge-made—where it is to be found in a decision rendered by Lord Thurlow, or by Lord Ellenborough—why need we wait for another Lord to deliver us from it?

Incompetent and inert judges clutch avidly at the rule of precedents. They cannot decide a case by resort to reason and principle, their legal understanding is mechanical; they must find a case in point. Together with reactionary judges, they overstress and abuse the rule of *stare decisis*. They refuse to follow the liberal and proper view that a former decision is a precedent only if it was right and only if its later application effects justice. They seek to uphold the "majesty of the law" without realizing that society's aim is not abstract perfection of legal process but a practical law enforcement that achieves rationalization and balance.

And yet it must be recognized that our system of check and balance requires a measure of judicial reaction to neutralize the emotional and impulsive tendencies which come from the legislature. Though there may be impatience with

# LOOK AT THE LAW

temporary quagmires, these should not be permitted to encourage anti-democratic methods and practices.

In discussing technicalities in a later chapter, we will point out the need for judicial realism. At present, it must be obvious that the twin problems of uncertainty and formality in the law require Solomons for their mediation; that the competent fulfillment of their tasks requires not only well-trained judges but intelligent ones. It must be apparent that we need (1) higher standards of legal education, and (2) better and less political selection of judges, to the end that the most capable men may be selected for the arduous tasks which confront them.

Capability in a judge presupposes intelligence; it must also include liberality and flexibility in thought and purpose. The late Justice Cardozo quoted a remark of Chesterton's to the effect that the most important thing about a man is his philosophy. And he added: "The more I reflect about a judge's work, the more I am impressed with the belief that this, if not true for everyone, is true at least for judges."

It is not enough for our judges to hold that damages for nervous shock unaccompanied by physical contact may now be recovered, in contravention of formerly accepted precedents, because medical science can now appreciate the tangibility of neurological injury and can guard against imposture. It does not suffice to hold that an automobile has become such a dangerous instrument that a manufacturer is liable for a defective wheel even if he did not manufacture it or know that it was defective, in violation of ancient judicial precedents. Our judges must go beyond these comparative trifles. They must rearrange their underlying social, economic and political doctrines; they must free themselves from the strangulation of accepted definitions. They can no longer take postulates for granted as though they were geometric or arithmetic certainties.

# LOOK AT THE LAW

It is not sufficient for our judges to realize that feudal precedents based upon the *droit de seigneur* will not deny a factory worker damages from her seducer because he owns the factory. They must begin to inquire whether the factory worker may not sue to restrain the factory owner from closing his factory and thereby arbitrarily terminating the employee's right to work. They must readjust their definitions of trespass, of ownership of property; they can no longer approach their judicial problems from the standpoint of a laissez faire philosophy.

Our judges must realize that, as Miraglia says, "the social theory of law is not separable from the juristic," that juristic theory cannot be built as a structure of "empty, abstract formulae," lacking "concrete and content," separated from life and the conditions of existence at a "bare mathematical form." Instead, they need to appreciate, as President Roosevelt recently wrote, that "the law is one of the living forces that guide organized society"; that it "cannot remain static but must be constantly molded to the requirements of passing generations and the changes in our social and economic structure."

We need courageous judges who are not awed by the legal cenotaphs of the historic past; judges who are unafraid of taking new and untried paths and who find them by impatiently brushing aside legal foliage and trampling down legal underbrush. Criticism of such judges by legal fundamentalists for ignorance of, or disrespect for, legal technique is a testimonial to judicial initiative so rare that one should gladly follow it and take the risk of error. We have enough examples of judicial reaction; we can run the risk of its antithesis.

# CHAPTER V

## *The Layman Says:*
## THE LAW IS TOO TECHNICAL

*1.*

THE LAW says that a man who breaks into a building is a burglar. The statement is simple enough, and to the layman seems susceptible of but one construction. But now look at the by-play going on in a courtroom:

A policeman hails his prisoner before a judge.

"What is the charge?" asks the judge.

"Burglary," answers the policeman.

"How do you plead, guilty or not guilty?" asks the judge.

"I move to dismiss the complaint," the prisoner's lawyer breaks in.

"Upon what ground?"

"Upon the ground that the complaint charges my client with breaking into a railroad car and that is no crime under the law," the defendant's counsel answers.

"Why not?" asks the judge.

"Because the statute refers to breaking into a building and a railroad car is no building," quibbles the lawyer.

What is the judge to do in this dilemma? If the defendant has broken into a railroad car with intent to steal, he ought to go to jail. On the other hand, if a building is an immovable structure, the judge cannot supply defects in a criminal statute to make a crime out of something the legislature has not expressly defined to be a crime. For the protection of our innocent citizenry, criminal statutes must be kept within the strictest limits.

Leaving this quandary for a moment, let us observe the

# LOOK AT THE LAW

next case. A defendant is charged in an indictment with stealing a pair of shoes. The prosecution produces the shoes which a policeman testifies were taken from the fleeing prisoner. They are marked in evidence.

Defendant's counsel takes the policeman for cross-examination.

"This is the pair of shoes you took from the prisoner?"

"Yes, sir."

"And the pair of shoes the defendant is charged with stealing?"

"Yes, sir."

"You recognize them?"

"Yes, sir."

"No doubt about their being the very pair?"

"Yes, sir."

"Now hand me the right shoe."

The policeman complies.

"Now the left."

The policeman looks at the remaining shoe, hesitates and then mumbles:

"There is no left; they're both rights."

"I move to dismiss, your Honor," says the prisoner's counsel. "We are charged with stealing a pair of shoes but two rights do not make a pair."

What is the judge to do with this obvious technicality, this quibble? If he sustains it, the law is cheated and made ineffectual. If he overrules it, he must violate the rule that a criminal indictment is to be construed strictly so that a man may not be convicted of a crime with which he has not been charged.

The conscientious judge ponders his problem in somewhat this fashion:

"The defendant ought to be jailed, if guilty. But if I break the rules or ignore the precedents in this case, it will

# LOOK AT THE LAW

stand as a precedent for further and continued infringements upon the rights of defendants until we find ourselves convicting the innocent. Is it better to let this guilty defendant go free and let the legislature fix the law, or to stretch my conscience to convict this defendant?"

How the judge solves his personal problem, despite our system of rule and precedent, depends on the judge and his bent. Return, now, to the case of the intruder who broke into the railroad car and whose lawyer moved to dismiss because the statute refers only to a building.

"Motion denied," says the judge.

"Upon what ground, your Honor?" asks the disappointed lawyer. "Upon the ground that a railroad car is a building," says the judge.

"But the dictionary does not say so," objects the lawyer.

"I don't look to the dictionary. We let the dictionary look to us," retorts the judge. "A railroad car is a building within the meaning of the statute; in my opinion the legislature intended it to be."

Thus, by the sophistries of statutory construction, to which we have made reference in a previous chapter, a Nebraska judge holds the prisoner in such a case, while an Arkansas judge, more concerned with the sanctity of rule, frees him. In consequence of the same struggle, a tent in Massachusetts and a corncrib in Iowa become buildings; and elsewhere, a partitioned or fenced-off space within a building is likewise defined as a building.

Thus we find a judge who frees a horse thief upon proof that he stole a gelding and the argument that a gelding is something less than the horse mentioned in the statute or the indictment. And we see a Missouri court set aside a conviction for rape because the indictment ends with the words that the act had been committed "against the peace and dignity of State" omitting the necessary article "the" be-

# LOOK AT THE LAW

fore the word "State." What may we say of the law when the thief we mentioned in the beginning of this chapter is turned out because he had stolen two right shoes instead of the pair of shoes mentioned in the indictment?

These are not exaggerations; they are typical of daily instances of unnecessary judicial blessing of technicalities that survive from a day when the penalty for crime conviction was so severe that judges were hard put to it to let technical offenders escape the dire fate of deportation or death.

The field of statutory construction is rife with technicalities, and with varying and contradictory results. When justice beckoned, one judge found a jackass to be a horse, while another judge said that jackasses were cattle in the legislative minds. Even the United States Supreme Court caviled with its conscience, in one case, in finding that a vessel on the Great Lakes was on the legislative "high seas."

Of course, it is not truly a question of what the legislative intent was, but rather what the court *thinks* the legislative intent was or what it should have been, that determines the result in these matters. Or it may be the judge's bias or leaning; his notion of what the particular result should be, based upon his notion of right and wrong; his judicial balancing of the equities, that determines his disposition of these technicalities.

For example, a defendant was charged with driving an automobile while intoxicated. The defendant proved he had been taking a drug upon a physician's prescription and that, inadvertently, he indulged in an overdose which intoxicated him. The court said that while the statute referred only to intoxication and while the defendant was doubtless intoxicated, the legislature meant voluntary intoxication; that since the defendant had taken an intoxicating drug into his system because he had to, he was not guilty of a crime.

In a recent case in the United States Supreme Court, the

## LOOK AT THE LAW

defendants were charged with smuggling and concealing alcohol. They were convicted on the testimony of Federal agents who testified to conversations of defendants they had overheard by tapping telephone wires. The defendants appealed to the Supreme Court, urging that Congress had ruled that no "person" should tap telephone wires and disclose what was overheard. The Government argued that Congress had intended that the word "person" should not include a Government agent; the defendants argued that by using the word "person" Congress intended to include everybody, even Government agents.

The majority of the Supreme Court held with the defendants and reversed the conviction. Justice Sutherland voted to sustain it. Apparently, the court divided on the definition of "person." Actually, they differed on the morality of the practice of wire-tapping, as the opinion of the Justices plainly indicated. The majority, including the known liberals, said: "For years, controversy has raged with respect to the morality of the practice of wire-tapping by officers to obtain evidence. It has been the view of many that the practice involves a grave wrong. In the light of these circumstances, we think another well-recognized principle ... leads to the application of the statute as it is written so as to include within its sweep Federal officers as well as others."

Justice Sutherland, dissenting, said: "I think the word 'person' ... does not include an officer of the Federal Government actually engaged in the detection of crime. . . . The decision just made will necessarily have the effect of enabling the most depraved criminals to further their criminal plans. . . ."

In some States (Alabama, Georgia, Vermont, among others) movie theater "bank nights" are held to violate the various constitutional and statutory provisions against "lotteries." In other States (California, Iowa, New York, among others) they are held lawful. Although the decisions apparently turn on what the judges think of the technical question of the presence or absence of "consideration to the operator of the game," the only way of reconciling the varying opinions concerning the same legal technicality is by understanding that the real bases of the decisions are the judges' estimates of the desires of the people or their paternalistic notions of whether "bank nights" are good or bad for the populace.

Technical differences and difficulties are bound to arise in construing statutes. No legislative enactment can avoid them.

This is particularly true in the precincts of criminal law, where, when he is fighting for life or liberty, the ingenuity of the criminal's lawyer knows no bounds, legal, ethical or moral. Here, the lawyer seeks to free his client, guilty though he may be, by resort to every available technicality.

We have had such examples in previous pages, and other cases are to be found in any law report.

When a defendant's guilt rests upon a technical violation of a criminal statute, the use of technicalities to evade it is not only common but is condoned. This is particularly true when the defendant's guilt is more technical than actual. Take, as an example, the crime of statutory rape. Because of the necessary theory that below a certain age a girl is incapable of legal consent, a man who has sexual intercourse with a girl under a prescribed statutory age is guilty of rape. This is so, whether the defendant knew the girl's age, whether she herself knew it, whether she consented to the act, whether she was of previous chaste character and, generally, whether or not the crime was committed through ignorance or mistake. Obviously, such a rule can prove to be a mere technicality in consequence of which a perfectly

# LOOK AT THE LAW

decent boy might be liable to a considerable jail sentence, loss of his citizenship and a world of other severe consequences. Imagine a technical rule of law condemning a man to a five-year jail sentence for having had sexual intercourse with a girl, with her consent, the day before her eighteenth birthday, while there would be no such consequence the day after! Imagine such a result where a man has voluntary intercourse with a prostitute living in a disorderly house, who turns out to be less than the statutory age. No one will be surprised when such statutes are construed in an effort to avoid their rigors.

Technical differences in the construction of civil statutes are of daily occurrence.

Take a recent civil case involving a dispute between two liquor dealers, each of whom wanted to operate a liquor store within 1,500 feet of the other in New York City, even though New York State has a liquor law which prohibits two retail liquor stores within that distance "on the same street or avenue." One man had his store at 398 Fourth Avenue just south of Thirty-second Street. The other had his at 2 Park Avenue, just north of Thirty-second Street. Park Avenue and Fourth Avenue both run north and south. Park Avenue starts north from Thirty-second Street where Fourth Avenue ends.

Four members of the court held that since one store was on a street called "Park Avenue," while the other was on a street called "Fourth Avenue," the stores could be within 1,500 feet of each other and the law did not apply. They admitted that Park Avenue was a mere continuation of Fourth Avenue, but held that since the Board of Aldermen of the City of New York had said that one street was to be known by one name and one by another, they were different streets in law though not, perhaps, in fact. They pointed out that the 1,500 feet provision was easily evaded anyway,

## LOOK AT THE LAW

for example, by turning a street corner, so they cut a legal corner.

A dissenting judge said that "difference in nomenclature" did not alter the factual situation; that a street by any other name was still the same street. He called the other judges' attention to a case they themselves had decided, holding that the premises known as 50 Union Square, located within 1,500 feet of other premises located and known as 52 Fourth Avenue, could not support two liquor stores. Whereupon the majority of the court retorted that Fourth Avenue runs through Union Square and that premises known as 50 Union Square are also known as 207 Fourth Avenue, leaving the two liquor stores on the same street.

It is interesting to note that behind this court controversy was the fact that Park Avenue started at 32nd Street only by a legal fiction. For many years it had started at 34th Street, but the owners of the property at 32nd Street, who felt that the address "2 Park Avenue" had a trade value, induced the Board of Aldermen of the City of New York to call the last two blocks of Fourth Avenue, the first two blocks of Park Avenue. Then, in a litigation with the man whose property at 34th Street had for years been known as 2 Park Avenue, the court decided that if the Board of Aldermen said Fourth Avenue was Park Avenue, it was Park Avenue, even if it was Fourth Avenue.

An almost humorous example of technical statutory construction occurred in Canada when two women schoolteachers refused to pay a house painter. The house painter filed a lien against their house. Through their lawyer, the schoolteachers moved to vacate the lien upon the ground that though the work had been completed November 14th, the lien had not been filed until December 15th, and they pointed out to the judge that the statute required the lien to be filed within thirty days after completion of the work.

# LOOK AT THE LAW

Whereupon the house painter's lawyer argued that the lien was validly filed because George VI, not Edward VIII, was King of England. He proved his point thus: King Edward abdicated December 10, 1936. George VI succeeded him. The new King's birthday was December 14th. Under the law, the King's birthday is a legal holiday. Likewise, under the law, anything that must be done on a holiday may be legally done the next day. Therefore, since his client's lien had to be filed on December 14th, and that day, being the new King's birthday, was a holiday, the lien could be filed on December 15th. The judge sustained the lien.

2.

But it is not only in the field of statutory construction that we encounter technicalities. The whole structure of the law is rife with them. In the domain of judge-made, substantive law the underlying struggle is manifested by the struggle between uncertainty and rigidity, as we have seen in previous chapters. On the administrative side, the law is shot with technicalities that produce "uncertainty, delay and expense and above all the injustice of deciding cases upon points of practice which are the mere etiquette of justice," according to Dean Pound of the Harvard Law School. Or, as Elihu Root put it, "Justice is entangled in a net of form."

The ubiquity of technicalities in the administration of our criminal law has held it up to public scorn. Applications for mistrials in criminal cases, motions in arrest of judgment, reversals of convictions of notorious criminals because of technical errors in the conduct of the prosecution, are of common occurrence. Examples are to be found throughout these pages. Here, two will suffice.

There is a rule of law that a man cannot twice be placed

## LOOK AT THE LAW

in jeopardy for the same offense, which means that having been once acquitted, he cannot be tried again, however guilty he may be.

Andrew Dowling was indicted and tried for having "burglariously entered a freight car . . . and stealing . . . therefrom." After the prosecution's evidence was in, his counsel moved to strike out the count for burglary. The judge granted this motion. Then he moved to strike out the charge of stealing, but the judge denied this application. After the jury convicted him of larceny, he appealed. The appellate judges held that since the prisoner was indicted for burglary and larceny in a single count in the indictment, the judge could not strike out the burglary charge without striking out the larceny charge, and since he refused to strike out the larceny charge, legally the burglary charge remained in the indictment, even though he said he had struck it out. The legal consequence was that when the jury convicted the defendant of larceny only, they were impliedly acquitting him of the charge of burglary and that having once been acquitted of burglary, he could not be tried again for the same offense, under the double jeopardy rule.

Though the court held he could be tried again for larceny, this was a futile gesture, because they were then engaged in reversing his conviction for larceny and it was obvious that the defendant could no longer be convicted at all.

There is another historic rule, grown out of centuries of persecution, that the accused is entitled to confront and to be confronted by his accusers. This rule has been enlarged by statutes which require that in a criminal case a defendant must be present in court during his trial or his conviction is invalidated.

Like many beneficent rules, this protection has been refined by technicalities to points of absurdity that jeopardize

# LOOK AT THE LAW

the very rule itself. As late as 1936, an appellate court reversed a conviction in New York because the defendant who had been charged with arson was not present in court when the jury, while considering the case, returned to the courtroom and asked that the testimony of a witness be read to it. It appeared that before the jury had retired a second time, someone had called the judge's attention to the fact that the defendant was not present, though his lawyer was. The judge turned to the lawyer and asked if he waived the presence of the defendant during the rereading of the testimony. He did so. The appellate court held that the court rule would not permit his counsel to waive his presence; that he had to be present even if his presence in no wise affected what was occurring. The court of final resort met this technicality by saying that the rule applied only in murder cases, since the defendant could plead guilty in any other case and could waive his right to a trial, and that if he could waive his right to a trial he could waive his right to be present at the trial.

"Though the defects in our administration of the criminal law are more striking and have attracted more attention, the conditions as regards the administration of the civil law are scarcely less satisfactory," says Willoughby in his *Principles of Judicial Administration*. Various analyses produce varying criticisms in which the phrase "maze of technicalities" is by no means absent. And the phrase is no exaggeration.

A civil defendant never hesitates to evade service of a summons, to challenge the validity of its service, to claim the complaint is insufficient and to ask for its dismissal on technical grounds, to seek to move the action from a State to a Federal court, to obtain extensions of time to answer, to require plaintiffs to serve bills of particulars, to take depositions of nonresident witnesses, to discover and inspect books

# LOOK AT THE LAW

and records — to mention only a few of many procedural complications. Every practice motion means delay until the matter can be heard and decided, each one offers an opportunity for appeal, each successful appeal means delay and expense. Before a plaintiff's case can be reached for trial, a reluctant defendant can tie the litigation into such a snarl of preliminary delay and expense that a plaintiff's patience and purse may be readily exhausted.

There are no bounds to the persistence of a defending suitor or to the ingenuities of his lawyer. The hallowed jury of one's peers, the hallmark of liberty, is favored by defendants when the jury calendar is far behind the nonjury calendar, while a desire for speedy trial is manifested by defendants when the plaintiff's witnesses become missing or incapacitated.

On the other side is often found the tricky plaintiff's lawyer who brings strike suits, examines defendants before trial, seeks discoveries and inspection of confidential books and records, subpoenas customers and friends of the defendant and otherwise makes technical procedural moves, all in an effort to harass or embarrass an innocent defendant into an extortionate settlement.

No class of lawyer is guiltless; each uses technical weapons of procedure, some legitimately, some malevolently, in the effort to level an opponent's defenses.

Even a Corporation Counsel of the City of New York, whose sense of civic responsibility is ordinarily strong, carried to an appellate court his objection to the application of the taxpayer for reduction of taxes because the taxpayer, owning thirty-seven parcels of land on which he wanted a reduction of taxes, included them all in a single petition. The Corporation Counsel wanted the taxpayer's lawyer to draw and file thirty-seven different petitions. Then the Corporation Counsel intended to draw thirty-seven differ-

# LOOK AT THE LAW

ent answers, after which thirty-seven different proceedings would appear upon the court calendars, each one requiring the taxpayer to pay a separate calendar fee. The court would then have to try thirty-seven different cases, witnesses and experts being called and testifying thirty-seven different times. The judges unanimously rejected such a contention and pointed out that the procedure which the taxpayer's attorney followed conserved the time of the court and litigants, brought about dispatch of the business and avoided the technicalities of an unnecessarily large number of suits, without injury to anybody.

Because of lawyer-practices of making technical procedural moves in every case, it has been estimated that mere technical matters of practice and procedure occupy one-third of the time of the courts.

In the Supreme Court of New York County, for example, each week-day finds over 400 lawyers and their clerks attending before the judge specially designated to hear practice and other preliminary and procedural matters. Another judge sitting in a different part of the same court has his own collection of similar applications, while a judge in still another part hears thousands of applications each week of which no notice is required to be given. Most of these are matters of technique and strategy — legal shadow-boxing.

A series of articles in the New York *World-Telegram* disclosed that the New York Supreme Court in New York and Bronx Counties handled 196,996 motions in 1935, while only 3,408 cases were being disposed of by trial, and pointed out that almost three out of every four cases brought in this court are disposed of without consideration of the merits. The writer found that there had been submitted to a single judge, in a 19-day period, 4,999 preliminary applications involving approximately 375,000 pages of affidavits and briefs.

# LOOK AT THE LAW

Such a volume of procedural business is accounted for by the fact that every practice rule, however beneficially intended, is perverted to a contrary use by the ingenuity of the legalist. When the legislature gives the plaintiff the privilege of examining the defendant before trial in order that the plaintiff may use the defendant's testimony in proving his case, a multitude of plaintiffs examine a multitude of defendants. Each plaintiff swears he wants to use the defendant's testimony on the trial. Ten, perhaps, out of a hundred are telling the truth. The other ninety want to find out what the defendant is going to say so their lawyers can prepare to cross-examine and so they can get additional testimony for the trial to overcome the defendant's story. And of the ninety, a considerable number who seek such testimony are prepared to fabricate answers to it, if necessary.

In some jurisdictions, if the defendant does not merely deny the plaintiff's story but advances a separate story of his own as a defense, the procedural rules will not permit a plaintiff to examine a defendant as to that story. For example, if Jones sues Smith to recover $5,000 under a written contract, and Smith admits the contract but pleads that Jones released him from making the payment, Jones cannot examine Smith about the release. But Jones' lawyer can get Smith's story of the release in advance of the trial just the same—by use of a little technical subterfuge.

In a great many States, in order to avoid the congestion of court calendars and the delay of trials caused by false answers filed by defendants, the law permits a plaintiff to move the court for judgment on affidavits. In those cases, the plaintiff files affidavits demonstrating that the claimed defenses are utterly false. This requires the defendant to file affidavits telling his story in detail to show that he really has a defense. If he thus convinces the judge that he may have a defense, the court orders the case to go to trial in

# LOOK AT THE LAW

the regular way; if he doesn't, the judge orders immediate, so-called summary judgment against him.

To get back to Jones, who can't examine Smith about the claimed release: Jones' lawyer makes a motion for summary judgment, claiming Smith is just lying about a release. He makes the motion with no hope of winning it, but merely to compel Smith to file affidavits telling the details of the release transaction—Smith does so and the motion is denied. The time of the court has been wasted, but resort to this tricky technicality enables Jones to get Smith's story in advance and to prepare, honestly or falsely, to meet it at the trial.

Other examples of the use of preliminary technicalities for purposes of delay and evasion are legion.

For example: If a man resident in New York sues a Delaware corporation doing business in New York in the New York Supreme Court for $3,000 or more, the defendant has the choice of filing an answer in the State Court or, at its option, of filing an application to remove the case to the Federal Court. In the State Court action, the defendant must answer within twenty days from the date the action was commenced. If it wants delay in answering, it can get it by removing the case to the Federal Court, for then it does not need to answer until twenty days have elapsed from the date the case was removed. If the Federal Court calendar is behind the State Court calendar, the defendant generally removes the case to the Federal Court.

It does not matter whether the case really belongs in the Federal Court or not; the moment the defendant files its petition, many cases hold that the State Court clerk can do nothing but remove the case; that if he claims the removal is unjustified, the plaintiff must apply to the Federal judge to send the case back.

If the Federal judge refuses to send the case back to the State Court, there is no appeal until the plaintiff has tried his case in the Federal Court and then, in appealing from the judgment, the plaintiff may claim that the case should never have been removed to the Federal Court in the first place and that it ought to be sent back to the State Court for trial. Then and only then, after a delay of years in some jurisdictions, can the plaintiff have the case sent back to the State Court.

But that is not all. The defendant who had the case removed to the Federal Court can petition that court at any time, before or after the trial, to send the case back to the State Court. Even after he is beaten upon a trial of the merits in the Federal Court, the defendant can appeal to the Federal Appellate Court and ask that the judgment be set aside upon the ground that he really had no right to move the case to the Federal Court, though he himself sought the removal in the first place.

There are cases where a defendant, over plaintiff's objection, removed a case to the Federal Court and then having been unsuccessful on the trial, succeeded in having the judgment against him vacated by the higher court, after years of fruitless litigation on the part of the plaintiff.

Such untoward effects come from the technical enforcement of a technical rule that the jurisdiction of the Federal courts cannot be conferred by consent—a rule finding its roots in the provisions of the Federal Constitution and in Congressional statutes dating back to 1787.

In matters of giving evidence upon a trial, an apotheosis of technique is reached. What is to be admitted in evidence upon a trial and what is to be rejected, is a subject of such abstruseness that volumes of law books are constantly being written and rewritten on the subject. *Greenleaf on Evidence*, a standard work written in 1899, consists of three volumes of 2,167 pages, citing perhaps almost 15,000 precedents. Wigmore, a more recent expert on the subject, has

# LOOK AT THE LAW

a text consisting of five volumes aggregating 5,500 pages, with 42,000 precedents.

With all this wealth of material and precedent, appellate courts are daily reversing civil and criminal verdicts and judgments because the trial court erred in admitting or excluding evidence. The rules are fine, and the refinements and exceptions numerous. Evidence may be "incompetent" or "irrelevant" or "immaterial." It may not be the "best" evidence. It may be hearsay. No proper foundation may have been "laid" for it.

The distinctions are so often unknown to the lawyer who makes the objection to the testimony that he usually rattles off all the objections he can think of, so as to cover every contingency.

The consequences of these technical objections, in expense and delay to the suitor, if the judge admits or excludes evidence to the disagreement of the higher court, is often a serious one, for reversal of the judgment often follows. And frequently such a result follows, even though the reason for upholding the technicality is difficult for even the legal mind to understand.

For example, in January, 1930, a Miss Kelly was a passenger in a taxicab which collided with a truck. She was severely and permanently injured, concededly through no fault of her own.

She sued the owner of the cab and the owner of the truck. The case ultimately came to trial. The question was which of the two was liable. Each blamed the other. The taxi driver took the stand and said the truck ran into his cab. The truck driver took the stand and said his truck was not in motion when the cab ran into him. A police officer testified that he had questioned the truck driver at the hospital to which the plaintiff had been taken after the accident, and that the truck driver had then told him that he had been unable to

# LOOK AT THE LAW

stop his truck because the pavement was slippery. The jury found a verdict for the plaintiff against the owner of the truck for $14,000. The trucking company appealed.

In February, 1937, seven years after the accident, the appellate court reversed the judgment and ordered a new trial because it held the trial judge committed error in allowing the policeman to testify to the truck driver's contradictions of his testimony. Why? Because Miss Kelly was not hurt? No. Because the truck driver was not at fault? No. Then why? Because, the Court said, the statements of the truck driver at the hospital were not binding on the defendant and should not have been admitted in evidence.

"Why not?" you ask.

"Because it was not part of the *res gestae*," answers the appellate court.

"What is the *res gestae*?" you ask.

The *res gestae*, roughly speaking, are the acts and declarations relevant to the matter at issue; but as a famous English judge said, "The question remains, what are relevant?"

What is a part of the *res gestae* is a variable quantity that has puzzled judges for years. As to that, the judges say that the law has a theory that if an incident occurs, everything one says and does immediately is probably done spontaneously and, therefore, honestly; that it really reflects what he really believes or really thinks; but that what is said or done later, after one has had a chance to think it over and be deliberate in his words or acts, may not be truthful.

What has that to do with the fact that the truck driver told the jury one story and told the police officer another, you ask. "Well," says the technical insurance company which insured the truckman's employer, "the truckman's statements at the hospital were not part of the *res gestae* and he can't bind his employer by any statement he may have made which was not part of the *res gestae*." That is a

# LOOK AT THE LAW

perfectly good legal point and there's good legal reason for it. "Then again," says the insurance company, "one cannot impeach a witness without warning him."

"What does that mean?" asks the layman.

"That's another sound technicality," must be the answer. "It means that before calling the police officer to testify that the truck driver had made a contradictory statement at the hospital, Miss Kelly's lawyer should have first asked the truck driver, while he was on the witness stand, whether he had not made such a statement to the police officer and then have called the police officer."

This is not easy to explain to the lay mind; nor is it easy for the lay mind to grasp these technical refinements or to understand their necessity. All the layman knows, after all the explanation, is that, because one jury was told that the truck driver made contradictory statements as to the cause of the accident (which was the very point it was called upon to decide), and because the jury might have been persuaded by such testimony that the truckman was lying at the trial, the appeal court, seven years after Miss Kelly had been hurt, concededly without fault on her part, threw the $14,000 judgment out and told her she'd have to try her case all over again before another jury.

Obviously these may be sound rules, but their application worked a poor result in this case.

One of the favored stamping grounds for technicalities is found in the practice on appeals. An appeal must be taken within a limited time and in many jurisdictions it is held that, regardless of reason, the time to take an appeal cannot be extended. In our Federal courts, a survival of the old Chancery practice, which bristled with technique, formerly controlled the manner of taking the appeal. One either went up to the appellate court by "petition to review" or by "writ of error." If the appellant went up by "petition to review"

# LOOK AT THE LAW

when his lawyer should have resorted to a "writ of error," the error was fatal and he lost his appeal. And vice versa. The risks of error and the difficulties of distinction were so great that lawyers finally went up both ways, so their appeal could be heard on the merits without risk of technical dismissal.

Another trifling technicality on appeal with dire consequences is found in the simple word, "Exception." When one appeals claiming error by the court below, ordinarily it is not enough to show that the judge committed error, but counsel must call the judge's attention to the error so that he may correct it. Clearly such a rule, if observed in spirit, would be a salutary one and might, except with obstinate judges, serve to avoid needless expense and delay of appeals. But like so many legal precautions, this rule in practice degenerates into a mere technicality that serves to deny the unwary suitor relief.

In the trial of a case, one lawyer asks a question. The other lawyer objects. The judge sustains the objection, or he overrules it and permits the witness to answer. Now is the time the lawyer who has been offended by the judge's ruling must call his attention to the fact that he believes the judge has committed an error. He does it by "excepting" to the ruling of the judge. He says, "I except to your Honor's ruling" or something equivalent; in some jurisdictions, he need merely say, "Exception." Theoretically, having had his attention called to his error, the judge will reconsider his ruling and perhaps reverse himself. Actually, this occurs faster than anyone but an expert stenographer can record it.

Q. What did you say to him?
Lawyer: Objected to, incompetent, irrelevant and immaterial.
Judge: Sustained.

# LOOK AT THE LAW

Other Lawyer: Exception.
Q. What did he say to you?
Lawyer: Same objection.
Judge: Same ruling.
Other Lawyer: Exception.
Q. What did you do then? . . . and *ad infinitum*.

But it is not merely that the rule serves no really useful purpose; it actually works injustice, because the appellate court, in the event of an appeal, will not disturb the judgment of the court below even if the court committed error, unless the aggrieved lawyer has snapped an "exception" into the record before the next question was asked.

This is illustrated by an amusing story (though not amusing in its consequences to the client) told by a lawyer who specialized in court work as trial counsel. The bulk of his work was done in one county where he was so well known to the judges that they treated him with courtesy, if not with some measure of deference. He had occasion to try a case in a neighboring county before a judge, since dead, who was no respecter of persons. In fact, the judge in question had little or no use for trial lawyers and made it a practice to bait them. His technique was skilled and varied, and included a habit of calling counsel "Mister" and ignoring his surname.

Jones had hardly opened his trial when he had occasion to object to a question asked by his adversary. This colloquy then occurred:

Mr. Jones: I object, your Honor, upon the ground that the question calls for a conclusion.
The Court: Objection overruled, Mister.

In order to claim on appeal that this ruling constituted error, the law required Jones to except to the judge's ruling by saying, "I respectfully except to your Honor's ruling,"

# LOOK AT THE LAW

or its equivalent. However, taken aback for a moment at the judge's discourtesy, to which he was wholly unaccustomed, Jones hesitated for a moment, and then, recovering, said, more or less impudently: "Jones." The judge completely ignored the retort.

Thereafter, and throughout the trial, the following occurred and recurred:

Mr. Jones: Objection.

The Court: Objection overruled, Mister.

Mr. Jones: Jones.

Finally the case went to the jury, which found against Jones's client. Jones appealed.

Months later, as Jones told the story on himself, Jones's partner, who had been working on the case in the appellate court, came into Jones's room in a state of consternation.

"We're licked on that appeal," he said. "I don't see a single chance of reversal."

"Why, what's the matter?" asked Jones. "I'm sure that judge committed a dozen errors in admitting evidence."

"So am I," said his partner. "But what good is that going to do us? You didn't take a single exception. I've gone through the whole record, and every place there ought to be 'exception,' I find 'Jones.' "

Jones said that he had occasion later to try another case before the same judge but, as he wryly admitted, "He called me Mister all through the trial and I meekly replied, 'Exception.' "

### 3.

No discussion of legal technicalities would be justified in omitting some mention of the subtleties employed by the law itself in binding together the rents in legal garments by the use of legal fictions.

Frequently, when the law finds it difficult to achieve a

# LOOK AT THE LAW

desired end by the use of accepted legal rules, it designs a fictional device in order to accomplish its purposes. This device is frankly and logically known as the legal fiction.

The legal fiction is a false assumption which the law makes. A prominent legal historian justifies the legal fiction as the first of three instrumentalities whereby the law is brought into harmony with society, although many law writers decry it and condemn its use as a lawyer's artifice and deception. However, it cannot be denied that needed change in the law has been obtained by surreptitiously using legal fictions to give lip service to conflicting legal precedents, customs and adages. And Tourtoulon, a noted legal philosopher, brands much of the criticism of legal fictions as superficial, since, he says, the law cannot be constructed upon objective realities.

As is usually the case, there is something to be said on both sides. But the danger of duplicity lies in its effect. Naturally, attack by subterfuge invites defense and counter-attack by technicalities; the combat becomes one of technique, with the substance frequently lost sight of (although it is the academic rule that no legal fiction shall be given weight to work an unjust result). One lie justifies another; resort to a fiction for a proper purpose paves the way for a battlefield strewn with combatants injured and destroyed by technicalities, pro and con.

We hear of the father who sues, claiming damages from the man who has seduced his minor daughter. The defendant answers: "Yes, it is true that I seduced your daughter. But you cannot recover damages from me because you contracted your daughter out to work for other people and therefore you weren't entitled to her services when I seduced her."

What sort of defense is this? Are the feelings of a father outraged any the less because his daughter was bound out to

# LOOK AT THE LAW

work for somebody else? What has that got to do with the seduction or the father's right to recover damages? Can a confessed seducer take refuge in such an evasion?

The answer is yes, and for extremely technical reasons. The common law has always denied the right of a plaintiff to recover damages where only his feelings were hurt and neither his person nor his property injured. For that reason the common law judges, willing to award damages against a seducer, and unable to permit the woman to sue, worked out a fiction that the father could sue his daughter's seducer for damages for loss of property, i.e., his right to his daughter's services. The ingenious theory of this was that the seduction put the girl in a state, mental or physical, which tended to deprive her father of her services, so that he could sue for the loss he sustained thereby. As a matter of fact the purpose of the judges was to punish the seducer, and once the parties got into court, the jury was at liberty to fix damages far beyond any fictional monetary loss of services suffered by the father. But before the court would entertain the action at all, the fiction of lost services had to be observed, and only the father (not the girl or the mother) could recover. So, no matter how outrageous the seduction, the seducer could avoid its consequences by pleading one of a number of technical defenses an ingenious legal mind could suggest which bore no real relationship to the offense.

A legal "presumption" is a technical legal fiction. "To presume" means to take for granted without proof; "presumption" is the noun that substitutes in the courts for legal evidence. A legal "presumption" allows the law to infer a conclusion from proof of a fact; a man was seen fleeing from the scene of a crime, he is found in possession of stolen goods, inferences of guilt follow.

When we hear of a man who has been unjustly found guilty on circumstantial evidence, we will frequently find

# LOOK AT THE LAW

that his conviction resulted from the fact that certain of the matters which the prosecution could not prove were "presumed" by the law. When we hear of an unjust result in some civil case, the chances are that it occurred because something was presumed by the law instead of being proven by the successful party.

For example, it was only after a once well-to-do New York State farmer had served three and a half years in prison on an arson charge, that the highest court, in July, 1937, reversed his conviction upon the ground that his guilt had been "presumed" and not proven, that the jury improperly "based inference upon inference" in finding him guilty.

In this case, the harm was done because the judge allowed the jury to infer that the defendant had burned his barn because the State proved, among other things, that he had bought four gallons of gasoline, and to base a conviction on that circumstantial evidence.

Under rules which are the foundation of personal liberty in a democracy, the law says generally that a man will not be punished unless he has been shown intentionally to have broken the law. This, in the law, is called "criminal intent," and without criminal intent, the law says a man should not be jailed. Manifestly, one cannot believe a man to have intentionally broken the law unless he knew what the law was. So to be a criminal, one must, first, know what the law is and, second, one must intend to break it.

Then there is another rule of law that requires every man to be proven guilty. We have an apothegm known to every school child: Everyone is presumed innocent until proven guilty. (Here, again, we find a presumption.)

Now, what does all this mean? It would seem that the law says that before it will jail a man it will prove he knew the law and deliberately broke it. But does it? It does not.

# LOOK AT THE LAW

Instead, it resorts to technicalities—it creates and invokes a fiction to gainsay the rules it has made.

Instead of undertaking to prove that the defendant who, seeking to evade punishment, wails, "I didn't know the law," the shrewd wit of the law suggests the rule that everyone is presumed to know the law. And, to clinch the matter, the law says this presumption is irrebuttable, i.e., not only will we not prove that you knew the law but we won't let you prove that you didn't know it.

So also with the rule that the breach of the law must be deliberate and that the defendant must have "criminal intent."

To prove a man's intent is a difficult affair at best. In his cups a man may speak his mind and announce his intentions; generally a man's intent must be read from what he does rather than from what he says.

But having announced that the guilty intent of the accused must be proved, the law must find a way to prove it. Again the law fears to be honest. It will not revoke the rule that guilty intent must be proved; it will evade it with a technicality—a legal fiction. Instead of being frank and saying, "We can't prove guilty intent, so we won't try," it says, "We will keep the rule but we will get around it; first, by a definition, and then by a presumption."

First, the definition: "When we say a man must have criminal intent," the law goes on to say, "that does not mean that he must have intended the consequences of his act. It merely means that he must have intended to do the act itself."

Now, the presumption: It says everyone is "presumed" to contemplate the natural consequences of his act.

The definition and that little word "presumed" promptly kill the budding hopes of those accused, for they mean that if the defendant is charged with endangering the lives of

# LOOK AT THE LAW

passengers by stopping a train, the State does not have to prove that he knew the train was a passenger train or that he intended to endanger the passengers' lives; all it needs to do is prove that he put up a red flag intending to stop the train, and even if it was for a perfectly proper and legal purpose, the "presumption" supplies the rest. It is for the defendant to convince the jury of his honest purpose.

So when a boy threw a rock at another boy and it hit him, it did not help the accused boy any to say he did it for fun or that he expected the other boy to dodge. Nor did it help when his lawyer said the boy had no criminal intent in throwing the rock, that he did not intend to hit the other boy; for the State trots out the little "presumption" that says "when he threw the rock in the general direction of the other boy it must be presumed that he knew what the consequences of his aim might be and he is chargeable with them."

At this point, let it be said that though there may be no complaint with the consequences of the application of these rules in particular cases, the unnecessary creation of rules in particular cases and their evasion by technicalities make of the law a technical maze that mystifies laymen and enables lawyers endlessly to keep remedies and reforms at bay.

But to resume consideration of legal presumptions.

Sometimes the law says that a man is guilty of a crime only if he does a thing maliciously. For example, if he commits a mischief he may be liable civilly; to be fined or imprisoned, he must do it maliciously. To prove a man did a thing spitefully or malevolently is ordinarily a herculean task, so the law again resorts to the evasion of definition and presumption. It says while "malicious" may mean "spiteful" to a layman, it only means "willful" to a lawyer; that "willful" means "knowing," and the law will presume an act is "knowing" if it was done by a man in his right mind who may be "presumed" to know what he is doing. Again a triumph of reasoning and technicality.

The general rule in a criminal case is that if it is proved that the accused committed the crime, the rest will be "presumed," and the accused must then "rebut the presumption." When it becomes too easy for the accused "to rebut a presumption" (as when the law presumes everyone to know the law, to which the accused can readily say, "I didn't know it," and no one can gainsay him), the law says the presumption is irrebuttable.

In short, in many cases, the rule of law that the accused must have criminal intent is a fiction because the rule is wiped out by saying the mere doing of the act presumes the intent and the defendant will not be permitted to deny it.

The criminal law is full of presumptions. The best known of these is the presumption mentioned, that every man is innocent until he is proved guilty. As a matter of fact this presumption is nothing, it is not even evidence; it is a mere fiction. It is merely the law's way of saying the burden is on the State to prove that a man committed a crime before he may be convicted of it.

There is a presumption that a defendant is sane, that he has ordinary human faculties. These are mere complements of the presumption of intent and knowledge of the law and are designed to put the burden on the accused of justifying the commission of a forbidden act.

In civil actions one also meets presumptions at every turn. There are natural presumptions and legal presumptions; there are rebuttable presumptions and irrebuttable presumptions; there are mixed presumptions and the law even admits that there are artificial presumptions.

A man who absents himself from his usual haunts, who cannot be located and who has not been heard from for a statutory period, is presumed to be dead. His wife may re-

# LOOK AT THE LAW

marry; the courts will probate his will and divide his property; they will enforce payment of his life insurance, though all the while he may be going his daily rounds in some other town, eating, drinking, fornicating and generally claiming the rights of a live citizen of one State while enjoying the immunities of a dead one in another.

A monument to presumptions is to be found in a Louisiana cemetery where inscribed on a granite shaft is to be found the simple inscription "105 La. 39." This designates the volume and page of the reports of the Louisiana courts wherein the court held that where it was impossible for a jury to determine the question of fact of whether a mother or her daughter, who were both lost at sea in a shipwreck, died first, the law would determine the question by indulging in a legal presumption that the mother died first. The result was to effectuate the daughter's will which provided for a monument in a cemetery and though there were no remains to be buried, the court required the monument to be erected. Fittingly, it was erected and inscribed to the omnipotent law that could presume facts indeterminable by jurors.

The capital offense of murder is an apparent exception to the rule of fictional presumption of criminal intent. Reams of judicial learning have been unwound in discussing what proof of deliberation is needed in order to sustain a conviction for murder. Yet even this grave crime finds the law enjoying its fictions and, in consequence, in many of our States one can be, and many men have been, executed for technical murder, for killings that one neither committed, intended or even knew about.

Murder, it is to be known, is a matter of definition. Killing a human being between wars may or may not be murder. Killing is homicide, and murder is a form of homicide to be distinguished from manslaughter, justifiable homicide

# LOOK AT THE LAW

and excusable homicide. Generally murder is a premeditated or depraved killing. But it may also involve an accidental killing.

Back in the seventeenth century when crime and capital punishment were affinities, Lord Coke, the famous English jurist, said that it was the law that a poacher whose arrow, aimed at a deer, was deflected by a branch and killed a boy, was guilty of murder, although the poacher had no notion of the presence of the boy nor any idea of hurting him. Lord Coke put this on the sole ground that the death occurred as a result of the unlawful act which the poacher was trying to commit. Later this technical crime was further refined thus: If Smith threw a stone intending to kill a bird and the stone struck a bystander to whom Smith intended no harm, Smith had committed no offense. But if Smith threw the stone intending to kill, in order to steal Jones's chickens (which was a crime), and the stone hit a bystander, then Smith was guilty of murder.

Another ancient application of this rule made it even more ludicrous. Sometime, in early England, a man was permitted to shoot game unless the yearly value of his lands amounted to less than one hundred pounds. When a poor man went a-hunting, and an accidental killing resulted, the courts were called upon to apply the poacher rule and to brand him a murderer. To their credit, they quibbled their ways out.

The consequences of these ancient rules led to the modern and generally accepted provision that homicide committed by a person engaged in the commission of any felony is punishable as murder; in some States, if the killing occurs while the killer is committing a major felony, a crime of violence, such as burglary, rape or arson, it is considered first degree murder. Here we find the law using a rule that makes it unnecessary to prove criminal intent in cases of

# LOOK AT THE LAW

murder and refuses to permit the defendant who wants to plead a lack of intent, or even a lack of knowledge of the presence of the person killed, to deny his culpability on those grounds.

The to-be-expected result of the artificial creation of technical murder, by definition, has been resort to technicality, not only by defendants, but by judges and jurors, in efforts to avoid the imposition of the extreme penalty where extenuating circumstances exist. No record of jurors' reasons are made; they are merged in their verdicts. But judges must give reasons and they must find refuge in legal technicalities.

So, the courts have been hard put to decide whether or not murder has been committed in given cases. Was the defendant still committing the burglary when he fired the shot that killed the deceased? If he was, however accidentally the shot was fired, he is guilty of murder and the law will listen to no excuses. If, however, he was no longer engaged in the commission of the crime he may be heard to urge his lack of intent to kill. If he was still working at his crime, his intent concerning the killing is immaterial; if he was not, the State must prove the killing premeditated.

So the court must determine what constitutes a completion of the original crime. Had the defendant fully escaped from the scene of the original crime when the killing occurred? To determine that question the courts sometimes ask whether the defendant still had his booty with him or whether he had abandoned it. Had he gone a reasonable distance from the scene of the crime? What is a reasonable distance? Next door? Across the street? Suppose the deceased died from fright. Is the burglar guilty of murder? Would the result be the same if the deceased was suffering from heart disease? These are not products of the imagination; they come from actual cases where the defendants'

# LOOK AT THE LAW

lives and liberties turned upon some such refinement of technique or language. So, where a defendant was found to have willfully set fire to a barn, he was charged with murder because of the death of a tramp who, unknown to the defendant, had been asleep in the barn. Charged with this constructive murder, the defendant countered with the quibble that the tramp came into the barn after the defendant had set the fire and not before; whereupon the court charged the jury that if this was so, the defendant was not guilty of murder. The jury acquitted the defendant.

In some cases, defendants have been charged with murder because of an unintentional killing, while the defendant was a trespasser, engaged in some technical offense; for example, while he was hunting out of season, carrying a concealed weapon, selling liquor in violation of law, driving past a tollgate while attempting to avoid paying the toll, throwing stones, etc. In such cases the courts have stretched legalisms to the utmost to avoid convictions for the major offense.

But this legal hairsplitting does not reach its zenith until we find these irrebuttable legal inferences or implications of intent to kill, regardless of the facts, in cases where a number of persons are engaged in the commission of a felony in the course of which someone is killed. Then, under the rule, all are subject to the implication of intent and all are equally guilty.

In other words, suppose the original poacher Smith was aided by Thompson and Doe, and Doe, when Roe tries to stop him from killing a deer, shoots and kills Roe. Is Smith guilty of the murder. The answer is, "Yes." Is Thompson? Again, "Yes."

But suppose Smith says, "I wasn't there when Doe fired the shot; I didn't even hear the shot; I didn't know Doe had killed Roe or was going to; he didn't tell me anything about it." The answer is still, "Yes," for the law presumes that it

# LOOK AT THE LAW

was the intent of all three to accomplish their purpose of poaching over any opposition, even to the point of murder.

This rule found modern illustration in a case in which five young men, spurred on by empty pockets and three or four drinks apiece, went off to hold up an elevated railroad station agent. Four went upstairs to the platform to do the job while one stood watch at the entrance down below on the street. The episode had originated in a dare for the boy-watcher downstairs, and for him it was in the nature of a liquor-stimulated prank. Wholly unknown to him, one of the young men upstairs carried a pistol and he used it with telling effect when the station agent resisted. The agent died and all five of the young men, including the downstairs watcher who had never gone near the upstairs platform, who had never had any intent to kill and who had never even known the man upstairs carried a pistol, were tried, condemned and ultimately executed.

Manifestly, such a technical crime encourages technical defense. So we have the rule that if, before a felony planned by several perpetrators is carried out, one of the participants withdraws or abandons his purpose, and so informs the actual killer, he is not guilty of murder for a killing that occurs subsequently in the course of the commission of the crime.

If, for example, two men set out to burgle a house and one quits before he reaches the house, he has committed no murder though the house is thoroughly burgled by his companion who kills someone in the course of the burglary. Clearly, there cannot be even a presumption of criminal intent to murder when the prospective burglar leaves his partner a block from the scene of the proposed burglary and goes home to bed. But suppose the dividing line is closer than that.

A young Italian woman, married off to an older man by

her parents, tired of bearing his children and suffering his brutalities. She found a lover of her own age and plotted with him to kill her husband, and, on the husband's insurance money, to remarry. The parties lived in a single family house in a somewhat isolated section. The husband made it a nightly practice to leave after supper for a drinking bout with his cronies at a neighboring tavern. He usually returned about 10:30, boisterous and drunk.

The plot called for the young lover to wait about 10:30 some night behind the hedge which fronted the property, and to shoot the husband as he returned home. The young man enlisted the aid of a young friend who had a double-barreled shotgun and who, for fifty dollars of the insurance money, promised to be paid by the wife when the job was done, sawed off the barrel of his gun and agreed to lend it for the purpose of the killing. In addition, the owner of the gun agreed to aid in the commission of the crime.

On the night appointed, the young man turned the gun over to the wife's lover and accompanied him to the scene of the crime. They both hid behind the hedge and awaited the husband. The lover had the loaded gun, he held it poised and ready to pull the trigger whenever the husband should appear.

However, the husband was late on this particular evening, which proved to be a chilly one. Furthermore, the sky grew overcast and it commenced to drizzle. Waiting grew unpleasant. The aide grew restive; after all, he had nothing against the old man and fifty dollars was not so much for a job like this, anyhow, and perhaps he wouldn't even get it. Finally, he rose to his feet, saying he was going home. The principal conspirator begged him to remain. He refused to be dissuaded from his purpose; he said he was tired of the whole affair and would have nothing more to do with it. Just then the old man was heard noisily coming along. The

# LOOK AT THE LAW

lover pulled his accomplice down beside him; both boys crouched behind the hedge. When the old man got opposite him, the wife's lover fired. The husband fell, dead.

The police had no difficulty in solving the crime. Both boys and the widow were indicted and, after trial, were convicted and sentenced to death. An appeal was taken. The appeal court reversed the judgment of conviction of the owner of the gun. It found that he had abandoned the criminal enterprise before it was executed; that no intent to continue it could be presumed against him because he had expressly quit it before the commission of the crime. He was freed.

One cannot avoid remarking the difference to this defendant had he said, "Aw, all right," when the other lad importuned him to stay, instead of, "Naw, I'm goin' home." On such trifles do life and death rest in the technicalities of the law.

### 4.

Unfortunately and inevitably, in attempting to govern ourselves by rule, we find ourselves ruled by technicalities, and words are the stuff of which they are made. Democratic government rests upon word-promises of the rule of law; we buttress and amplify them by statutes and judicial pronouncements that consist of words. These rules, so fabricated, we challenge with words. So, in the law, as in many of its kindred branches that govern communal living, struggle is epitomized by technical questions concerning the meaning, the arrangement, in short, the use of words. This is inescapable.

Where the field of contention rests on words, in the very nature of things, subtleties and sophistries are bound to have their play, however well-intentioned the opposing forces. Careless statute making, ignorant decisions, a wealth of both,

# LOOK AT THE LAW

reconciliation of conflicting statutes and decisions, as well as natural difficulties of construction and definition, are bound to produce controversy.

We cannot escape technicalities, pro and con, in any human system that is so dependent upon spoken or written language. Whether a democracy be defended or despotism be advocated, the weapons are words. And the words used are invariably the same; only their connotations differ. So it is with the law, the handmaiden of government, where dependence upon words reaches its zenith.

Aside from inevitable controversy, it must be remembered that lawyers and judges work with words; they are their tools. They dress their ideas and cloak their purposes with them. They bend them to their wills. For purposes of exposition, they select words that sparkle with clarity; for purposes of mystification, they choose mystifying and apocryphal hog-Latin terms.

For these reasons alone, our law must find its way through a morass of technicalities, with diverse and unpredictable results.

Beyond this, we suffer from pretensions to which we subscribe in theory and which we seek to evade in practice.

We base our democratic form of government upon fallacies of equality which the natural sciences deny as completely as they do the historical metaphors of the Bible. And, in practice, we deny the ones as we do the others.

To insure equality we promise a rule of law. But we are not content with a rule of law. We are not content to suffer the individual hardship which flows from inflexible rule, in order to preserve the academic, or even the practical, sanctity of rule. The sufferer invariably rebels and, with rare exception, the law administrator, being human, also seeks a way out. The consequence of both is resort to technicality, to quibble, as means of evasion.

# LOOK AT THE LAW

When we seek to adopt rules that abate the rigor of existing rule, we simply add disabilities to existing ones. No rule can temper the rigor of rule; only human intervention will avail, and that through a process of evasion that avoids the rule, without denying it.

Government by rule is an academic extreme that would, if carried out strictly, be so rigid that it would destroy itself. Like political reformers in power, it would so antagonize its constituency that they would emulate the Athenians who tired of hearing Aristides called the Just. Democratic government subscribing to rule needs a moderating human influence to secure the balance so necessary in a social state.

The struggle is symptomatic of democratic government, with its high pretensions and grave ambitions. It is the same conflict that is waged between uncertainty and rigidity in the field of judicial precedents, between legislative rule and the social need in the domain of statutory construction. Inflexible rule serves the standards of equality which democratic government professes, while its open denial gives impetus to movements that seek dictatorship or anarchy. Law administrators must advocate the faith they profess; they can deny it only surreptitiously. This they do by resort to legalisms, a necessary face-saving process that saves inflexible rule by making it flexible.

In addition, life as we live it is an endless struggle between oughts and wants. The individual struggle is intensified in the community where our individual wants are pitted against the communal oughts. We seek to accomplish our selfish purposes and do not hesitate to evade the most beneficent and necessary law when doing so. This again means resort to technicalities.

The litigant, of course, wants to win at any cost. The man who complains, in the abstract, of the technicalities of

# LOOK AT THE LAW

the law today, does not hesitate to avail himself of them, in the concrete, tomorrow. It is a most exceptional lawyer who would refuse to take advantage of a technicality in order to win his client's cause; indeed, he might be chargeable with his client's loss if he failed to do so. His resort to technicality is usually limited only by his skill.

The individual litigant, however, is not the principal malefactor. His jousts with the law are but sporadic. It is the corporate defendant that is the American personification of efficiency, whether it fabricates a nation-wide steel trust (with whatever variations of spelling or arrangement it thinks justified), or whether it fabricates evasions that make it the less trustworthy in its dealings.

Nor does democratic government itself hesitate to further its ends by the use of quibbles and evasions.

When it becomes too difficult to break through the political and legal webs behind which premier racketeers entrench themselves, the Government itself seeks to find some more convenient stature which the racketeer has technically violated. Thus, when Al Capone proved too hard a nut to crack by ordinary means, the Government got technical and charged him with violations of the income tax law, and having been indicted on one charge he was sentenced on another, or upon many others. Similarly, when a murder charge fails, the defendant is often charged with the illegal possession of a weapon. When a businessman cannot be convicted of grand larceny, he is charged with some technical violation in issuing a credit statement. Bankers guilty of embezzlement are often dealt with in this way: they are readily found guilty of a violation of some technical provision of a banking law. It is not difficult, with so many laws, to find one almost any banker has violated, consciously or unconsciously, at some time or other. The recent prosecution of Hines, New York City Tammany leader, offered

# LOOK AT THE LAW

a good example of an indictment for engaging in a lottery and a conviction for "fixing" public officials.

The Federal Mann Act, designed to prohibit the commercial white slave traffic, has proved a convenient instrument by which elderly married men have been made to suffer for transgressions other than sexual ones. The Lindbergh kidnaping law, designed for honest-to-goodness kidnapers, has been used as a means of prosecution, though the forcible detention was technical and for purposes other than ransom.

A striking example of the technical use of antiquated statutes designed for other purposes is to be found in the recent Harlan County, Kentucky, prosecutions, where the government, to punish antilabor terrorism, resorted to an 1870 statute which made it a crime for two or more persons "to conspire to injure, oppress, threaten or intimidate any citizen in the free exercise or enjoyment of any constitutional right." (Imagine the consternation of the 1870 legislator had he been told that he was passing a law that would be used to further labor organization activities, and the dismay of Carnegie, *et al.*, had they been indicted under such a statute in the days of the Homestead steel strike!)

The use of such a device to punish offenders who should be punished for their real offenses is applauded when the purpose is a laudable one. In fact, the extension of the practice is advocated by well-meaning people in the interests of "justice." So, for example, the use of the 1870 statute employed in the Harlan County prosecution has been advocated by representatives of labor to curb Mayor Hague of Jersey City in his attempts to restrict the exercise of civil liberties. While the letter of the statute readily lends itself to such use, the danger of official sanction upon the technical use of criminal statutes is not without its threat to the very interests the labor representatives seek to further. For example, the Harlan County trial was still under way when the

# LOOK AT THE LAW

Michigan Supreme Court held that the maintenance of a picket line was an interference with the free exercise of the right of a nonstriking employee to work, and laid judicial basis for prosecution of the officers and members of every labor union that undertakes to strike and picket; and it furnishes Messrs. Girdler, Weir, *et al.*, with a ready means of seeking the indictment and imprisonment of Mr. John L. Lewis and his associates.

Similarly, resort to technical statutes by labor in an attempt to collect damages of $7,500,000 from the Republic Steel Corporation finds the defendants cross-claiming for an equal amount under statutes which obviously were never intended for such use.

The effect of such practices was the ground announced by a Baltimore judge (according to an Associated Press dispatch in the New York *Times*) for acquittal of a State Senator of the charge of having entered into a conspiracy to transport two girls from Baltimore to Annapolis during the preceding legislative session for purposes of prostitution. "A verdict against the Senator," the judge said, "would open the way for a wave of 'consummate blackmail.'"

We decry technicalities when they are permitted to produce untoward results. Yet who will say that we do not welcome them when they enable us to effect a desired end?

We doubt that man wants such certainty in his law that a Portia cannot quibble the unpopular Jew out of his forfeit while exacting from him the uttermost toll of the letter of the law. Is not the public ire aroused only when the result is at variance with the popular emotion? Doesn't the newspaper and movie audience applaud the skilled shyster who vindicates "virtue" with his sophistries? Does the public condemn the judge who upholds the technicality that avoids enforcement of a hypocritical sumptuary law?

Laws against drinking, gambling, prostitution; statutes

# LOOK AT THE LAW

prohibiting the use of contraceptives—all meet the same fate. Either they are ignored as dead letters or, if sought to be enforced by a too zealous prosecutor, they are nullified by judicial sanction of legal hairsplitting evasions.

The New York anti-race-track betting statutes have been evaded for years by judges who have upheld technical and quibbling bookmakers' and race-track operators' lawyers. For instance, when the New York statute prohibited possession of a device "for gambling" and the police picked up a bookmaker at the race track and charged him with illegal possession of a racing program, his lawyers got the court to acquit the defendants upon the ground that while a race-track program might be used for gambling, it was not "a device for gambling under any of the definitions which we (the Court) have been able to find."

While pruning unnecessary law and exercising greater care in the formulation of statutory law will aid in reducing technicalities, the task is essentially judicial. No legislative rule of law can help, for it is the function of the judge to moderate rule without abating it. He may not permit hard cases to make bad law and, conversely, he must not permit bad law to work individual hardship.

Every judge must tolerate the technicalities inherent in the law. But he can refuse to uphold those that deny just result, while being tolerant of those fictions whereby the law seeks to adjust itself to the needs of life. Much of the discredit visited upon the law is caused by judges who are unable, by lack of perception, knowledge or ability, to turn the ubiquity of legalisms to needed social ends.

The judge's problem is to balance abstraction, theory, against realism, life. The task is not always simple, no matter how enlightened the judge. In fact, the more intelligent the judge, the greater the number of contending forces on each side his vigilant mind will summon. But no human

## LOOK AT THE LAW

institution works without some modicum of error; and the intelligent and competent judge can readily avoid results that today hold the law up to discredit.

Speaking of the technique of statutory construction, a Rhode Island Circuit court judge said:

"All laws should receive a sensible construction. The reason of the law in such cases should prevail over its letter. The common sense of man approves the judgment mentioned by Puffendorf, that the Bolognian law which enacted 'that whoever drew blood in the streets should be punished with the utmost severity' did not extend to the surgeon who opened the vein of a person that fell down in the street in a fit. The same common sense accepts the ruling, cited by Plowden, that the statute of the first Edward II which enacts that a prisoner who breaks prison shall be guilty of felony does not extend to a prisoner who breaks out when the prison is on fire, 'for he is not to be hanged because he would not stay to be burned.'"

In a recent case an enlightened New York judge said:

"There seems to be at present a strong tendency to revive imprisonment for debt. Its horrors seem to have been forgotten since best sellers have crowded out Dickens. This trend should be resisted. . . . By clever sophistry the plaintiff seeks to bring him (the defendant) within the body execution statute. Legalistically that argument may seem able but it does not appeal to the conscience of this court."

No one would criticize a judge who held that a blind man could testify to what he had heard concerning an accident, though the statute under which he sought to testify referred to an "eyewitness."

Concerning procedure, our judges themselves point to its technical defects and their remedy. Chief Judge Crane, of the New York Court of Appeals, said recently in refusing to heed technical pleas of counsel for Luciano, a notorious

# LOOK AT THE LAW

and convicted gangster: "We must not be so backward as to make our procedure a hindrance instead of a furtherance to justice."

Justice McReynolds of the Supreme Court said recently: "Unhappily the enforcement of our criminal laws is scandalously ineffective. Crimes of violence multiply; punishment walks lamely. Courts ought not to increase the difficulties by magnifying possibilities."

How the judges can magnify or minimize the inevitable difficulties of technical procedure is readily illustrated.

After a long and arduous trial, a notorious criminal had been convicted of murder. The case was a cause célèbre. There was no doubt of the defendant's guilt. But, as is invariably done in capital cases, the defendant appealed to the highest court of the State. The appeal was argued and the appellate judges retired in consternation. They would have to reverse the judgment of conviction, though they were convinced of the defendant's guilt, because the judge who had tried the case had committed undeniable error in refusing to admit in evidence a letter which had been offered by counsel for the convicted defendant. The law was clear; the judge should have received the letter and should have permitted it to be read to the jury; his failure to do so, under a long line of established precedents, was error that required the conviction to be set aside and a new trial to be ordered.

The appellate judges were about to order a reversal of the judgment of conviction when an appellate judge with common-sense tendencies asked to see the letter. To the amazement of the judges, it was not available. Due to an oversight, it had not been marked for identification and included in the record, as is customary in such cases. The skeptical judge insisted on seeing the letter before he would vote for reversal. Others of the judges remonstrated; it was highly irregular; the appeal judges, under the law, were

# LOOK AT THE LAW

bound by what was in the record; they had no legal right to consider anything else; the cases and precedents were clear on that subject. The dissenter stood his ground. Finally, the chief justice sent for the district attorney who had prosecuted the case. He came to the State capital from the distant city where the case had been tried and brought with him the letter that was causing all the difficulty. The letter was opened and read. It was utterly innocuous; there was nothing in it which, by any stretch of the imagination, could have caused the jury to have changed its conclusion respecting the defendant's guilt. The lawless judge then insisted that the judgment of conviction be affirmed; he argued that there was no point in reversing the judgment on a useless technicality and thereby hold up the law to public reproach. Finally, he won his point and the murderer's conviction was sustained.

In a civil case, a lawyer asked an appellate court to reverse a judgment which the plaintiff, a widow, aged fifty-five, had obtained for damages which she sustained when she was struck by an automobile, because the witnesses at the trial were permitted to testify that while at the time of the accident she had chestnut hair which was just beginning to turn gray, a day or two after the accident her hair had turned snow-white.

The defendant's lawyer objected that the jury had considered on the question of damages the fact that plaintiff's hair had turned white immediately after the accident, even though there had been no testimony that the change in its color was due to the accident.

The appellate court, in rejecting this technical plea, said that it had no difficulty in surmising that any medical man, had he been called on and asked a hypothetical question, "What caused the change of hair?" would have said that in his opinion it was due to the accident; that any intel-

# LOOK AT THE LAW

ligent juror had a right to know, without expert medical testimony, that one's hair may turn white from shock or fright.

The court compared the situation with that of plaintiff who testified that after he was struck in the eye he had had what is vulgarly known as a black eye and said that in that case it would be unnecessary to produce an expert witness to say that "an extravasation of blood resulting in ecchymosis" might follow such a blow; the theory of the court's decision being that every man, though he be a judge or juror, had at least one experience as a boy that taught him that doctrine of cause and effect.

On every side, liberal rules for the protection of citizens are sought to be turned into technical instruments of protection to the guilty. But alert and intelligent judges can prevent such consequences.

The struggle is between blind judicial habit and a skeptical judicial approach; between accepted legal rules, fatalistically applied, and comprehending analyses, repeatedly made and constantly renewed.

That that is frequently the struggle was pointedly illustrated in a case wherein one Liedeker and wife sued Sears, Roebuck & Company because Mrs. Liedeker tried out a sample collapsible beach chair in a Sears, Roebuck store and, true to the promise, the foot-rest of the collapsible beach chair collapsed. The appellate court reversed a judgment for the plaintiff because the majority of the court found that, under established legal rules, the chair was not inherently dangerous. The chief judge and the trial judge held with the plaintiff.

This case is indicative of the difference between logic and experience, between the academic law and the law in practice. Four appeal judges concluded that logically and under rules of law, the chair was not inherently dangerous.

# LOOK AT THE LAW

But Mrs. Liedeker sat in it and fell down. So she sued. The trial judge evidently sat in it and he also fell down. So he found for the plaintiff. And the chief appellate judge either sat in and fell down, or concluded that discretion was the better part of valor, for he said, "The experiences of the trial justice with the chair, and an examination of it by this Court indicate that the trial court was fully justified in finding the chair was not reasonably safe for use." So he held with the plaintiff.

But by weight of numbers of judges, the plaintiff lost; a triumph for the law of logic.

This case is akin to what a Kentucky court, speaking of the fallability of academic tests, said:

"Take the bumblebee. Apply to him the recognized aerotechnical tests. From the points, shape and weight of his body in relation to total wing area, he cannot possibly fly. But the bumblebee does not know this and he goes ahead and flies anyway."

In the very nature of things, we cannot avoid technicalities, quibbles and legalisms. Since the year 4000 B.C. we have had approximately sixteen different legal systems, of which about one-half still survive. Of these, our own is about 400 years old, as against the Chinese, which has survived, in one form or another, for some 5,000 years. None of these systems has been able to avoid technicalities or to work out an effective method of administering exact justice between man and man. Such a system cannot be woven out of the materials with which we must work.

However, we can minimize technicalities by improvement of the quality and character of our legislators, of our lawyers and of our judges. Intelligent laws, intelligently drawn, will lessen the fictions of statutory construction; judges will not have to strain themselves to repair obvious statutory defects, and lawyers will not be offered the so-

# LOOK AT THE LAW

frequent opportunity to find convenient legal refuges. More intelligent and more realistic judges will more readily dispose of sophistries, so that lawyers will be loath to advance them. More courageous and more public-spirited lawyers will interpose before their defense of a client and the client's greed a barrier of self-respect that will deny the temptation to further the client's cause by underhanded subterfuge.

Above all, if we could instill a greater morality in our suitors; if a man wouldn't do in a court of law what he wouldn't do in a drawing-room, or better still, in a gaming-room, we might find less technicality and more morality in the law.

Until we attain these Utopian goals, we must concentrate on the improvement of our judges—for it is their task to alleviate the rigor of rule and to avoid the evasion of beneficial rule. The means of so doing are discussed elsewhere.

Meanwhile, the need of avoiding existing technicalities tends to make the law hypocritical.

# CHAPTER VI

## *The Layman Says:*
# THE LAW IS HYPOCRITICAL

*1.*

WHEN the Smiths endeavor to be the social equals of the Joneses, inconsistency becomes the pattern of their lives. They go to boring parties though they prefer to be home in bed; they eat rich food in public that disagrees with them in private; they pretend to a bookish or musical culture they do not possess; they spend money they cannot afford.

So it is with the law. When it represents that it deals equal justice to all; when it guarantees the equal right of all to life, liberty and the pursuit of happiness, without distinction of race, religion and color; when it defines "justice" as the practice of treating all alike before the law, it is forced to deny its origins, to make false claims of being scientific and logical, and to hide a much worn biologic undershirt behind a shirt-front dickey of pretense.

In the adoption of laws, lawmakers frequently discriminate between the powerful and the weak, the privileged and the humble. When the rich are in control of the government, legislators curry favor with the wealthy and pass the cost of government on to the poor through sales taxes on necessities. When business is in the saddle, legislators enact anti-labor laws calculated to reduce production costs and pass high protective tariff laws designed to increase profits. We still have poll taxes where landowners' psychology still preponderates, and there are today no small number of advocates of the denial of the vote to those on relief.

When the masses control at elections, lawmakers exploit

# LOOK AT THE LAW

the rich. They surtax the upper bracketeers, their furs, their superpowered automobiles and their other luxuries. They curry favor with the underprivileged with doles and bonuses, and cater to labor with wage, hour and similar class measures.

In the ranges of the criminal law, the distinction between the potent and the impotent is often glaring. Poor men's crimes, assault and robbery, rape and murder are unequivocally prescribed and proscribed. The theft of a loaf of bread or of a bottle of milk is defined by the statutes without complication or refinement. But the instruments of fraud and deceit by which the rich take from the poor, the practices of monopoly and chicanery, the methods of big business and finance—these are often found to be without recognition in the statute books or, when found there, are the subjects of such indirection and ambiguity that highly paid lawyers can readily perceive byways and exits.

The discrimination is obvious, for rich men do not need to steal purses, while poor men have no chance to steal millions.

In many States the laws still regard women as men's intellectual inferiors. In some States discriminatory legislation excludes married women from civil service positions; in others their pursuit of certain occupations is forbidden. Many protective laws for women workers are found, in practice, to cause employers to hire men instead of women. So much so in some instances that the intent of the legislators who pass them might almost be considered ulterior. In consequence, Senator Radcliffe of Maryland recently announced his intention of supporting the National Woman's Party and clubwomen in their demand for passage of an Equal Rights Amendment of the Federal Constitution.

However, it is in the administration of the law that its hypocrisies most glaringly appear.

# LOOK AT THE LAW

Many of our Southern States have laws on their statute books to insure to Negroes the equal rights secured to them by the Fourteenth Amendment to the Federal Constitution. Yet only recently, in the Scottsboro cases, the United States Supreme Court was called upon to reverse judgments of conviction for murder because, in their practical administration, the State laws permitting Negroes to serve on juries were completely ignored. Recently, a Northern Negro Congressman, forced to travel "Jim Crow" after his train had crossed the Mason-Dixon line, had more trouble than satisfaction when he sought legal redress for the deprivation of the civil rights guaranteed him in no uncertain terms by the Federal Constitution.

A conference recently held at Birmingham condemned the South's "Jim Crow" laws and called for "full citizenship for all persons, regardless of race, abolition of poll taxes and equal educational opportunity for all children."

Even more recently, the United States Supreme Court denied the right of the Missouri legislature to refuse Negroes admittance to State law schools even though the State subsidized them to go elsewhere.

No class is free from fault in seeking to protect and perpetuate vested rights by unjust and undue discrimination that violates our basic democratic tenets of equality of opportunity. The 1939 New York State Senate found it necessary to pass a bill to exclude from the benefits of the State Labor Relations Act any union which denied membership to persons because of race, creed or color. Labor representatives opposed the bill.

Though religious freedom is promised to all, schools, colleges, clubs and even hotels exclude or restrict Catholics, Jews and Negroes, while juries, called upon to redress violations of Civil Rights Law, support flimsy defenses based upon perjured facts.

# LOOK AT THE LAW

In this late day our Federal courts are called upon to vitiate an ordinance forbidding the distribution of handbills (and we are reminded of the freedom with which the eighteenth century Englishman distributed much franker "broadsides," and wonder about our much vaunted progress in democratic government). Our Supreme Court is moved to prohibit "deportation" from a boss-ridden community, and to enforce the right of assembly and free speech therein to punish anti-union terrorists in their efforts to intimidate union mine workers, and in other ways to uphold, in a small way, the civil rights standards we so optimistically enunciate.

The rich and the influential are almost invariably favored in the administration of our civil and criminal laws. A motor-cycle policeman often hesitates and lets the speeding Rolls-Royce go by, particularly when it bears a favored license plate, and it is an unusual prosecuting attorney who will not appreciate the extenuating circumstances which someone with power or influence urges on behalf of a defendant.

The principal instrument that denies our pretensions of legal equality is usually the lawyer. The rich man gets a lawyer who wields the powers of wealth and influence through a large, well-equipped and well-connected organization. The poor man gets a lawyer who fits his purse, if he gets one at all.

The late Justice Cardozo of the United States Supreme Court, in a recent address, told of the time in New York when there were so few lawyers available that the City Council passed a statute to forbid a rich man from hiring all of the lawyers and thereby preventing his adversary from finding one to represent him. He told the story jestingly to illustrate different and more paradisiacal days for lawyers than the overcrowded ones in which they now suffer. He might have mentioned another ordinance, more in

# LOOK AT THE LAW

keeping with the times, modeled upon an imperial ordinance of Rome, wherein it was declared to be the duty of the presiding judge to see that an unfair number of the leading advocates were not engaged by the same side, and wherein it was also provided that if one side was prevented from obtaining adequate legal assistance, this should be considered proof of the injustice of the other side's cause.

In a civil case, the poor man often appears without a lawyer; in a criminal case, counsel is assigned. The rich man fights a case to the final court; the poor man who can find no money for his lawyer, and who has neither relatives nor friends, is usually advised to plead guilty. The rich man's lawyer renders arduous services for swollen fees; the poor man's lawyer usually makes an effort in keeping with the meager fee he hopes to receive.

This has always been so. Juvenal said of counsel for the Roman poor:

> "The court has met; with pale and careworn face
> You rise to plead some hapless client's case,
> And crack your voice, for what? When all is o'er,
> To see a bunch of laurel on your door.
> This is the meed of eloquence; to dine
> On dried-up hams, and cabbage, and sour wine."

Sitting in the front row of benches in almost every criminal court of the land at ten o'clock Monday morning, when the judge enters, may be found a number of lawyers.

"Oyez! Oyez! Oyez!" intones the bailiff. Once the judge is seated, the officers bring into the barred pen a batch of prisoners who have been recently arrested. They are being arraigned for pleading.

The clerk calls a name. The officer unbars the door of

# LOOK AT THE LAW

the pen and a scared and miserable-looking Negro youth steps out. With an officer beside him, he moves forward before the bench.

"Rufus Smith," intones the clerk, "you are charged with the crime of grand larceny. Anything you say will be used against you. You are entitled to an adjournment of forty-eight hours in which to obtain a lawyer. Have you retained counsel or do you want counsel assigned to you before you plead? How do you plead, guilty or not guilty?"

The scared Negro swallows his Adam's apple in fear and confusion. He hasn't understood a word.

"He's askin' you have you got a lawyer?" whispers the officer beside him.

"No, suh, Ah ain't got no lawyer," answers Smith.

"Do you want to get one?" asks the officer.

"Ah ain't got no money, boss," says the Negro.

The officer turns to the waiting judge. "He says he wants a lawyer assigned, your Honor."

"Very well," says the judge. "I'll assign Mr. Thompson to defend this man. We'll call this case again."

Mr. Thompson, himself a Negro and a member of the bar, has been sitting in the front pew. He strolls over to the side of the pen and interviews his new client.

"Got any money?" is his first question.

"No, Mr. Lawyer," says Smith.

"Where do you come from?" asks Thompson.

"N'Orleans."

"Got any relatives here?"

"No, suh."

"No relatives anywhere?"

"Well, Ah got a brother-in-law what's cookin' on the Pennsylvania."

"Don't he come into New York?"

"Yes, suh, sometimes."

# LOOK AT THE LAW

Finally Thompson arranges to seek out Smith's brother-in-law and meanwhile pleads the prisoner "not guilty." Smith goes back to jail to await trial.

If Smith had been charged with murder the counsel assigned to defend him would have been entitled to an allowance from the State for defending him—$500 to $1,000; hardly an inducement to have the life of a man on one's hands. For lesser crimes the lawyer must fend for himself, and unless he can find some relative or friend who will lend the defendant some money, or put it up for him, the defendant generally finds himself pleading guilty. If someone can be found who will beg, borrow or steal the money for a fee, the assigned lawyer devotes his talents to the defense.

The abuses of this system were pungently described by District Attorney Dewey of New York at a recent Legal Aid Society dinner:

"I should like to take you also to the Court of Special Sessions. There, before a bench of three judges, cases are tried for crimes ranging from bookmaking to unlawful entry, from liquor law violations to possession of burglars' tools and from impairing the morals of a minor to malicious mischief. One-third of these defendants have no lawyer and there is no lawyer to take their cases. They stand before a criminal court without representation except such as the court itself provides for them. The judges are forced to interpose objections themselves and rule on them for the preservation of the record for appeal. In all 27,900 residents of this city passed through the Court of Special Sessions in the year 1937. Of these a total of 16,000, or more than half, were in New York County, and of this number approximately 5,000 were without benefit of counsel.

"More than 1,200 other felony cases were assigned to a collection of lawyers who sit more or less regularly on the

# LOOK AT THE LAW

benches. The result is a tragedy and a farce. These bench warmers, most of whose offices are in their hats, represent our profession in Part I of General Sessions. You are entitled to know how the profession is represented there.

"Not long ago, one of these lawyers was assigned to a case in Part I. In violation of his oath as a member of the bar, he squeezed $25 in fees out of the defendant. Difficulties arose between them and the Voluntary Defenders took over the case. They soon learned of the fee and reported it to the court, who ordered the attorney to return the fee. A week passed and he returned $12.50, stating that he had spent the balance on 'expenses.' These expenses, it developed, amounted to carfares for two visits to the Tombs. Again the court was advised and finally, after protracted delay, the lawyer gave up the other $12.50.

"Only last month a lawyer who regularly makes his office in the Magistrates' Court came out of the courtroom at the end of the morning session well satisfied. He confided to a friend that it had been a good day. He was assigned by the magistrate to defend a woman on charges of vagrancy and at the end of the case she was convicted. But she so aroused the magistrate's sympathy that he suspended sentence and gave her five dollars out of his own pocket. Said the lawyer to his friend: 'This was just enough to complete my fee and when we got downstairs I made her turn it over to me. It was a good day's work.'

"Too often the very livelihood of the lawyer who sits on the benches accepting assignments from the court is made up of money extracted from the impoverished relatives of an unfortunate defendant. I have seen case after case of this kind. While the defendant waits in the Tombs for his trial, his own lawyer demands and procures adjournments so he can put pressure on the defendant's family to raise money to pay him for services he undertook to perform as an officer of the court. There have been cases where the assigned lawyer abandoned his client when he found there was no money in it.

"Only recently one of these lawyers was assigned to represent a sixteen-year-old defendant under indictment. Immediately he began writing letters to the boy's family in another State, demanding $250 for his services and threatening that unless he was paid, the defendant would be sentenced to thirty years in prison. While every lawyer and social worker would know that no such thing was, as a practical matter, likely or possible, this lawyer delayed the trial for weeks until he completed his efforts unethically to extort a fee.

"Last month a new all-time low was reached. A defendant in the Tombs had all his money on deposit with the cashier at the City Prison, a total of twenty-five cents. A member of the New York Bar was assigned to defend the case and his first act was to procure an assignment of the twenty-five cents from the defendant and collect it from the prison cashier."

Besides skillful and diligent counsel, the rich man has at his command trained accountants, investigators, medical and other experts. The poor man has none of these things. The rich man can buy delay and technicalities. For the poor man justice is swift and sure.

In criminal cases money buys political-legal influences which obtain continuances until witnesses die or disappear, intimidate witnesses and bribe prosecuting officials and jurors.

Even after final conviction and affirmance, hope is not dead for those with money. Pardon boards, commutations—there are always moves that can be made so long as they can be paid for. Even executive clemency may be obtained, if not for a political price, then by use of highly-paid doc-

# LOOK AT THE LAW

tors, alienists, or other experts, guided by the astute and resourceful hand of a lawyer. We shall not soon forget the pardoning of Morse, the shipping man, after doctors had testified that he was about to die, and his survival for many years thereafter, once his prison doors had been unlocked. We cannot help but contrast this with the protracted incarceration of Mooney and of the Scottsboro Negroes.

As a rich man keeps alive with the aid of doctors and nurses long after a poor man would have died, so money enables the rich man to avoid the clutches of the law long after the poor man would have succumbed. The career of the notorious Harry K. Thaw offers a striking example.

On June 25, 1906, Thaw killed Stanford White. At his first trial the jury disagreed. On a second trial Thaw was acquitted on the ground of insanity. He was committed to an insane asylum and later escaped. He was found in Canada. When he was deported from Canada he was indicted in Dutchess and New York counties for conspiracy in escaping. Meanwhile, he was released on bail. Thereupon he obtained the appointment of a lunacy commission which found him sane.

Subsequently his mother petitioned for the appointment of another lunacy commission; he was adjudged insane. All this continued from 1906, when the killing occurred, until 1924, when he was finally adjudged sane.

It is said that these various legal complications cost the Thaw family more than a million dollars; without money his case would have been dealt with summarily and settled, once and for all, many years before.

Though we use the term, "rich man," more practical usage suggests the term, "influential man." Though money can and does invariably buy influence, much influence is exerted without wealth. Everything that has been said about the ability of men of affluence to deny the equality of legal

# LOOK AT THE LAW

processes may as readily be said about men of influence. These include, among others, politicians, gangsters, employees of moneyed corporations and officers and agents of labor unions; in short, anyone who may control money or influence votes.

The influence of the influential is not direct, but subtle. It is not overt, but surreptitious. Indeed, when two litigants must face a jury, the poor man is the more likely to get a favorable verdict (largely because of the personnel of jurors —especially in urban centers). Thus a forty-eight-year-old tailor obtained a substantial verdict against the chairman of the Standard Oil Company of New York upon a charge that he had had him committed to an insane asylum for writing letters to his (the defendant's) daughter, while a pedestrian obtained a verdict against J. P. Morgan for injuries resulting from an automobile accident. And, too, when public attention is directly focused upon the rich man accused of crime, as in the case of Richard Whitney, ex-President of the New York Stock Exchange, the glare of publicity often compels summary treatment.

Still, when money can bring delay, finance flight and avoid examination or extradition, as in the case of Insull, who went to Greece, of the oil executives Blackmer and O'Neil, who went to France, of Stewart, who went to South America, of Bergdoll, who went to Germany, the delay is not usually compatible with the trend of public opinion.

It may safely be said that wealth and influence directly or indirectly mold the processes and administration of the law. Whether it be on the criminal or the civil side, the result is no different, though on the civil side it is less widely known or publicized.

This is no new complaint. Bonner quotes Demosthenes as saying: "The bulk of us, O Athenians, have no share of

# LOOK AT THE LAW

common or equal rights with the wealthy; indeed we have not. They have what time they please allowed them for answering complaints and their offenses come before you stale and cold; whereas, if anything happens to one of us he is tried immediately after the act."

Nor is it an uncommon one today. An old Russian proverb advises: "Do not wrestle with the strong; do not go to court with the rich."

In Mexico, according to an article in *Esquire*, law administrators are more brazen and less hypocritical than are ours. "Justice," according to the writer, "is still a rich man's prerogative, a commodity you buy in a limited market with the judge as jobber and the lawyer as broker. Like in the days of Hammurabi, the rich strike a deal while the poor go to prison. . . . A rich man in prison is 'an accident,' not a proof of equal justice for all. . . . If you are poor, you are punished and that is all."

### 2.

The fiction of equality in the law is carried out by the injunction, "Let the punishment fit the crime." Here again, even assuming that such a standard would serve equality, we find an implied promise of equality, largely unperformed.

A scared, starving, unemployed baker holds up the cashier of a cafeteria, grabs five or ten dollars from the till and runs. A howling mob follows at his heels, a policeman brings him down with a shot and captures him. He is indicted summarily for robbery, tried and convicted, and subjected to imprisonment at hard labor for a term of ten years and, if he has been previously convicted, perhaps for life.

Yet sleek stock manipulators and bankers take tolls of millions of dollars, cause poverty, misery and suicide of men, women and children, and the law shrugs its shoulders, saying: "*Caveat emptor*—let the buyer beware." When the

# LOOK AT THE LAW

law does work, it punishes a scheme to defraud, though it may impoverish thousands, as a mere misdemeanor, while the larceny of a rich man's purse is made a felony. Thus, in Pennsylvania, the statutes make embezzlement a felony if committed by a servant, whereas it is only a misdemeanor when committed by a banker, or by a corporate officer or director, or by a trustee.

The law lays heavy sanctions upon the convicted felon, though the cause of his crime be poverty, with its degrading youthful associations and environment. Attempts to palliate society's offense by treating the transgressor as a first offender come too late—the damage has already been done.

The attitude of the law respecting the punishment of the mental, physical and moral defective gives little heed to the relationship between the offense and its punishment. Our jails are full of mental cases, men with weak and diseased minds and bodies who have been convicted of offenses which are defined by the law as crimes and who are being punished just as though they were of normal mentalities and physiques.

An elevator man, in a wild fit of rage induced by the boss's refusal to give him the afternoon off, maniacally filed down and weakened the elevator cables, plunging a half-dozen innocent people to injury and possible death. His diseased mind figured that the injured persons would hold the boss responsible.

A middle-aged mail clerk committing arson to see the fire engines run; a sadist killing a woman; a pervert exposing his person—these and thousands of others inhabit our jails because they are not "legally" insane.

In dealing with the mental defective, the punishment neither fits the criminal nor does it fit the crime. Here the law makes symbols and rule the measure of its hypocrisies. Under a tender physical age, assumed to be an outpost of

# LOOK AT THE LAW

irresponsibility, a criminal is a juvenile delinquent, his act juvenile delinquency. Beyond it, regardless of the mental age of the delinquent, he is a criminal, his delinquency punishable as a crime. A mental, physical or moral delinquent, even unto the medically insane, is of a piece with the sane, knowing, and deliberate law-breaker.

The defective cannot escape punishment as a criminal unless he is "legally" insane. In the middle of the nineteenth century an English judge defined insanity as being a state of mind that does not permit one to know what he is doing or that what he is doing is wrong. This remains the definition of "legal insanity."

The judge will illustrate the difference by charging the jury as follows: 'If you find that the defendant's mental state was such when he killed this young man that he did not know what he was doing or did not know that what he was doing was wrong, you may find him 'not guilty because insane.' If, however, you find that he did know what he was doing when he killed this young man, or he did know that what he was doing was wrong, you must find him 'guilty' regardless of whether you believe that he was medically insane or whether you believe that he was moved to kill by an impulse which he was mentally incapable of resisting."

Examples of this rule show untoward consequences, not merely to the "criminal," but to society.

The pickpocket is punished for his deliberate act; the kleptomaniac is punished just as though it were his deliberate act. Meanwhile, a perfectly sane woman defendant who kills her lover pleads momentary "legal insanity"—for a blinding moment she did not know what she was doing—and a sympathetic jury finds her "not guilty because insane."

Not alone are congenital and other defectives unfairly treated by being put in jails where there is no chance of

# LOOK AT THE LAW

cure, but society is subjected to recurring danger of their presence by treating them as criminals, jailing them for specified terms and then turning them loose again to ravage and prey. There is some excuse for parole commissioners who are deceived into believing a criminal to have reformed so that he may be returned to society. There is no excuse for a system that turns unfortunate animals out of jails to commit new crimes instead of committing them to asylums until cured. Many of our most notorious capital crimes within recent years have been directly attributable to the legal definition of insanity and the treatment of the defective as a criminal.

A twenty-four-year-old upholsterer, named Fiorenza, after having been arrested four times for irresistible-impulse crimes, was freed on probation in the face of the psychiatrist's report indicating that he was a dangerous person. Finally, he attacked and murdered a young married woman and was electrocuted for the crime.

A farm boy, one Alexander Meyer, free after one attack on a girl, ran down another, ravished the body and threw it down a well.

A nine-year-old child was ravished and beaten to death by a Brooklyn barber named Ossido, who was out on bail awaiting trial on another sex crime and who had a criminal record for similar crimes.

Veronica Gideon, a young artists' model, her mother, and a waiter who boarded with them were murdered by Robert Irwin, a young sculptor who had been released from an asylum and whose criminal tendencies were a matter of official record.

A thirty-year-old man was sentenced to a fixed term in state's prison for molesting a girl and will be turned out to prey on society though, in addition to other miscellaneous crimes, he had been arrested and convicted for rape at dif-

# LOOK AT THE LAW

ferent times, for annoying children and for impairing the morals of children. Another, a fifty-three-year-old laborer, is serving a fixed term for impairing the morals of a five-year-old girl, and will be freed at the expiration of his term to repeat other offenses such as these, which his criminal record discloses: indecent assault, carnal abuse of a child, molesting a six-year-old girl, molesting an eight-year-old girl, molesting another six-year-old girl.

If imprisonment is designed to punish and deter, how futile it is in these cases to take revenge on the diseased! How little deterrent is to be found in clapping up one mental deficient, without attempt at a cure, as an example to another!

The punishment of the diseased and the weak is as logical today as was the practice of trying domestic animals for crime in a former day. A law writer says that "the record of the criminal tribunals of France discloses ninety-two such juridical processes between 1120 and 1741." Oxen and pigs were tried and condemned to death for goring or otherwise maiming, killing or devouring young children. Formal trials were held which were followed by a solemn form of execution, even to the extreme of fastening a pig to a cross in the cemetery where all condemned criminals were executed.

Without going into the subject too fully, our entire system of punishment for crime may be said to be based upon a series of unscientific subterfuges, evasions and shams. We fine and jail persons convicted of criminal offenses as punishment and as deterrents to others. This means that we fix punishments so that the next person may feel it in his interest to pass up the opportunity for criminal gain in the face of possible punishment.

In truth, the sentence, within the defined limits which the law sets, fits not the criminal or the crime but the judge, his personality and his particular state of mind on the day in question. Some judges are severe, some lenient. Some condemn one type of crime and condone another. Some are liberal in their social views; others take a most charitable view only of the defections of the rich. Professor Frederick J. Gaudet, in a recent monograph based upon a study covering a ten-year period, concludes that the wide variance in sentencing habits of various judges can be ascribed only to variance of personalities.

Yet some judges are honest; others are reachable. Some yield to the call of money; others to the influence of votes. Some are put on the bench by political organizations linked to gangsters; others are mercenaries of corrupt business corporations.

James V. Bennett, Federal director of prisons, in a recent address to judges, gave a list of "horrible example" contrasts between sentences in analogous criminal cases. While urging more consistency in sentences, he told of an inveterate counterfeiter, sixty-three years old, with a thirty-year criminal record, who had received a year and a day as his sentence; while a thirty-two-year-old first offender of poor environment had received seven years for attempting to pass a single bad bill.

The defendant's sentence may also vary with the judge's humor. A judge's wife's temper may readily add years to the permanency of abode of the criminal population. At Christmas time, when the judge is "high," sentences are low. When the judge is low, the converse may hold true.

Yet a mere conviction and suspended sentence with consequent social ostracism may be greater punishment to a decent person who has made a single mistake than a severe prison term to a hardened criminal.

The whole subject of criminal punishment (which we do not here attempt to discuss at length) is such a survival and retention of anachronisms of hatred and revenge, of

# LOOK AT THE LAW

punishment, of inabilities to face realities and to make honest valuations, of unwillingness to pay the burden of dealing properly with poverty and ignorance and their consequences of crime—in short, the system of criminal punishment is so strait-jacketed by medieval legal custom, dogma and myth, practices shutting out modern scientific thought and discovery, that it may be summed up as a tissue of legal hypocrisies. Certainly it denies any pretension that the law deals equality. Instead it adds to the punishment of the punished, while mitigating the penalties upon the strong and influential.

All this is so, in the absence of political intervention. When politics takes a hand (and the criminal courts offer a favorite stamping ground for lesser political lights who maintain the liaison between political and criminal rackets), then hypocrisy becomes venality.

The attempt to reconcile criminal punishment with justice rests, under modern methods, upon our probation system. Unscientific at best, it becomes a corrupt farce when the politician takes it over. Hardened and habitual criminals trade gangster aid in corralling, intimidating and stealing votes in exchange for probation favors that justify dishonest judges and fool honest ones, while the balance of punishment is preserved by excessive severity towards unfavored offenders.

In New York recently, the State Department of Correction, after public demand, finally released (after it had been withheld for eighteen months for "editing") a report criticizing the personnel and methods of the Probation Department of the Kings County Court as inadequate and inefficient and stating that the "major motivating force" in the department appeared to be "largely political."

Manifestly, even a bad system can be made worse in this fashion.

# LOOK AT THE LAW

And civil sanctions share these faults. Frequently the consequence of infractions of the civil law surpass those of the criminal law.

If Jones steals less than $25, the law limits his sentence to a misdemeanor term in jail. Only if he commits murder, or some other ranking capital crime, may he be executed. In between these offenses, penalties are at least supposed to be designed to fit the crimes. At any rate, for a crime, the convicted criminal gets a defined sentence with a maximum term fixed. For a civil offense, one may be imprisoned at the pleasure and during the displeasure of the judge. For a refusal to obey the order of a judge, whether it be to answer questions or to execute a deed, to pay money to one's wife for alimony, or to return money taken from an estate (even though in the latter cases one may be financially unable to do so), an offender may be kept in jail indefinitely. Often the real offense is offending the judge, who may dislike the offender rather than the offense; or it may be, and often is, the dignity of the bench that is offended. The judge masks vengeance, which sometimes is exaggerated far beyond the actual offense, under the legal pseudonym of contempt.

In a recent case, a judge had so severely charged a jury against a defendant that he had been convicted. A few weeks later while another criminal case was being tried before the same judge, the trial was interrupted so that he might hear an application by the District Attorney to set aside the prior conviction, the District Attorney having meanwhile become convinced that the defendant was innocent. Later, while summing up in the case on trial, the defendant's lawyer was tactless enough to call the jurymen's attention to the scene they had just witnessed as proof of the possibility of unjust conviction. The judge, smarting under the knowledge of his unwarranted contribution to the unjust result in the prior case, held the lawyer in con-

# LOOK AT THE LAW

tempt and fined him for attempting to "befuddle the jury"— a practice for which lawyers have been hired and in which they have been engaged since ancient Roman days.

Juries have no small power to fix exorbitant punishments. When they dislike a litigant or his lawyer, or if they overlike his opponent or his lawyer, they may fix an amount in reaching a verdict out of all proportion to the offense charged in the complaint. This is particularly true in actions where women claim damages for breach of promise, seduction and other affairs *de coeur*. A breach of promise to a good-looking blonde with a nice pair of ankles is a much more serious offense than it would be if the plaintiff were less to the jury's fancy.

In personal injury cases, the whole scheme of assessing damage is faulty.

Suppose, while driving an automobile, Jones's attention is diverted for a moment and he hits a passer-by. The injured pedestrian sues to recover damages for his injuries. The judgment he recovers is designed to compensate him for his losses—his loss in wages, the cost of his medical treatment, the impairment of his future earning ability—and to give him compensation for any suffering or injury he has sustained.

While the law seeks to compensate the injured party, it does so only if Jones, the automobilist, is found to be at fault. In that case, it punishes Jones by compelling him to compensate the injured man for his injury. If Jones was not at fault, if neither party was at fault, or if both were at fault, the pedestrian is not compensated, nor is Jones penalized. Obviously, the situation carries with it a curious admixture of effort to compensate and effort to penalize.

If Jones alone is at fault, the penalty he is assessed depends not upon what he has done, but upon the conse-

# LOOK AT THE LAW

quences, however little he intended them. But it does not reckon with his ability to pay.

If Jones has merely bruised the passer-by who has been agile enough to get almost clear, Jones may be called upon to pay some nominal sum, such as $100. If the pedestrian's reactions are slower and he is seriously hurt, the judgment against Jones is likely to be $10,000 or more. If the injured man happens to be a laborer earning $4 a day, the amount he is awarded would be a hundred times less than if he happened to be a banker earning $100,000 a year. If the pedestrian is an actress whose face is considered beautiful, a scar on her face will subject Jones to greater penalties than if she happens to be a salesgirl in a five-and-ten-cent store, whose face bears no relationship to her fortune. Yet Jones's momentary lapse—his offense—is the same.

Why should Jones give up the savings of a lifetime of labor in paying a judgment to a person he struck with his automobile, just because his attention lagged for a single moment? Nobody can keep his eye on the road all the time. To do so is a physical impossibility, even if one's attention were not constantly diverted by road signs, other automobiles, pedestrians, shop windows, and a hundred and one other things which naturally divert the attention and are legally put there for that express purpose.

Jones drives for an uneventful twenty years; once a passer-by is injured through his lagging attention, and Jones becomes a wrongdoer. A jury visits judgment upon him, and the injured man sends the sheriff to take his house and his lands and his savings, even to garnishee his salary. One moment Jones was comfortable and well-fixed, owned his own home, had money in the bank, with his old age provided for; the next minute he finds himself a potential bankrupt and pauper. Clearly, the apothegm that the law makes the punishment fit the crime is a delusion in these cases.

# LOOK AT THE LAW

The injured pedestrian is gambling too. If the offending motorist is a J. P. Morgan, the injured man may be in luck, however slightly he is hurt; if the driver is a day laborer with a car but no liability insurance, the unfortunate victim may as well not be hurt at all for all the monetary reward he may expect.

Academically, the basis of an award in a negligence suit is not to have the punishment fit the fault; it is retaliation, punishment of the one who has been most at fault. Practically, it often works out as an effort to charge the one better able to bear the loss, either as between the parties themselves, or as between the wrongdoer and the State, which would have to support an injured pauper. Or it may simply be the expression of the jury's sympathy or resentment, or the fruit of the jurors' own experiences. The conflicting bases account for many of the compromise verdicts for which juries are frequently, and often unjustifiably, criticized.

*3.*

In many situations, the law can do little or nothing to moderate the gap between our virtuous preachments and our nefarious practices, the hypocrisies of our great American mores. Take those that flow from the concepts that man is a civilized, ethical, soulful creature, celestially bred, with a divine mission on earth. How is the law to reconcile the moral inhibitions against gambling on the statute books, or to fit the call of the flesh to the proscriptions of the sexless, the inhibited or the uninitiated? In short, how is the law to solve the problems created by moral injunctions with amoral desires for wine, women and wrong?

From time immemorial, in these fields of human diversion, we have preached one form and practiced another.

# LOOK AT THE LAW

A recent Gallup poll showed that fifty per cent of our population gamble, the ventures ranging from church lotteries, twenty-nine per cent; punchboards, twenty-six per cent; slot machines, twenty-three per cent; card-playing for money, twenty-one per cent; betting on elections, nineteen per cent; sweepstake tickets, thirteen per cent; betting on horse races, ten per cent; to numbers game, nine per cent.

To paraphrase Victor Hugo, this must be a great crime or none at all, since all are guilty of it. Yet we seek to restrict by law our natural tendencies to take a chance and to try to get something for nothing.

Having committed our legislators to a policy of hypocritical statutes against gambling, we pursue a hypocritical policy of enforcement. We arrest the little policy player who gambles a few cents on what the last numbers of the Stock Exchange clearance figures show; we pick up the street-corner crap-shooter and we fine the card-playing frequenters of the back room of the cigar store and saloon. But we wink at the race-track bettors and the bridge, poker and roulette players, playing for far higher stakes at their homes, in their clubs or in gaming rooms at Saratoga, Newport and Miami. Ofttimes the judges who sentence little gamblers to jail during the week patronize Saratoga, Palm Beach and French Lick casinos over the week-end.

Though the constitutions of many of our States expressly perpetuate our colonial inhibitions against gambling, our legislatures pass evasive statutes designed to let down the bars for horse and dog race tracks and other forms of escape for a commerce-ridden people. The results are sometimes shocking.

In New York, for example, in 1934, the legislature, desiring, in the face of a constitutional prohibition against gambling, to legalize race-track betting, ingeniously removed the criminal penalties of bookmaking by reiterating

# LOOK AT THE LAW

that the loser at a race track could recover his money. Since, under a judicial precedent, one cannot be subjected to double penalties, the courts must find that since the winner is subject to a civil penalty, i.e., the loss of his winnings, the criminal penalty goes by the board.

The practical result was, before the recent change in the constitution, that a bookmaker could make book and a bettor could bet at a race track in New York without being arrested, with the following contradictions:

(1) The constitutional provisions prohibited the pari-mutuel system (which has since been adopted by vote of the people) so the State could not make the tremendous profits other States made out of horse racing.

(2) One was guilty of a crime if one took bets at a place other than a race track.

(3) One could bet on horses but could not bet on dogs.

(4) A loser could sue to get his money back though everybody knew an average jury would not give it to him.

In the horse-racing business, before this expedient was devised, various other devices were utilized to evade the law. They were successful chiefly because of the cooperation of the authorities, including at times the judges (many of whom are regular attendants at the race tracks), who reasoned realistically that the people wanted to go to horse races and to bet, and there was nothing inherently wrong about it anyway.

In the dog-racing field, where the sponsorship is not so rich and so influential as in the horse-racing field, the operators have had a harder row to hoe. There, for a time, they were conducting betting operations "under an ingeniously devised scheme, deliberately contrived to avoid the pitfalls" of the law, under which they sold purchase options upon each dog in a race, which, if exercised, were repurchased at prices fixed to give winning bettors their profits.

# LOOK AT THE LAW

The scheme was a palpable one to permit betting; but the late Judge Bonynge, recognizing the sham, defended the practice in words and sentiments which are worthy of perpetuation:

"The district attorney urges that these purchase options are a mere subterfuge and that the man who buys one of them for two dollars merely intends, in truth and in fact, to lay a bet of that amount. Very possibly this is true, but a wrongful intent on one side is not enough to satisfy the requirements of the law. Here the uncontradicted evidence shows that the plaintiff is actuated by the bona fide intent to give each and every patron a valid option to buy a particular dog. If such patrons choose to flaunt his good intentions and buy options to line their pockets with unholy gains, they cannot thereby make a criminal out of him. Were the rule otherwise, every cotton and commodity broker or dealer in the land would be in jail before nightfall. Does anyone suppose that the delicatessen dealer who buys an option on 500 bales of cotton ever intends to take delivery of it, or that the salesgirl who acquires a future in 1,000 bushels of wheat will ultimately bake bread or make pancakes with the resultant flour? Let the vendor of an option establish that he is pure in heart and the law takes no account of the base motives of those who may deal with him.

"In the course of his opinion dismissing the writ of habeas corpus to which allusion has already been made" [that was in the criminal case which had been dismissed the year before] "Mr. Justice Steinbrink observed, after strongly hinting the guilt of the present plaintiff, that 'it may be that the trier of the fact is more naive and will find otherwise since what is here stated is not controlling. . . .' Has not my good brother overlooked the fact that a certain amount of naïveté is an essential adjunct to the judicial office? Does not the Supreme Court grind out thousands of divorces annually upon the stereotyped sin of the same big blonde attired in the same black silk pajamas? Is not access to the chamber of love quite uniformly obtained by announcing that it is a maid bringing towels or a messenger boy with an urgent telegram? Do we not daily pretend to hush up the fact that an offending defendant is insured when every

# LOOK AT THE LAW

juror with an ounce of wit recognizes the defendant's lawyer and his entourage as old friends? More than half a century ago P. T. Barnum recorded the fact that the American people delight in being humbugged and such is still the national mood. Nowhere is this trait more clearly shown than in the field of gambling. A church fair or bazaar would scarcely be complete without a bevy of winsome damsels selling chances on bed quilts, radios, electric irons and a host of other things. If the proceeds are to be devoted to the ladies' sewing circle or the dominie's vacation, no sin is perceived and the local prosecutor, whoever and wherever he may be, stays his hand. But if a couple of dusky youths are apprehended rolling bones to a state of moderate warmth, blind Justice perceives the infamy of the performance and the law takes its course. Sweepstakes and lotteries are unspeakably vile and yet through them we have contributed so many millions to the Irish hospitals that it is rumored patriotic Irishmen cheerfully volunteer to have their tonsils and appendixes removed just to keep the hospital beds occupied and the nurses employed. For a generation or more betting at horse races was unlawful. After this prolonged burst of morality the Legislature suddenly discovered the need of 'improving the breed of horses' and enacted article 20 of the Membership Corporations Law, followed later by chapter 440 of the Laws of 1926. In a backhanded way this legislation restored race track betting by removing the criminal penalties. But let no one suspect that our best citizens repair to Belmont Park and other near-by tracks for the purpose of betting or gambling. Perish the thought, for their minds rest on higher things. Improving the breed of horses is their aim, and their conversation, aside from formal greeting, deals solely with sires and dams, foals and fillies, blood lines, consanguinity and inherited characteristics. These things a judge must believe, even at the risk of being chided as naïve, because they are contemporary America."

In a dozen different ways, the law reflects hypocritical life. Recently in Vermont, citizens paraded on the Sabbath, some bearing arms in pursuance of antiquated, unrepealed, Sabbath laws requiring citizens to go armed to church,

# LOOK AT THE LAW

others driving in vehicles at less than five miles per hour to obey hoary anachronisms still on the statute books, all in an attempt to bring disrepute on Sunday closing laws that were being invoked against movies, drug stores and gasoline stations. In many of our cities, theaters operate on Sundays under the guise of "sacred concert" halls. Recently in New York City "burlesque shows" were terminated and "superior vaudeville" substituted.

Though many of our States permit prize fights, films of prize fights held in other States may not be shown without violating a Federal law which forbids the transportation in interstate commerce of prize-fight films.

We need no reminders of the shocking accompaniment of the late, unlamented 18th Amendment to our Federal Constitution. The spectacle which lay hypocrisy made of the law during the Prohibition period requires no elaboration. It is matched, though not so glaringly, by the manner in which the law at present reflects the hypocritical attitude we take when "sex rears its (so-called) ugly head."

We have criminal statutes in many of our States which prescribe a criminal penalty for adultery. Daily our courts grant divorces based on that offense. Yet no one ever prosecutes any of these defendants. On the contrary, a person who went to a prosecuting officer with a request to prosecute in such a case would be considered prima facie a blackmailer.

Thirty-one of our States have similarly unenforced criminal statutes prohibiting fornication.

The treatment of prostitutes belies admission of their necessity and their unavoidable ubiquity. An infected prostitute who has been arrested is charged with "soliciting" and turned out with a fine or, after a perfunctory workhouse sentence, to continue the spread of venereal disease, because, except in isolated instances, the law isn't allowed

# LOOK AT THE LAW

to recognize the problem and to deal with it medically.

We find hypocrisy rampant in the field of matrimonial relations. Some States, such as New York, will not permit divorce for anything short of adultery. The consequence is that people who are incompatible must get divorces in Mexico or Paris, or in Nevada or Florida, based on false statements of intention and residence. Or they must connive at perjury, which is a crime, to get a New York divorce for a fake and planned act of adultery.

That they do this is attested by a recent survey made public by the National Divorce Reform League which reported that although adultery is the only ground for divorce in New York, infidelity actually accounts for only 1.8 per cent of New York divorces. And that this is not peculiar to New York appears from a statement lately made by Justice Denis E. Sullivan, of Chicago, who denounced Chicago divorces, saying, "A great number of divorces are tainted by collusion, perjury and fraud."

A judge who sits on a divorce calendar must not appear shocked or surprised when witness after witness, each called in a separate case, follow each other and say, with slight variations, as noted:

"I am a private detective. On the ⌉14th day of ⌉December / 19th day of / August, at about eleven o'clock in the evening, I followed the defendant to the ⌉Grand / Victoria Hotel. He was with a lady; she was a ⌉blonde / brunette, but was not the plaintiff. I saw him sign the register Mr. and Mrs. John Smith; he was assigned to ⌉317 / 818. I waited a little while and then went to the room. I knocked. A man's voice said. 'Who's there?' I answered,

# LOOK AT THE LAW

"A bellboy with {ice-water.' / a telegram.'} He opened the door slightly It was the defendant. I forced my way into the room. He was {in / without his underwear.} The {brunette / blonde / pink} lady was in the bed. She wore a {blue} nightgown."

The judge knows very well that if the lady was really a lady, the defendant was just being a gentleman and was giving his wife an easy divorce; while if she wasn't a lady, the defendant was merely figuring that having the name, he might as well have the game.

Invariably, the law requires the divorce plaintiff to take the stand and swear that he or she did not collude with the defendant to permit a divorce. This is usually a palpable lie and everyone knows it—plaintiff, defendant, lawyer and judge.

However, the judge must listen to the stock testimony and go through the forms the law requires in many of our States, because strong religious groups prefer to make perjurers of the parties and hypocrites of their lawyers and the judge, rather than allow an honest couple to obtain a frank and honest divorce for incompatibility. The judge has his choice: to refuse a divorce and invite bigamy, adultery and illegitimacy, or to nod at evasion which promotes natural desire and perhaps may ultimately result in another and more successful marriage.

Because of the difficulty of divorce, people often resort to collusive and fraudulent marriage annulment actions.

A boy and girl elope and marry secretly, or after seven or eight drinks, or on a dare. Or perhaps, with deliberation and premeditation on one side, a Follies girl and a callow scion of a rich father, or a male night club entertainer and some

# LOOK AT THE LAW

father's spoiled darling, contract a midnight marriage before a town clerk or justice of the peace. In any of these situations, a few mornings after convince one or the other, or both, of the truth of the marry-in-haste maxim. Thereupon father gets a lawyer and the child or children receive some instruction in the intricacies and hypocrisies of the law of divorce. They are told that to obtain a divorce there must be adultery by one of the parties; to obtain an annulment there need not be adultery, since the law permits a marriage which was void in the beginning and which was never consummated, to be annulled.

The lawyer is asked what the law means when it says the marriage must be void in the beginning. He answers: "If either party was induced to consent to be married by fraud or by duress, if either party did not know what he or she was doing as a result of intoxication, if either party was physically or legally incompetent to consummate the marriage, etc., it can be annulled."

The parties and the lawyer put their wits to work. All that is needed is a story and to have both parties swear to it. If they are both of a mind, there is no obstacle, once a story is agreed upon. If the marriage is a rich girl-poor man, or a poor girl-rich man seduction, the fortune seeker will be glad to swear to anything for compensation.

For the ordinary sort of hasty marriage, where intoxication is not available, the ingenuity of the lawyer is called into play and ordinarily it does not fail. Fraudulent misrepresentations inducing marriage can be readily conceived. The fact that the husband once had a venereal disease is a good ground for annulment, although he has apparently recovered from it; that the wife misrepresented her age or the husband his business or his earnings; that the wife falsely claimed she was pregnant, or that she was a virgin, or that she had not previously had children; that the husband concealed the fact that he had a heritage of inheritable disease, or insanity, or that the wife agreed to go through with a religious, as well as a civil ceremony, but afterwards refused. Any one of these claims or some variation thereof suffices, and the one that most closely fits the facts is adopted by the parties to meet the hypocritical requirements of the law.

There is another point which must be overlooked by the tolerant judge in these cases. The law provides that an annulment may not be granted if the parties have cohabited with each other after the facts have become known. While this is no great stumbling block where the parties are conniving to annul a marriage for fraud, since the plaintiff can usually defer the date of his knowledge to a time when he tired of the connubial couch, the matter is not so easy when an amorous couple marry for fun and decide after a week of it that the time has come to claim they had been drunk, or had married on a bet, or the like. In those cases, it is sometimes difficult to find a judge who is willing to be credulous to the point of believing that the unconscious couple remained unconscious for a week, or spent a week in a hotel room saying their paternosters.

While it is true that even in these candid camera days there are usually no eyewitnesses to the act of consummating a marriage and there is ordinarily no oral testimony that can gainsay the cooperative oath, the law does not require judges to have a moronic belief in the spoken word. Even judges have a right to believe, as one judge expressed it, from experience and observation, without further proof, that "when a chicken cock drops his wing and takes after a hen his purpose is sexual intercourse."

In a recent case in Kings County, New York, the judge tired of the incredible. He had tried, at one term of the court, four or five of these annulment actions. In each one the bride wanted the marriage annulled because the husband

# LOOK AT THE LAW

refused to go through with a religious ceremony after a civil marriage and in each one the bride "solemnly avowed that there was no cohabitation following the civil rites." The next couple, with the same claims, were an actress and her former manager. Just what there was about them to make them the unfortunate victims is difficult to determine, but in any event, the judge selected them as the vehicle to take his expression of strained patience to posterity. After hearing their case, he wrote an opinion referring to the claim that the defendant had agreed to a religious ceremony without which plaintiff would not stay married.

"Such a recrudescence of religious fervor in the present age tends to tax the credulity of the court," his opinion stated. "Nor are its doubts allayed by the extraordinary lack of ardor and curiosity manifested by these young benedicts, or the quite exceptional fortitude and virtue displayed by the female of the species. In a word, the stories sound fantastic and unbelievable. However, truth is sometimes stranger than fiction and it may well be that the nuptial couch has ceased to serve its time-honored function. In the face of recent warnings, old-fashioned jurists must not permit their antediluvian ideas to impede mankind's headlong progress toward the almost perfect state. Hence, if plaintiff will submit to a physical examination by a physician to be designated by the court, and his findings corroborate her claim that the marriage was never consummated, the court will defer to his superior wisdom. Otherwise the complaint will be dismissed."

The fact that the plaintiff announced after the decision that she would seek a divorce in Reno, rather than submit to such an examination, does not necessarily prove her bad faith, and this, unfortunately, demonstrates the judicial test as a fallible one, for plaintiff may have been previously married, or may have had sexual or medical experience to which

# LOOK AT THE LAW

she was unwilling to confess, or she may have been unwilling to undergo the humiliation of such a test.

The law's hypocrisies in the field of sex relations are closely allied with the fictional "temporary insanity" defense which is most commonly employed by love-triangle participants who have killed lovers or spouses.

This branch of the law is rampant with hypocrisy. As we have already pointed out, a medically insane defendant is treated as a criminal, with dire consequences to himself and society. In that connection, we referred to the ease of establishing fictional temporary insanity in sex cases, and the difficulty of establishing legal insanity in less sensational situations.

The determination of these matters, where the case goes to trial, is left to lay juries with no medical knowledge or training and with no ability to assess them. However, this is not due to legal incompetency but to necessary legal hypocrisy. The law doesn't want a jury of experts; it doesn't want to ascertain whether or not the defendant is actually medically insane. It knows the standard of legal insanity which it sets up is a false one — particularly when the plea uses the stock phrases: "everything went black — or red, or blue — and the next thing I knew. . . ." That might be really important, if true, in determining whether the killing was deliberate and cold-blooded, or whether it occurred because the defendant got angry and suffered a rush of blood to the head. (Getting angry and being mad — in the technical sense — are two different things, and ordinarily the law notes the distinction.)

What the law is really saying to the jury in these cases is, "We can't openly sanction such killings but if you think they're O. K., we'll give you a chance to say so." As Denys Wortman, Scripps-Howard cartoonist, put it, supplementing a cartoon showing two women discussing a tabloid head-

# LOOK AT THE LAW

line of "Not Guilty," "Not guilty doesn't mean she didn't kill her husband, it just means it's O. K. to kill him."

In short, the trial of the defendant is often converted into a trial of the decedent, and when the latter is found guilty the former is thereby automatically acquitted.

The advantage of this unsanctioned system is that a jury may find a balance between a rigid standard of legal conduct and a rational application of that standard.

A medical board would not serve the desired purpose; only a jury can suffice, influenced in its decision by its conceptions of right or wrong, by its notions of justification, by its sympathy, horror or anger, false or colored, all of which would play no part if the decision were left to experts. The proceedings are dressed up in legal garments. Experts take the stand and testify in response to long hypothetical questions that embrace every fact testified to during a long and arduous trial — questions which sometimes take a day to read and which the jury neither listens to nor understands. One expert testifies one way and one the other. And then the jury disregards them all and determines whether in its opinion, for its own reasons, the deceased should or should not have been speeded on his way.

The verdicts in such cases must follow a necessary hypocritical strain, or complications ensue. It is not enough to find the defendant "Not guilty," nor is it enough to find him "Not guilty because insane." To be freed, he must be found "Not guilty because insane at the time of the commission of the crime." If he is merely found "Not guilty because insane," he is supposed to be held in an asylum for the criminal insane until a medical board (or another jury in some jurisdiction) certifies him as legally sane, and then and only then is he released.

The legal point is that insanity is no defense unless the defendant was insane when he committed the act; it is no defense if he became insane later. But juries do not take this hokum seriously. They are turning the defendant out because they do not think he ought to be punished, for one or more of a variety of reasons, in which his legal insanity may not figure at all. Consequently, in spite of the judge's careful instructions, they often ignore the fictional legal hair-splitting.

In a case in Queens County, New York, involving a sixteen-year-old boy who killed a girl of his own age in a suicide pact and then failed to take his own life, the judge criticized the jury for the delay and expense required to free the boy after the jury upheld his plea of temporary insanity, because the jury merely found him insane and failed to limit his insanity to the time of the commission of the act. However, a medical board remedied the defect a few days later.

In three hours a Los Angeles jury convicted one Paul A. Wright who killed his wife and best friend; it deliberated eighteen hours more before it found him innocent by reason of insanity. Then the Court said: "It appears to the Court that the defendant has regained his sanity. I therefore remand the defendant to the custody of the Sheriff until his sanity has been decided in the manner prescribed by law."

Though juries do not take these subtle legal distinctions seriously, the law does. If a lay jury finds the prisoner legally insane at the time of the commission of the crime, he is freed. However, if, after the commission of the crime and before he goes to trial, a commission of experts finds him medically insane, his trial is deferred. The law will not try him until he is "cured."

For example, the New York *Times* of November 23, 1937, reported the case of John Keough, thirty-one, who shot and killed James Heaney in a Brooklyn speakeasy in

# LOOK AT THE LAW

June, 1932. Eight months after the killing, Keough was arrested for robbery. Then he was indicted for murder and put on trial. Soon after the trial had commenced, he was found to be insane and was committed to the Asylum for the Criminal Insane at Matteawan. In August, 1936, he was released from the insane asylum as cured and returned to Brooklyn for trial on the murder indictment. He was convicted by a jury on March 1, 1937. His counsel then appealed to the Court of Appeals, which granted him a new trial to determine the question of whether or not he was insane at the time of the killing.

Suppose a killer is tried and convicted, and then suppose that some morning, pending sentence or execution, the prison guard walking by his cell sees him banging his head against the cell-door, while muttering incomprehensible gibberish. The prison doctor examines him and recommends to the warden that a medical commission be impaneled to determine whether the prisoner has become insane since his conviction. The doctors examine him and report that he is insane. When this occurs, sentence is deferred or the executioner is sent back home and the prisoner is transferred to an asylum for criminal insane. There all the efforts of the physicians are devoted to curing him of his insanity. When he is cured, he is sent back to the condemned row to be executed.

The law sets different standards for conviction and for execution. It lets a lay jury determine whether a man was insane when he committed the crime, while it resorts to doctors when it seeks to put his sentence into execution.

The law will execute a man who was medically insane when he committed a crime, but will not try, sentence, or execute one who becomes medically insane after he is committed. It will cure him first and try and execute him later. Meanwhile it won't let him execute himself or let God exe-

# LOOK AT THE LAW

cute him, if it can avoid it. It takes his belt and shoestrings from him and cures him of appendicitis that he may not cheat the law by dying. Physicians at Sing Sing Prison in New York recently rescued a prisoner from a diabetic coma so that he might be electrocuted. This attitude reminds one of the man who was halted in his attempt to jump off a roof while crossing the parapet leading to the roof by being warned that if he didn't come in off the parapet, he would fall off.

### 4.

Sifted, the charge of hypocrisy in the law is found to rest on fundamental bases. We have seen how the law grows from and is molded by habits and customs; how it reflects our human virtues and vices. Similarly, it mirrors and exposes our hypocrisies.

The law exalts property and its owner, not only because it is rooted to habit and custom, but because we ourselves still cling to those concepts of ruder ages. While we still worship possessions and honor their possessors, we cannot charge the law with fault when it continues ancient sanctions upon violation of property rights while it disregards ravishment of human rights. The law has had centuries of experience in dealing with crimes of violence which the ruling classes have naturally and invariably condemned. It cannot determine as readily new lines of demarcation between admired modes of money-making and rapacious business larcenies. Until society determines that its own crimes should not charge the unfortunate victim with criminal intent, that sharp business practices are not to-be-rewarded virtues but sanctioned crimes, the law can do little in obtaining greater equality of treatment between rich and poor, except to rely upon the good sense of jurymen.

# LOOK AT THE LAW

This, it must be remembered, is one of the most important functions of the jury. When the judge tells the jury to base its verdict upon what it believes a reasonable or a reasonably prudent man would have done under all the circumstances, it is merely seeking to take up the slack between accepted static rules of law and current standards of conduct.

"The morals of any given society at any given epoch are determined by the totality of its conditions both from a static and dynamic viewpoint," says an eminent French writer. One would hardly want a judge so to instruct a jury unless he did not want the jury to understand what he was saying. But when a judge says to the jury: "Hold these men to the standard to which you believe a reasonable man would conform," the law is saying what the French legal philosopher says. It is saying: "The law doesn't always mean what it says; it must sometimes be hypocritical; you go and make a mistake in this case, if you think you ought to, and bring the law down to the level of life; do what you think society ought to do, not what it says it ought to do." And it does not say, as some seem to think: "Do as you please without restriction." On the contrary, it says: "Do as you think society wants you to do."

In an editorial comment upon the acquittal, perhaps legally unjustified, of one Montague, who had been picked up in California a half-dozen years after his indictment in New York for a robbery, during which time he had gone straight, the New York *Times* pointed out that we sometimes needed juries so that they might make mistakes.

Nor is there any method by which the law can keep selfish political, economic, social or other forces from molding legislation to their own ends or from administering it for their own purposes.

Government flows from the cooperation of minority groups, and each group in power invariably is able to push

# LOOK AT THE LAW

some of its own pet measures through the legislature. For example, needing the support of the Church, other groups will vote for the enactment of Church measures though they do not believe in them. Thus sumptuary legislation finds its way into the statute books and remains there, though only a minority favors unenforceable and unpopular governmental censorship.

The failure to enforce such laws is evidence that there is strong popular dissent, and since democratic government cannot function by coercion, passive popular resistance negatives statutes which contain false definitions of criminality. Laws against poaching and smuggling, laws imposing taxes, sumptuary laws, have always been in this category. Attempts to define as criminal, i.e., violations of the will of the majority in a democracy, acts which are not truly violative of the existing social order, if successful, would make persecution out of prosecution, and persecution ultimately defeats even its own purposes. Such statutes prove not that human perversity is a crime, under any proper definition, but that the law is perverse and needs readjustment to fit the needs of the community. Non-enforcement is the administrative method of adjusting the statutory law to the social order.

The law cannot counteract biologic impulses, and it is beyond the reaches of the law to enforce the Ten Commandments among racial, religious, social and economic groups. Equality of treatment must rest upon a conception of a paramount selfish need for such treatment in a democracy, and an understanding that without such treatment democracy cannot survive. It is only when the Jew realizes that his safety depends on the equality of treatment afforded the Negro, and the Catholic realizes that for his ultimate protection he must maintain the sanctities of the Jew, that the law will be enabled to maintain these pretensions.

# LOOK AT THE LAW

As between the rich and the poor in the administration of the law, the problem is again basic. The preference of the influential, whether it be the landed gentry under a vestigial feudal system, or the political job holder, when the people are in power, whether it be the factory owner in a Hoover day or the labor politician-leader in a Rooseveltian era, is part of any human system.

If we could eliminate the influence of money or demagoguery from our politics and the influence of politics from our judiciary, some of our difficulties would be avoided. If we could eliminate unneeded technicalities and improve the standards of selection for our judges and lawyers, as we suggest elsewhere, much would be accomplished. But until there is a change in the underlying social viewpoint, neither judges nor lawyers can do more than salve the wounds.

We can seek to provide free justice to the poor, as we do, by charging the cost of administration of our courts to the tax-paying public; we can permit the impoverished to resort to our courts *in forma pauperis* and thereby avoid even the lesser direct costs we charge to the suitor; we can sanction the "contingent fee" system and encourage legal aid associations so that the poor man can get a lawyer without charge unless he is successful; we can provide public defenders for the impoverished defendant charged with crime. But these are expedients which do not, and cannot, reach the roots of the difficulties.

When we build our institutions upon a false premise of equality; when we say, "We hold this truth to be self-evident, that all men are created free and equal" (somebody said that when a lawyer says "self-evident" he is confessing that he is asserting something he can't establish by proof), we are wishfully asserting a biologic untruth that lays the foundation for many of our later hypocrisies. Though we know something of the inequalities of heritage and birth,

# LOOK AT THE LAW

the accidents and incidents of mind and body, of tangible and intangible muscular, glandular, and nervous differences, of later inequalities consequent on station in life, of breeding and environment, of wealth and of poverty, of education and of training, of disease and of accident, we seek to mold legal practices and dogma to these basic assertions of equality, without sufficient attempt to equalize the known inequalities.

What are the inevitable consequences? The minority in power passes laws that seek, by discrimination, to increase the inequalities, and insists upon administration that heightens its selfish advantages. The owners of property fashion a social system that calls for laws to protect property and to aid in its accumulation. Conversely, lack of property is made an offense against the system, and is punished when manifested by any attempt, direct or indirect, to acquire the property of others, whether it be by contracting unpaid debts or the more direct method of committing theft.

Based on an assumption of everyone's equal opportunity to acquire property, the law cannot recognize poverty as a justifiable motive for an attempt to equalize the inequalities in the opportunities to acquire property, for such a recognition would disclose the basic hypocrisy of the whole structure. The common law would not recognize poverty and ignorance and could not recognize glandular and other mental and physical disturbances as a source of crime. The law cannot do so today unless our citizenry is willing to bear the cost of crime eradication.

We know now that the phrase, "Let the punishment fit the crime," is often a mere bromide that treats the victim as the offender and the effect as the cause. We know that the crime for which we punish the victim is society's failure to provide treatment needed to equalize natural inequalities. But until the people are willing to pay the cost in housing

# LOOK AT THE LAW

and parks, education and training, physical and mental medical treatment, the law must continue to punish poverty, ignorance and disease as crime.

Where, as here, the law is hypocritical because of public ignorance and apathy, because the bases of the problem are more social, political and economic than legal, law administrators should seek to coordinate their efforts with those in the allied fields, first, to enlighten public opinion and, second, to formulate and seek to effectuate a program of enlightened and gradual change. If we have hypocritical divorce laws because of what lawyers consider an unenlightened viewpoint of the Church, let the problem be tackled at the source by cooperation between lawyers and the clergy. If congested juvenile delinquency criminal court calendars are caused by malnutrition in delinquents, let lawyers cooperate with medical agencies in seeking the cause and with social and governmental agencies in eliminating it.

There is little logic in expecting the law to recognize mental disabilities as a source of offense when it ignores the more tangible and recognizable physical disabilities.

Of course the legal definition of insanity is archaic and belongs in the museum where the legal definition of witchcraft is stored. The man who truly suffers from an irresistible impulse has no more criminal intent than the man who has no mental conception of right or wrong. Yet one goes to jail while the other goes to an asylum, though there probably is no real difference in the punishment except that the insane man doesn't know when, if ever, he will be released.

However, the law clings to its definition, not because it believes in it, but because it has no choice under the present system. For example, in the case of Robert Irwin, who killed two women after having been released as "cured" from an

# LOOK AT THE LAW

asylum, the State could hardly have afforded to have a jury find him "not guilty because insane." So the defendant, admittedly suffering from dementia praecox and with less than five years to live, was persuaded to plead guilty to second degree murder, while making statements which indicated clearly his mental irresponsibility. Then, to preclude the possibility of the prisoner being released as cured at some future date, as he had been in the past, the judge sentenced him to a term of from 139 years to life. He was therefore confined in Dannemora prison, where insane criminals, not the criminally insane, are confined.

Likewise, in the case of Joe Arridy, a twenty-two-year-old youth with the mentality of a child of six, who escaped from an institution for the feeble-minded and raped and killed Dorothy Drain, aged fifteen, Colorado executed the defendant, after its Supreme Court held that though mentally deficient, he could comprehend the difference between right and wrong. An Associated Press dispatch told graphically how he went to his death "happily," "grinning," "hardly able to wait," obviously unable "to comprehend the nature of death" but "anticipating an exciting and novel journey."

These equivocations are forced upon the law because it is dealing with problems not within its scope. They belong primarily to the medical profession. The lawyer has no ability to deal with the mentally afflicted. The legal definition of mental incompetency is no protection to the individual or to society. Nor should it be a lay jury's function to pass upon matters involving psychiatry or other medical questions.

Several years ago, Mayor La Guardia of New York recognized the social, political and medical nature of these problems and sought to meet them, in part, by requiring that men guilty of sex misdemeanors be given psychiatric exami-

# LOOK AT THE LAW

nations while in prison so that upon their release they might be committed to institutions for mental defectives, where necessary, instead of being turned out to renew their perverted activities.

Only in such fashion can the law be freed from these inadequacies. Meanwhile it must do the best it can to protect society against lack of ethics of many criminal lawyers and their medical "experts" who unscrupulously use "insanity" defenses to free the guilty, while rigid legal laws punish the mentally incompetent.

Civil penalties, as has been pointed out, smack of the hypocrisies of criminal sanctions. We labored for years under a system that required a workman to "assume the risk" of his employment (as though working at an unguarded machine or having his family starve offered a free choice) and to sue and starve if he was hurt while at his job. It took years to convince employers of the public need for a mutual fund for the protection of injured workmen, regardless of fault. Today, we are undergoing the same process in the personal injury field. Because of the claim of added cost to the automobilist, unfortunate defendants are being assessed the full cost of undivided reparation instead of making the cost a mutual and proportionate one for all who share the risks of driving, although the insurance system in force tends to that result. Whether or not the suggested remedy is practicable, at least the failure to adopt it drives the law to hypocrisies and marks it as a helpless target for abuse.

Judges recognize the deficiencies of this system but they can do little about it, as they can do little about the hypocrisies of our sumptuary laws except to commit the law to derivative hypocrisies.

The problem goes back through the legislator who adopts hypocritical laws. Yet he cannot be wholly to blame for

## LOOK AT THE LAW

the infirmities he shares with us. We cannot criticize him for yielding to the forces that influence his nomination and election. We cannot ask him to do a political death-defying act in the face of a phalanx of ladies of the church auxiliary or of a convocation of clergymen.

We have laws against prostitution often fostered by church-going gentlemen who rent their properties in the red-light districts for disorderly houses. Lincoln Steffens, Judge Lindsey and others have revealed these conditions. Yet it is said, in defense of these lay hypocrisies, "We admit that prostitution is inevitable and perhaps we even profit by it. But why dignify it with open recognition and invite its increase?"

"Face the problem, control it and eradicate its evils," argue protagonists.

The law can do nothing but follow the dominant element (except as it is diverted by improper influences), and since the reform element is most strongly organized and most vociferous, while the liberals are not organized at all, the former is usually successful in foisting hypocritical and unenforceable standards on the populace. And when the abuse becomes too glaring, the judges resort to the evasions of statutory construction. As one judge put it:

> "The pathway of judicial literature from the earliest period down to the present is literally strewn with cases which, like beacon lights, have guided the hand of justice in preventing unjust, unrighteous, absurd, unreasonable and abhorrent results from the use of general words and expression in statutes."

Thus, a liberal Baltimore judge recently acquitted a bookmaker because the police had gained entrance to the bookmaking establishment illegally. The judge had to hold that "Come in" might be a sufficient social invitation to enter, but it did not justify a police officer in breaching the

# LOOK AT THE LAW

paraphrased rule that an American's home is his castle.

Sometimes the necessity of hypocritical statutes cannot be gainsaid, as in the case of our criminal laws which prohibit murder. When the law is charged with hypocrisy in denying an unwritten sex law, or in condemning a mercy killing, it must admit the charge. "But what of it?" asks the legal technician. "Are we legally and openly to make every man or woman the judge and executioner of those who have wronged them? Shall we throw the lists wide open and invite the avengers to take their toll? Or shall we leave the murderer to uncertainty and thereby dissuade murder?" The law here is consciously hypocritical in an effort to keep pliable without becoming wholly ineffectual.

Based on a "naturalistic" philosophy of law, the law must be hypocritical, for it must save our faces as best it can and in the process must be ready to act as a whipping-boy. It must allow us absolution for transgressions which are human and to-be-expected, without putting a premium on them. It must hold the fear of punishment over the prospective offender, while being tolerant of his breaches when he offends. In this, its policy does not differ from that of religious groups whose strength of survival over the centuries have been due to an underlying and sometimes undeclared tolerance of the weaknesses of their communicants.

The law, hypocritical in its pronouncements, can only administer these hypocritical laws in such a way as to reconcile private vice with public pretense of virtue. Generally, far from being condemned for its hypocrisies, it should be praised for its ability to reconcile law and life, for its effort to obtain a balance between the requirements of Justice and the calls of Mercy.

# CHAPTER VII

## *The Layman Says:*
## THE LAW IS TOO SLOW

*1.*

"INNUMERABLE children have been born into the cause; innumerable young people have married into it; innumerable old people have died out of it. Scores of persons deliriously found themselves made parties in Jarndyce and Jarndyce, without knowing how or why; whole families have inherited legendary hatreds with the suit. The little plaintiff or defendant who was promised a new rocking horse when Jarndyce and Jarndyce should be settled, has grown up, possessed himself a real horse, and trotted away into the other world. Fair wards of court have faded into mothers and grandmothers; a long procession of Chancellors has come in and gone out; the legion of bills in the suit have been transformed into mere bills of mortality; there are not three Jarndyces left upon the earth perhaps, since old Tom Jarndyce in despair blew his brains out at a coffee-house in Chancery Lane."

So wrote Dickens of the leading case he immortalized, the case that so thoroughly established the familiar apothegm that "Justice delayed is justice denied."

Justice has always been denied by delay. The law has always emulated the tortoise. Bonner, writing on "Lawyers and Litigants," mentions the euphonious Athenian case of Nausimactus et Xenopeithes v. Aristaechmus, a guardianship suit that took eight years. And Demosthenes, in ancient Greece, complained of his inability to get to trial in an

# LOOK AT THE LAW

ejectment suit which had been pending for sixteen years.

The pre-Victorian chancery suit was notorious for its prolixity and delay, and Bentham, Romilly, Dickens and others focused public attention upon it and finally compelled official action to expedite legal proceedings. There were many horrible examples of delay in Victorian cases which received less notoriety than did Jarndyce vs. Jarndyce. For example, in 1827, a dispute occurred concerning $1,200 which had been put in the hands of an English stockholder. By 1882, the fund had grown to $15,000. But that was the only thing that had progressed. All the parties to the suit were long since dead; all the lawyers—and there were many of them—who had figured in the case were dead; all the judges, except one, who had ever made a decree in the case were dead, and that one venerable man was long since off the bench. All the clerks who had ever recorded decrees and all the commissioners who had made reports were dead; the very courthouse in which the case had been originally heard had been pulled down and a new courthouse facing another direction had been built on the old site. By reason of the deaths the case had long since lost its original name; by reason of delay and neglect it had been taken off the docket and forgotten until it was revived by a descendant of one of the original parties who learned of the existence of the fund by accident and finally obtained its distribution.

To this day we are not free from fault, though generally it is not so grievous.

"I.R.H. Wins $381,472 in Sixteen-year-old Suit," reads a headline in the New York *Times*. The article revealed that the suit was instituted in 1921, and though the case was tried prior to 1933, the decision was not rendered until 1937. Incidentally, this was a lower court decision, which is a mere introduction to the numerous appeals which con-

# LOOK AT THE LAW

stitute the real litigation in a matter of any importance.

Another headline of October, 1937, reads: "1908 Suit for $106,152 Settled by City for $325."

A third New York City headline reads: "Hearst Pays $30,000 for Fireworks Claims; City Collects for Many Hurt in Garden in 1902." It appeared that after the explosion of the fireworks, eighty-one suits were commenced against the City of New York. The city retaliated by bringing six actions against Hearst in 1909. After a long legal battle the city collected $32,000 in one case, and thereafter started negotiations for settlement of the others in 1932, finally completing the settlement in 1936.

The Circuit Court of Appeals in Philadelphia (the judges then sitting have since been superseded) stayed the operation of an order directed at Mayor Hague of Jersey City in a labor case, pending appeal, and then held up the determination of the appeal for almost two years, the stay continuing and meanwhile tying the hands of the plaintiff.

An action brought in a California Federal Court in December, 1936, was still pending two years later; during the intervening time, the court was considering the single question of whether the complaint was sufficient in law; defendants had not yet been compelled to file an answer.

The law's delays are, as they have always been, the subject of public and private rebuke. "Failure to secure expedition"; "the delays of litigation"; "uncertainty, delay and expense"; "antiquated and cumbersome"; "unjustifiable delay"—these are some of the characterizations that leading lawmen apply to the administration of the law. In the public mind, law and lag are synonymous.

There are, of course, no available records showing how many plaintiffs, discouraged or unable to bear further expense, quit and took what they could get rather than pursue endless litigation. Nor have we any statistical data con-

# LOOK AT THE LAW

cerning the litigants who died in poverty, as a result of interminably delayed law suits.

The causes of the law's delays are not unknown. Nor are they wholly irremediable. They occur wholly in the field of the administration of the law, responsibility for which rests upon the legislature, in the first instance; upon the judges, their subordinate officers and agencies, and the lawyers in the second; and upon executive and other administrative agencies, in the third.

The administration of the law rests upon the adjective law, as distinguished from the substantive law. The latter is the body of rules which delineates rights and duties, as between man and man; the former prescribes how these rules are to be enforced. Constitutions and legislative acts create and organize courts to administer the law, and make basic rules which prescribe their functions and powers, their personnel and their methods of procedure. Having been so organized, the courts themselves make further rules for their own guidance, to the extent permitted by the legislature. Thus it would appear that the responsibility for the functioning of the courts rests upon the legislature which determines their organization, and upon the judicial personnel which is charged with the duty of carrying out the powers and duties charged to it by the legislature.

Of course, if the legislature fails to provide sufficient courts or sufficient judges and other needed personnel, or if it fails to adopt liberal rules of procedure and leaves antiquated common law and equity ritual in effect, or if the people fail to elect or the Governor or other appointing officer or body fail to nominate proper judges, there is little remedy in altering the law.

Likewise, unless the administrative branch of the law, the Executive, the District Attorneys, the Sheriffs and other law-enforcing officers and bodies, enforce the law, there is

# LOOK AT THE LAW

little the law can do to make itself effective. But if the courts are properly organized and sufficiently and completely manned; if they are implemented with liberal and elastic rules of procedure and the judges are themselves given power to make needed supplementary rules, then the failure of the law to function expeditiously must be laid at the doors of the courts. Federal Circuit Judge (formerly Dean) Clark said recently in this connection that legalistic construction by judges of the new, liberal Federal procedure rules was tending to resurrect the technicalities of old common law pleadings.

On the other hand, if the judges make adequate rules and lawyers pettifog in an effort to evade them, the consequences should be charged to the lawyers.

At present, the New York City Bar Association says, "The judicial structure is needlessly complicated through inertia and for historical reasons no longer valid. We now have a mass of separate constitutional provisions, legislative acts, sets of rules, judicial and administrative control, or no control, all leading to needless disorganization, confusion and inefficiency."

Whether or not there is insufficient help in the corner grocery store depends primarily on the volume of its business. The courts have not been so much undermanned as they have been overpatronized. We are a litigious people, and a litigious citizenry always spells congestion in the courts. Any enterprise organized for normal business finds difficulty in providing sufficient help for its peak loads.

We are not unlike the Athenians. There, as here, "litigation was the handmaid of politics." While their courts were considered congested by a delay of a year, some of our jury calendars are more than four years behind.

Our citizenry goes to law upon the slightest provocation. A day in court in any large city witnesses a succession of

# LOOK AT THE LAW

controversies submitted to a judge that a kindly or tolerant word would have avoided, or a fair or honest attitude would have obviated. Indeed, the tenacity and pertinacity of litigious neighboring farmers, quarreling over a border line between barren fields, has become an accepted concept in our American way of life.

Our civil courts are deluged with damage suits praying judgment for thousands of dollars, based on trifling causes and feigned mental suffering. Every physical hurt is claimed to be permanent in an effort to enhance the amount of a judgment; accidents are framed and injuries trumped up, not only by individuals but ofttimes by concerted co-operation of rings of lawyers, doctors, litigants and witnesses. The result is an impenetrable congestion that delays legitimate suits and honest suitors.

Besides, we rely on our courts too heavily. We charge them not only with judicial functions but with a wealth of duties that more properly belong to the executive and administrative branches of our government. And we leave to law-suits many matters that might more properly be determined by other means.

By reason of the judicially-made rule that the judges may pass upon the constitutionality of our laws, the Supreme Court is enabled to legislate. It may determine constitutional questions by asking whether it thinks legislation passed by Congress is wise or justified, and when it thinks not, it may hold it unconstitutional.

By injunction or mandamus, the courts supervise the legislative function of taxation. They interfere in election contests. They supervise the acts and conduct of administrative officers and bodies. They speak the last word in matters of labor relations; in matters of licensing the conduct of business and professions; trade practices; compensation for personal injuries; conduct of, and prices charged

# LOOK AT THE LAW

by, public utilities; regulation of issuance of, and trading in, securities; handling of, and prices charged for, produce, education, public health, pensions, town planning, etc., etc. They are charged with the duty of administering, reorganizing and distributing estates of insolvents, incompetents and infants, of supervising the handling of corporate and trust properties, of naturalizing aliens, of supervising appointment of guardians, the dissolution of corporations, of changing names, of performing marriage ceremonies, all matters almost wholly administrative. Willoughby points to provisions of statutes vesting in judges the power of appointment of administrative officers such as steamboat inspectors and members of the Board of Education of the District of Columbia; Dodd refers to local laws which give the judges power to remove administrative officers; and in Chicago, according to Martin, judges had the power of appointment of members of the Park Board in whom were vested wide administrative powers.

We leave to lawsuits so many matters that are extrajudicial that an extraordinary increase of business in any one of the manifold subjects of the court's jurisdiction can clog the entire judicial machinery. So, in times of depression, the courts are flooded with insolvency proceedings, time of the judges is taken from the other branches of the court's business and clogged calendars result.

When there is a boom in the real estate market or a crash in the textile market, a torrent of resultant damage suits overloads the courts. A government investigation may lead to an overwhelming number of anti-monopoly suits or a large increase in the number of minority stockholders' suits. For years, the failure to make provision for injured workmen's claims flooded the court calendars with such suits until the whole judicial current was dammed.

Currently, the litigiousness of the personal injury suitor

# LOOK AT THE LAW

and the evasive tactics of personal injury insurance companies overwhelm the courts with such litigation while other suits are unduly delayed. The New York Commission on the Administration of Justice recently estimated that approximately one-third of all the cases pending in the Supreme Court of New York State were for personal injuries resulting from automobile accidents.

The consequence of failure to make adequate provision for such periodic peak-loads has resulted in a tendency away from the courts to administrative agencies, to an accompaniment of criticism of the law. While such a tendency should be encouraged where proper, it should not be encouraged solely because of undue delay in the conduct of the courts. In cases of public service commissions, trade commissions, securities commissions, commerce commissions, where independent fact-finding facilities and technical experience beyond the judicial scope are necessary; or in cases of compensation commissions, where the theory of a lawsuit is fallacious; or in cases of labor boards, where the object should be accomplished by regulation and not by litigation, administrative bodies should regulate and fact-find, subject to protection of legal and constitutional rights by the courts. But there should not be unnecessary reference of matters properly judicial to administrative bodies, where political, untrained, unethical or dependent personnel, lacking judicial scrupulousness and responsibility, may make a mockery of the legal and constitutional rights of our citizenry. The administrative tribunals, to which we look for so much in these days, have already proved that there is no panacea in taking matters from the courts. The Interstate Commerce Commission has already demonstrated its ineffectiveness to speed railroad reorganizations. The Federal Communications Commission took under advisement a controversy between written and spoken communications

## LOOK AT THE LAW

companies in May, 1935; more than four years later its sphinxlike silence was still unbroken. Within recent months, the National Labor Relations Board was criticized before Congress for an inexcusable nineteen months' delay in a single case, which meanwhile left employer and employees suffering inconvenience and financial loss. Obviously, no legal forum has any monopoly on delay.

The two principal points of congestion in the administration of litigation are, first, getting a case to trial, and second, making a judgment stick through the processes of appeal. Calendar congestion is such that in urban centers the trial of criminal cases, where prisoners are out on bail, may be delayed as much as a year; while in civil cases, it is not unusual to find a trial calendar three or four years behind.

This is particularly true in the trial of cases by jury. Jury trials, with their greater formality of procedure, take more time to try than non-jury cases. Plaintiffs demand juries to get larger verdicts in cases where sympathy may play a part (such as in personal injury cases); defendants demand juries where the jury calendar is congested to get more delay; and plaintiffs who start strike actions (which they have no desire to try) put their baseless suits on a jury calendar so the defendant may suffer the fear and embarrassment of a pending claim and a threatened judgment as long as possible.

We have discussed in preceding chapters the technicalities to which resourceful defendants and their counsel resort to defer the judicial day of atonement. We have pointed out how Harry K. Thaw was able, by the use of money and ingenious counsel, to continue litigation for many years. Intermediate proceedings designed to delay a trial are some of the resorts of defendants, while a succession of appeals, once a plaintiff has succeeded in going to trial, is

# LOOK AT THE LAW

often effective in bringing all but the most persistent of plaintiffs to heel.

As an example, though an extreme one, Judge Baldwin tells of a personal injury action brought by a brakeman against a railroad company. The case was first tried in 1884. Upon the trial the plaintiff recovered $4,000 damages. The company appealed. The judgment was reversed on appeal in 1886. Upon a second trial the plaintiff recovered $4,900. The company appealed. The judgment was affirmed. The company appealed to a higher court. The judgment was reversed and a new trial ordered. The company succeeded on the third trial held in 1889. The brakeman appealed, without success, in 1894. He went to the higher court, which now, in 1897, reversed the company's judgment. A fourth trial resulted in a judgment for the plaintiff for $4,500. The company appealed and the judgment was again reversed. A sixth trial resulted in the plaintiff's favor. Again the company appealed and again the judgment was reversed. In 1902, upon a seventh trial, the brakeman got a verdict for $4,500 and, upon appeal, the judgment was finally affirmed.

Another instance of much delay with little excuse occurred in a case which arose out of the stopping by the British Admiralty of an American ship carrying foodstuffs, in 1915. The ship was delayed in a British harbor for several weeks, as a result of which the cargo was damaged. The ship owner claimed freight charges from the shipper; the shipper claimed damages for injury to the cargo from the ship owner. Though the parties retained counsel promptly, the ship owner's counsel did not serve his complaint until 1920, and then extended his adversary's time to answer and counterclaim until 1922, with the result that it was seven years after the occurrence that the shipper's answer and counterclaim were filed, and ten years had elapsed before the case could be reached for trial. Then, because of a technical oversight of plaintiff's counsel, the plaintiff lost its case. It then appealed, and started a supplemental action in another State. When the appeal was denied, the plaintiff's counsel made a new application to reopen the case based upon the new suit. This was denied and he appealed, won a second trial on his second appeal, and then obtained a decision on the second trial appointing a master to ascertain his client's damages. By now it was 1929. The master held hearings for a year and then filed his report awarding damages to the owner, but without interest. The shippers appealed to the court from the master's award of damages; the ship owner appealed from his failure to allow interest. By this time it was 1932 — seventeen years had elapsed — and the parties finally decided that a settlement would be preferable to further litigation.

The ship owner, who had been awarded $48,000 by the court, now had a claim for interest which brought the total to $96,000. This amount the shippers paid to the ship owner's lawyer, who claimed $50,000 as his fee, more than the principal of the recovery. This amount he deducted from the settlement and sent the client a check for the balance, which represented less than the interest on the claim. The client objected to the amount of the fee, but the lawyer was adamant. So the client hired a new lawyer to sue the old lawyer. In 1936 this case was tried and decided in favor of the old lawyer. The client then appealed, but since by now over twenty years had passed, he decided that he had had enough of litigation. He paid the new lawyer for suing the old lawyer, abandoned his appeal and the case and sought surcease from the technicalities of the law and the lassitudes of the lawyer.

There is something about a lawsuit that makes for delay. A lawsuit means combat, and it is not given to humans to

# LOOK AT THE LAW

fight continuously at high pitch. Periods of rest are required — time between rounds — respites back of the front lines — so that the combatants may return to the fray refreshed.

For reasons or without, the lawyer and the processes of the law are snail-like. Fair dealing requires that everything be done on notice to all parties and then only after hearing. The result is a pattern of notice and hearing, hearing and notice, that makes progress deliberate and result slow.

Every lawsuit consists of a series of phases, each of which is largely independent of the other. Pleadings must be prepared, and the rules governing pleadings are unique. There must be preparatory proceedings to enable a preparation for trial to begin. Preparation for trial cannot commence until after all the information needed for it has been obtained. Then the trial itself takes time, after it has been set by jockeying calendars, litigants, judges and witnesses into a semblance of concurrence.

The processes of a trial are slow; picking a jury, opening to the jury, examination of witnesses by question and answer, objection, discussion, argument and exception, summation, charging the jury, requests to instruct the jury, jury deliberation, motions to set aside verdicts, arguments and rearguments, are endless in time consumption.

In the recent trial of public officials of Waterbury, Connecticut, charged with grafting, over four weeks were consumed in selecting a jury, mainly because of the fact that since there were a great many defendants, the peremptory challenges of jurymen allowed to each defendant aggregated a total running into the hundreds. The trial started in November, and did not end until the following July.

During the trial of James J. Hines, newspapers commented upon the very considerable portion of time taken during each trial day by court and counsel in discussing

# LOOK AT THE LAW

and determining technical questions concerning the admissibility of evidence. One newspaper artist showed judge, counsel, witnesses and jurors bound round in a welter of red tape and technicalities.

After a trial come appeals, each of which involves its own components; preparation of the stenographic record of the trial and of the exhibits, preparation of briefs, of argument, consideration by the appellate court, etc., etc.

There may be one or more appeals following a single trial; then if the action is dismissed, particularly by reason of some technicality, new actions may follow. If the judgment is reversed or modified, a new trial may be ordered and then the process begins afresh.

Years may elapse between the conclusion of a trial and the conclusion of a litigation in consequence of appeals, ranging from those made in good faith for reasons of substance or for technical reasons, to appeals in bad faith for purposes of delay or extortion.

"Hague lost at the law but he is winning by delay," said the New York *World-Telegram* in an editorial entitled, "And Now Delay." "Delay has been Hague's one hope. Delay has served him well. Doubtless he will seek other delays by which to cling onto his dictatorship to the very last minute."

But lawyers do not dislike delay; time spent is one of the elements that go to make up their bills, so that the theory is, the longer the delay, the greater the charge. Besides, delay, as has been pointed out, is the lawyer's weapon, as it is the instrument by which the erring client evades the grasp of the law.

However, a ray of light may be seen in the announcement by the Securities and Exchange Commission that it will approve compensation in utility reorganization cases upon a basis of greater compensation for greater expedition

# LOOK AT THE LAW
—a shocking departure from the old-line legal techinique.

*2.*

An important cause of inefficiency and consequent delay in the courts is found in the character of its administrative personnel.

It should be readily apparent except to over-enthusiastic idealists that there is, in general, an apathy and a lack of initiative in public service as compared with private enterprise. There are many underlying reasons for this. The man who seeks safety in a small but assured salary, the man who seeks the haven of civil service protection and a later pension, lacks the spur and the fear that drives men in private enterprise. The lack of the profit-making motive usually lessens initiative and stems energy. Where, in addition, personnel is politically selected, a measure of inefficiency is added to a standard of lassitude.

This is too frequently true of the judicial administrative personnel. The judges, actuated by varying motives — a sense of service, personal ambition, vanity, desire for re-election — generally try to make good records. But, on the administrative side, judges play little part; it is the enlisted personnel, the clerks and the attendants, upon whom the public must depend for expeditious and efficient administration.

Judges have not sufficiently appreciated the importance of their administrative functions. It is usually considered that the determination of disputes is the principal excuse for the existence of the judiciary. The truth is that the judges are charged with a very considerable portion of the task of administering the law, and its prompt and efficient administration requires not only recognition but adequate provision by the courts. This it does not receive.

Administration, the problems of function, powers, or-

## LOOK AT THE LAW

ganization, personnel, and procedure are often left almost entirely to the legislature and judges approach them in a half-hearted way, as a sort of necessary evil. To the senior judge, regardless of his lack of administrative ability, is allotted the supervision of the administrative tasks, and he exercises it unwillingly, grudging the time it takes from the exercise of his judicial functions and feeling aggrieved because, as a result, he is overworked.

The judge who seeks to interest himself in the administrative side of the work of the court gets little cooperation, understanding or sympathy from other governmental agencies or from the public. The legislature feels that he is treading on its toes in advocating reform, while the public gauges the judge's working time by his appearances on the bench. Like the school teacher whose hours are popularly supposed to end when the children go home, so with the judge; time spent in administration does not count.

Even judges look askance at one of their own who takes his administrative tasks seriously. Current in many courthouses is the judicial gibe: "Oh, yes, he's a good judge, a good calendar judge," meaning that the judge referred to may be good at disposing efficiently of lawyers and litigants who seek delay, but he's not so much of a judge at "judging."

We could do with a few more good administrative judges. Unfortunately, many judges lack this ability. The judge who is best versed in the substantive law is often the least capable on the administrative side. Legal training does not make for business efficiency. The lawyer, like the doctor, is too often a poor business man. All of which makes the judges reluctant to exercise their administrative tasks, makes them hesitate to broaden them, and renders the results of little moment.

Ordinarily, there is little regularity, little system, in court

# LOOK AT THE LAW

administration. Courts, like legislatures, adopt rules and then neglect to overhaul them. They plod along under antiquated rules, without realizing the necessity for a periodic check-up to see if the old organs are still functioning, until some glaring abuse visits condemnation upon them. Although the Michigan Supreme Court had the constitutional power to do so, it did nothing to bring its rules up to date for sixty years.

In making rules, the judges call to their aid local committees of lawyers. Since lawyers, however well intentioned, share the administrative vices of judges, rule-making is generally conservative and slow and many years elapse before needed changes are adopted.

Sometimes it is the legislature that is at fault. For example, our Federal courts had been shuffling along under rules of procedure reminiscent of early Victorian days. Although the various State courts had been slowly discarding their ancient garments over a period of years, it was not until 1934 that Congress authorized the Supreme Court to revise the Federal practice to conform to standards generally adopted and prevailing all over the country. It was not until 1938 that such changes became effective, and then only after a twenty-year campaign by the lawyers comprising the American Bar Association.

Some of the delay in legal administration results from the inefficiency or incompetency of some of our judges. For this, the principal fault lies in the political influences which color the selection and election of our judges.

A lawyer, however able, must be politically fortunate if he would successfully aspire to the bench. Even Justice Cardozo is quoted as having said: "I would never have been elected had I not received the support of a group of Italian-Americans who voted for me on the supposition that since my name ended in 'o' I was one of their own race."

# LOOK AT THE LAW

We take it for granted that a capable lawyer, particularly one with trial experience, will make a capable judge. We require of him no special education or training, though in fact he should have qualifications, education and training far beyond those which the average lawyer possesses.

Were no considerations but legal and judicial ones permitted to enter into the selection of judges, were the best possible men selected, it would be difficult enough to satisfy the onerous demands made upon them. We indicate in these pages the complexities of their tasks. The qualities needed for their proper performance are almost godlike. The best of men can only fall short.

When, however, men are selected at political random, by geographic or religious accident, they are bound to have defects not only of training and experience but of knowledge and temperament.

And judges politically selected are frequently not permitted to select efficient administrative personnel, but must take and cannot interfere with an inefficient administrative organization also politically selected. Such judges, however well intentioned, cannot cut red tape when to sever it means a diminution of political patronage.

Likewise, an inefficient judge may readily become an inert one and thereby promote delay. This transition is not a difficult one.

Patience is one of the most necessary, as it is the commonest, of judicial virtues. Untrained spectators writhe in their chairs while a judge sits and listens to the unending drone of filibustering lawyers. And not without reason, for an impatient or hasty judge is anathema to the promise of a fair hearing and a just solution of a controversy. But while patience is needed, the judge may not succumb to the anesthetizing effect upon his mental processes of the protracted pleas of prolix lawyers.

# LOOK AT THE LAW

A story is told of a boring lawyer who, having made a tiresome argument, asked the judge who was about to adjourn court when it would be the court's pleasure to permit him to finish. The judge said, "We are bound to let you finish, but as for pleasure, that has been long since out of the question."

Overpatient judges invite and give lawyers unrestricted time to prepare endless factual and legal arguments in affidavits and briefs, and then take days to read and deliberate upon them, while they reserve decision and stop the clocks of legal time.

It is often difficult to ascertain when a judge stops being overpatient and when he becomes inert. One mark of the latter is bad attendance; another, long delay in decisions; another, an unwillingness to handle business and an overwillingness to grant continuances.

Under a heading, "Magistrates Loaf on Needless Jobs," the New York *Times* of April 16, 1934, reported:

"The city magistrates are underworked, and if a centralized court system could be established, the city could get along with half the present number, according to a report made to Mayor La Guardia by Commissioner of Accounts Paul Blanshard. Many magistrates have more than three months of vacation. It is the common practice for magistrates in Manhattan and the Bronx to come late in the morning and leave early. Twenty-six magistrates of Manhattan and the Bronx each worked an average of 214 days in 1933 which gave them, after all Sundays and holidays are allowed, an average vacation of almost thirteen weeks. On the same basis, the sixteen magistrates in Brooklyn have an average vacation of only six weeks, the Queens magistrates of ten and a half weeks and the Richmond magistrates of eleven weeks.

"The Manhattan and Bronx courts open habitually at ten

# LOOK AT THE LAW

o'clock instead of nine o'clock and some magistrates frequently close their courts and leave their chambers before the legal time limit. Three magistrates were off duty more days in 1933 than they worked. On the particular day we made a check of all thirty-seven parts of the magistrates' courts in all five boroughs that were then supposed to be in session (at 2:45 P.M.), magistrates were on the bench in only nineteen of the thirty-seven parts. Seven magistrates had left for the day and three were still out to lunch. Seven of the magistrates were in chambers presumably doing official work. There is no reason to believe that the day was exceptional, and a check showed that fifteen out of thirty-six magistrates assigned to duty on that day had completed their daily calendars by 2:45.

"Magistrates, unlike judges of the higher courts, have very little occasion to study the law after court hours. The Homicide Court, which is supposed to be open each weekday from ten to four, had an average in 1933 of less than three cases a day. The Women's Court of Manhattan had an average of less than seven cases a day. In all our tabulations of work we have given the magistrates the benefit of every doubt. In Queens the records of only four magistrates were considered last year, because only four worked all year."

Inert judges throw an undue burden upon their conscientious and competent brethren, who work diligently. The severity of the gentle Judge Cardozo, when Chief Judge of the New York Court of Appeals, was described by a colleague, who said that in his effort to keep the calendars up to date, he not only required judges to work every evening, but would not permit them to go home to dinner. A Federal bachelor judge is known to inhabit his chambers until midnight each night and to resume his labors before eight o'clock each morning. One judge was heard to remark that

# LOOK AT THE LAW

if he was called upon to determine the constitutionality of a forty-hour week, he would find anybody who merely abided by the law guilty of vagrancy.

However hard-working he may be, an inefficient judge delays the law's processes by his errors. Such judges cause mistrials, retrials and appeals with consequent duplication of effort and expense and loss of time.

In one case, an appellate court in setting aside a jury's verdict, said that the judge's charge to the jury was "too prolix to be understandable"; that the mere fact that it took eight hours to deliver justified the conclusion that the "jurors were not clearly or concisely instructed"; and, the the Court added, "It seems incredible to us that twelve laymen could intelligently comprehend and apply what the Court said."

There are judges whose qualifications for office are so slim that they are assigned by their colleagues to sit only in jury parts where negligence cases are being tried, and then other judges give them stock forms of charges to the jury which they may read as their own. When their cases are appealed, the appellate court judges are tempted to follow the lead of one of their number who, after a lawyer about to argue an appeal to reverse a judgment rendered against his client in the court below had begun, "This is an appeal from a decision of Mr. Justice Jones," interrupted the lawyer, saying, "Yes, counsellor, and what is your second ground for appeal?"

A judge in a Midwestern city is said to have been reversed on appeal so many times that all a lawyer who wanted delay needed to do was to walk into court with law books under his arm and pile them on the table in front of the judge, whereupon the judge found some excuse to adjourn the case or to transfer it to another judge.

A criminal judge sentenced a prisoner to three and a half

years in prison. The next day he had the prisoner brought back and reduced his sentence to fifteen months. A newspaper reporter came to the judge and asked the reason for the reduction, so that he could print the story. The judge asked him to withhold the story and told him that he had sentenced the prisoner under the wrong law, but added that such an error was not uncommon among the judges of his court.

The ungifted magistrate is subject to no check. No record of his successes and failures is published. He is one jobholder who may be incompetent and still keep his job, for the importance of permitting judges to be independent makes it necessary to put difficulties in the way of their removal. Recall of judges by popular vote is advocated and sometimes practiced, but the existing method of impeachment, or its practical equivalents, is designed to make removal difficult. Usually, a judge must be guilty of corruption or moral delinquencies before he may be removed. Some judges have slept during most of their "waking" hours on the bench, some have lost their mental faculties through age or accident, many have demonstrated incapacity and unwillingness to perform their duties, but almost all have played their parts until the final curtain was rung down. All such judges contribute to the drag in the administration of the law.

### 3.

The law's delays will yield to intelligent attack.

When delay is caused by congestion of court calendars, due, for example, to a large volume of personal injury or matrimonial cases, examination of the underlying social causes will supply needed remedy at the source. If an excess of matrimonial cases is caused by hypocritical divorce

# LOOK AT THE LAW

laws or by social or economic conditions, speeding up litigants and lawyers and denying them fair hearings offer no real solution. The remedy lies in dealing with the problem in other fields, be they social, economic or political. So, when an excess of personal injury cases indicates need for compensation statutes, the task goes beyond the lawyer's scope and requires cooperation with allied forces, in an effort to obtain such legislation. When, for example, the problems of debt collection delay impoverished litigants, cooperation with social and political agencies will suggest small claims tribunals. Likewise, an excess of contract claims requires cooperation with businessmen to promote better ethical standards or arbitration.

Beyond such problems of substance, delay will best yield to more efficient administration. Revision of the adjective law should be periodically and constantly dealt with by the legislature in cooperation with the judges. Permanent bodies, law revision committees and judicial councils should be set up and kept at work. Broad rule-making powers should be entrusted to the judges who should and who can keep practice in the courts modern and flexible. Simplification and liberalization of procedural rules are essential for understanding, and understanding is necessary for expedition.

Recently, coincidence furnished a good example of how the usual inordinate delay in the selection of a jury may be avoided by simple reforms. Two judges, Federal Judge Manton and County Court Judge Martin, went to trial almost concurrently for alleged misfeasance in office. Manton's case was heard in the Federal Court, where the judge questions the talesmen; Martin's case in the State Court, where counsel do the questioning. In consequence of this difference of procedure, the Federal prosecution was well into its case before the State Court jury had been selected.

The increase in the tasks entrusted to administrative

# LOOK AT THE LAW

agencies makes coordination and simplification of their adjective law essential. The present confusion and its consequent delay in this branch of the law is emphasized by a recent investigation made by Professor John H. Wigmore who reports that there are, at the present time, forty to fifty administrative bureaus, boards and commissions in Washington today, and that each has its independent regulations concerning procedure and practice.

Manifestly, such intricacies can only lead to confusion, which must retard progress, while, conversely, codification, simplification and standardization of rules and regulations will avoid delay in the disposition of legal matters under administrative control. An example of this is found in the New York City Magistrates' Courts which, while manned by appointees of Tammany Hall mayors, were the subject of considerable and justified criticism. Since the advent of magistrates appointed by Mayor La Guardia, "the calendars of the courts were kept up to date and the adjourned cases pending at the end of the year represented the work of approximately one court day."

Proper administration of justice in the courts lies between the judges on the one hand and lawyers on the other. On the judicial side, there is needed a conception of greater dignity for, and understanding of, the nature and problems of judicial administration, and improved training and technique to meet them. An administrative head of the court, a layman with a business man's point of view, of a stature equal to that of the judge, would be of vast aid in making the administration of courts businesslike and efficient. Failing that, a judge with executive ability should be designated to supervise judicial administration and his tasks should not be incidental.

The United States Supreme Court has just appointed a General Administrator (though unfortunately a lawyer)

# LOOK AT THE LAW

for the Federal Courts pursuant to authority granted by the last Congress.

On the side of the bar, a greater sense of responsibility for efficient administration is needed. Lawyers must realize that their ability to survive must rest upon the efficiency of their institutions; that the public will turn from the courts to administrative agencies, from litigation to arbitration, unless the courts can and will serve them effectively. Recent events demonstrate that, through economic pressure, lawyers are beginning to respond, realizing that injustice, though resulting in a fee from one client, will, in the long run, put an end to all fees. This is evidenced by clamor within the profession for liberalization of rules of procedure, which is already becoming effective in many places.

Judicial efficiency must, of course, rest upon effective judicial personnel. Court attaches should be selected by examination and should be protected from removal by civil service regulations. They should not be mere products of a political spoils system.

The selection of judges, of course, is the most important part of the whole problem.

The weight of intelligent opinion favors appointive judges, but the people are jealous of their power to select, and perhaps with good reason. The vice of the present situation does not lie so much with the election as with the political nomination of judges. Various methods to obtain nonpartisan nomination have been suggested: appointment of nonpartisan nominators, selection by bar associations, nomination by the Governor, by judges, and the like.

In Michigan, it was proposed that the State Constitution be amended to provide for a judiciary commission to nominate and the Governor to appoint judges. Ohio also considered a similar constitutional amendment, calling for election by the people. Both were rejected, however, in

# LOOK AT THE LAW

the 1938 election. The Baltimore, Maryland, Bar Association proposed a plan to permit sitting judges to run for re-election without nomination, to avoid party nominations or labels for other candidates.

Whatever the means, the present method of nomination by irresponsible political parties should be changed so that the influence of a responsible agency may be exercised. Even in New York City, where the Democratic machine rules the nomination of judges, the present Governor, Herbert H. Lehman, has been able, by exercise of his power of interim appointment, to influence the nomination and election of a number of able and nonpolitical judges, including Samuel Rosenman, President Roosevelt's friend and adviser; Charles Poletti, Lieutenant-Governor of the State and a young liberal of note; and Ferdinand Pecora, ex-president of the liberal Lawyer's Guild. In the Federal courts, in the same city, the caliber of the appointed judges has been noteworthy; where politics has played a part, it has not been permitted, with rare exception, to lower the quality of the appointees.

In the lower criminal courts in New York City, Mayor La Guardia has, single-handed, installed a system of appointment and promotion by merit that tends to make judicial office a career, and furnishes example of how many of the evils of our present politically-ridden judicial administrative system may be eliminated.

Of course, in the election of judges, political emblems should be eliminated and the tone of the contest otherwise freed from the heat and emotion of general political campaigns. But beyond that, judicial or other councils should keep and publish a record of the judge's work and its results, and the qualifications of the judges for promotion, demotion and removal should be judged thereby.

Judges should be more readily removable, preferably by

# LOOK AT THE LAW

action of higher court judges familiar with their work.

Such measures as these would not only be in the public weal but would be of invaluable aid to the majority of efficient, hardworking judges, whose efforts to remedy conditions in the courts are hampered by their weaker brethren. We discuss these matters at greater length in a subsequent chapter.

However, even with efficient judges, a change of judicial approach would be of great help in expediting judicial business.

The aura of formality with which the judge surrounds himself is not only used by unqualified judges to mask their ineptitude, but serves to discourage any attempt to do judicial business in a businesslike way. The judge's robe encases him in a factitious dignity; his dais raises him above the common level and makes him remote from common man. However necessary it be that he command respect (and a good judge, though he be found in shirtsleeves in his chambers, never fails to get it), the trappings of his office give the little man sitting at the bar of justice a false sense of his own importance and enable him to conceal an inability to understand behind a veneer of silence and reserve. How often has a lawyer writhed at his inability to talk it out with an intelligent judge, as man to man!

This factitious dignity ofttimes carries into the judge's work and into his reasoning. He finds it difficult "to get down to brass tacks," to penetrate the veneers and get down to the realities of the situation. Instead, he finds himself surrounded by unreal emblements of sovereignty and subconsciously he carries these into the realms of his reasoning.

A Missouri judge, Judge Ewing Cockrell, has experimented for years with a method of informal trial which he calls "trial by lawyers," the judge merely acting informally

# LOOK AT THE LAW

as arbitrator. The method has proved highly successful in expediting trials and avoiding appeals.

Unnecessary formality causes delay. It keeps a judge from deciding today an issue not before him, though he will be called upon to determine it tomorrow. Thus, an appellate court will frequently be heard to say, "It is not necessary to decide this question now," or, "Having determined to reverse the judgment upon the first ground, it is not necessary at this time to go into the others," although a new trial means a new appeal on the remaining undecided points.

We have discussed the speeding up of trials and the limitations of appeals by obviating technicalities. We must be careful to limit the pruning of technicalities so that matters of substance are not emasculated. One common expedient for cutting down calendar congestion and delay, for instance, is the limitation of jury trials. The right of trial by jury is secured by constitutional provisions but through various devices, including express consent and implied waiver, this guaranty is disregarded. Such methods, whenever employed, have proven successful in speeding up trials and unbinding court calendars, but they should not be pressed too far because the petty jury is an important institution, not merely to protect us against abuse of executive and judicial power, but also to avoid the rigidities and hypocrisies of the law.

We need no such extreme measures, if we can put the dispatch of business in our courts on an efficient plane and provide efficient personnel to handle it.

Delay should dissipate before such an approach, and with delay should go much of its concomitant, undue cost and expense.

# CHAPTER VIII

## *The Layman Says:*
## THE LAW IS TOO EXPENSIVE

*1.*

"Look at this," says Smith, opening the morning's mail. "Here's a notice from the bankruptcy court, saying that they're ending the Parker Shoe Company bankruptcy. The trustee is asking for a fee of $2,500; the attorney for the trustee, $5,000; the attorney for the bankrupt, $1,500; three appraisers, $750 each. That makes a total of $11,250, besides referee's fees and disbursements, including filing fees and stenographer's fees, which aren't fixed."

"How much for us creditors?" asks Jones.

"Doesn't say," answers Smith, "but it does say the trustees' report shows a balance of $12,000 on hand, and creditors' claims amount to $65,000. That means $750 left to pay the referee, the stenographer and the court clerk, the balance to go to the $65,000 of creditors."

"Which means the lawyers get the assets and the creditors get nothing, as usual," says Jones, in disgust.

This is the average creditor's conception of a bankruptcy liquidation. Nor is it without justification.

Under the New York State practice, an indebted businessman who wants his assets distributed to his creditors, but does not seek a discharge from his debts, makes what is called "an assignment" of his property "for the benefit of creditors" to some person he selects as "assignee." The assignee "administers" the estate and ultimately files an accounting which he asks the court to approve. Ordinarily, by the time of the accounting, little, if anything, is left for the creditors, as the following opinion of Mr. Justice Wenzel, a realistic judge, illustrates:

# LOOK AT THE LAW

"Matter of Union Dyeing & Finishing Works, Inc. Motion denied. This account is not approved. It is a classic example of the inherent inequity and iniquity of the so-called assignment for the 'benefit of creditors.' At the time the assignment was made, the assets of the assignor were actually worth $22,290.54 and its liabilities $24,665.37; today, after eight years, there is left the sum of $130.20, which the assignees ask in payment of their services. Certainly the ingenuity of the astute American businessman can evolve a more suitable method of meeting such contingencies."

The expense of bankruptcy and corporate reorganization proceedings is generally considered excessive. Since a bankrupt estate is potential prey, precautions adopted to compel honesty in administration (even though they are not wholly effective) take time and cost money. No matter how small the case, or how few the assets, there is a minimum of expense that cannot be avoided. It is only when assets exceed this minimum that there is a possibility of return to creditors.

As the assets increase, expense mounts. According to a report of the United States Attorney General for 1937, the expenses of administration of 42,396 no-asset cases was $496,276.92, an average of $11.70; while the cost of administering 12,719 asset cases was $14,891,431.42, an average of $1,170 per case—or 100 times greater.

When the assets are sufficient, it is not unusual for the cost of the reorganization of a large corporation to run into millions of dollars.

"The way in which companies in receivership or bankruptcy are drained by lawyers, auditors, trustees, etc., etc., has become a joke in business circles. But it's no joke to the creditors," states an article in the New York *Evening Post* of June 13, 1935, in commenting on the application for allowances submitted to the Federal Court in Delaware in the matter of the National Department Stores, Inc.

# LOOK AT THE LAW

"If National Department Stores weren't bankrupt before, the fees would be enough to put it into bankruptcy now," comments the *Post*. "What the creditors and stockholders will get remains to be seen. The fees asked are 14% of the corporation's capital."

In another article, entitled, "The Bankruptcy Racket" (New York *American*, November 1, 1935), Julius G. Behrens, financial editor, comments upon the decision of the Federal judge who allowed fees and expenses of $1,026,711 for reorganizing the affairs of the Paramount-Publix Corporation, although the judge had pruned the requests of lawyers, experts and protective committees who had originally asked for $2,841,031.

In the matter of American Bond and Mortgage Company, a group of half a dozen law firms shared some $530,000, one Chicago firm receiving over $150,000, and a New York law firm over a quarter of a million dollars. The Chicago firm received, in addition, almost $150,000 more as counsel for the trustees, while another New York firm received, as counsel for the receiver and the trustee under a number of mortgage issues, an additional total of $464,000, making a grand total of over a million and a quarter dollars.

Excessive fees for bankers, engineers, auditors, trustees, committees and counsel have been glaring in cases of corporate reorganization where cooperating and controlling bankers and lawyers select a complaisant or trusting judge who appoints (though frequently in the best of faith) a suggested or friendly receiver or trustee. Such a proceeding is known as a "friendly" receivership.

When, for example, the New York City Interborough Rapid Transit Company wanted to reorganize, their counsel, according to his own statement, "arranged for the receivership."

When it was decided to reorganize the Chicago, Mil-

## LOOK AT THE LAW

waukee and St. Paul Railroad Company, the company's bankers, who desired to control the reorganization, chose Chicago as the place for the reorganization, although the railroad was organized in Wisconsin and had financial and operating offices in New York and various other cities and States. The bankers in this case chose a method of which it has been officially said that, if they were not tacitly bargaining with the judge, they were able to go "shopping" among the Federal judges in order to obtain the appointment of the men they wanted as receivers.

Since "friendly" receiverships are so arranged as to achieve a maximum of cooperation between those in control, while excluding dissentients, there is little or no real opposition to the efforts of the cooperators to obtain unduly large fees, making the proceedings unduly expensive to the creditors and security holders.

In reorganizing the Chicago, Milwaukee & St. Paul Railroad (according to Lowenthal, "The Investor Pays"), the bankers, in concert with the chairman of the bondholders' committee (whom they had selected), "discussed and agreed upon compensation of about $1,000,000 for the bankers (they actually received $1,044,000) and between $500,000 and $750,000 for their counsel." Before a Senate Committee, the bankers testified that the expenses of the reorganization were fixed at a minimum of $5,000,000 and a maximum of $6,500,000. These are the emoluments in the upper brackets; in less important matters compensation is more moderate but volume is greater.

Under our practice, judges are called upon to appoint receivers, committees, commissioners, conservators, guardians, administrators, custodians, trustees, appraisers, of insolvent or mismanaged corporations, of banks, of trust estates, of businesses that fall within the reach of the courts, of bankrupt or other insolvent persons, of incom-

# LOOK AT THE LAW

petents, of children, of decedents' or aliens' estates, of real estate and of a multitude of other forms of property. And many such appointments carry with them a vast diversity of additional patronage, involving the appointment and employment of bonding and insurance agents, auctioneers, appraisers, collectors, mechanics, brokers, lawyers, and other agents and employees.

When, under the prevailing system, a judge is expected to allot such appointments to the political organization to which the judge owes his nomination and election, or where judicial nepotism or favoritism governs the selection of appointees, the litigant is usually charged with the expense of unnecessary, inefficient or even dishonest appointments.

A recent report of the law reform committee of the Chamber of Commerce of the State of New York said, on this score:

"Favoritism extends not only to individual appointees with sufficient influence, but also to groups centered around a single dominant figure. . . . There were certain closely integrated groups which secured a large amount of patronage. . . . The groups were so integrated that direct appointees in the group passed on the sub-appointments which they controlled to other members of the group. To take one situation as illustrative, one group of eleven persons related to or associated with a leader, secured a total of 413 appointments (including 271 selections of one member as insurance agent). In fifteen of these cases some one member of the group was appointed as receiver; in substantially each instance he appointed another member as attorney, a third member as real estate agent and a fourth as insurance agent. The net result was a little empire of patronage developed for all these appointees, obviously through their association with the leader."

A recent investigation in New York City of appointments by Supreme Court judges in mortgage foreclosure cases over a period of time was summarized thus by the New York *World-Telegram:*

Of 106 appointees who "earned" fees of $2,500 or more, sixty-six were identified definitely as active political workers; that the majority of appointees were named for no apparent reason except that they were active political workers and that the appointments were used by the courts deliberately and consciously as part of an established system to build up and maintain political organizations;

That although there were some 1,200 attorneys in Queens County of New York City, a group of thirty-one persons, of whom twenty-one were identified directly with politics, received thirty out of every 100 appointments made by one justice in the period from July 1, 1935, to December 31, 1936;

That one judge's brother received a good deal of the auctioneer patronage, that one judge's son and his office associates received 106 appointments as referee, worth not less than $10,000, in a period of a little over a year, that the brothers of the Queens County leader received sixty-six references, as well as a considerable amount of the auctioneer patronage.

The system of foreclosing real estate mortgages carries with it, in many places, an amount of unnecessary and wasteful patronage. When the owner of real estate defaults in making payment on his mortgage, the mortgagee must start a foreclosure action. In some jurisdictions the court appoints a referee to "compute the amount due" on the mortgage, an arithmetical computation that the judge could make himself in five minutes. For this the referee gets a fee. Later the judge appoints a referee to sell the property. The referee then hires an auctioneer to sell it; the auctioneer gets paid and so does the referee. The sale is advertised in

# LOOK AT THE LAW

little-known but politically recommended newspapers (a racing form paper, for example, carries a considerable amount of this advertising), and finally after months of delay and unnecessary expense, the mortgagee gets the property upon paying the legal costs. Meanwhile, a receiver appointed by the court has been collecting and expending the rents.

As a result of a recent survey of foreclosure actions in New York City, it was claimed

"That of $1,713,472.73 in fees awarded by judges, at least $1,422,792 was 'sheer waste so far as any benefit or service to the plaintiff-mortgagee was concerned';

"That in thirty-four out of each 100 Manhattan (New York) foreclosures and in thirty out of each 100 in the Bronx (New York), the mortgage holder recovered less than ten cents on the dollar."

These practices are common in many parts of the country. They are deplored by real estate interests which seek to simplify legal processes and to cut legal costs in such matters, urging that excessive costs tend to discourage mortgage lenders and to slow housing reform.

The conveyance of real estate titles is, ordinarily, similarly burdensome. No matter how many times a real estate title is conveyed, it must be searched for defects each time; and searching, legal and often guaranty charges are assessed against the seller or the buyer, though the same ground, literally and figuratively, is covered on each occasion. Years ago a system known as the Torrens system was devised to enable the permanent registration and certification of land titles by the State, at small cost, but the adoption of this system has been effectively fought by banks, lawyers and title-searching interests which prefer more cumbersome, expensive and lucrative methods.

Other stock items often make recourse to the law a highly

# LOOK AT THE LAW

extravagant pursuit. The highest paid judges receive $25,000 a year; our United States Supreme Court justices get $20,000 a year; our District Court judges $10,000 a year. A referee or master designated to sit as a judge may receive in fees, in a single case, a sum in excess of the judge's annual salary.

A Federal judge allowed his former partner a fee of $116,000 for his services as master in a rate case. The master had served 282 days of an average of five hours each, which made his compensation $85 an hour. A higher court reduced the fee to $49,250, or at the rate of $35 an hour.

A former New York Supreme Court judge sitting as referee in litigation involving the estate of the late Jay Gould over a three-year period was paid at the rate of $65 per hour.

Guardians who are appointed to protect temporarily the interests of infants in a pending litigation are sometimes the recipients of large sums. Such guardians (a total of ten) in the estate of Jay Gould received a total of $200,000 for their services. Of this amount, one guardian received $52,000.

In a contest over the will of Amos F. Eno, two special guardians were appointed and each received $17,500. The expense of preliminary administration of the estate was $431,000.

Executors and administrators, trustees and their counsel, frequently find their commissions and fees taking them into the higher tax brackets.

Accounting proceedings in the Jay Gould estate resulted in total charges for counsel and disbursements of $3,000,000, of which corporate trustees received $300,000, one counsel received $580,000, and another received $530,000.

Since trust companies have gone extensively into these realms of the dead, they have succeeded in inducing the New York legislature to double the compensation of estate representatives.

# LOOK AT THE LAW

Even minor appointees become afflicted with clutching hands when they embrace the property of the dead.

In a recent case in New York, the judge appointed appraisers who "spent the whole or part of nineteen days" in appraising the personal property of a decedent which consisted of twenty-four bonds and mortgages, listed corporate stock and a furniture business. The appraisers, in turn, employed two experts and one certified public accountant. For their services, each appraiser claimed $3,580 (exclusive of the charges of the experts and the certified public accountant), which would be compensation at the rate of $188 per day, assuming they had spent all the time they claimed to have spent. The judge allowed them $2,500 each. The Appellate Court said, "We consider the amount allowed in this case as unreasonable and excessive and that $1,000 each will be ample compensation."

Nor do the insane escape. A brother of a New York State Supreme Court Justice was charged with income tax frauds. The prosecution charged that he had failed to account for $55,250 in fees for lunacy commission appointments, and that in 1937 he had received $10,140.24 in payment for fifty-three appointments as an examining physician in court cases and lunacy appointments.

And many of such allowances are sheer waste.

The New York *World-Telegram* recently commented editorially, "In Kings County alone in the last five years reports of eighty-five lunacy commissions costing the city approximately $75,000 have been rejected by the court as not reliable."

2.

"Consider my case," said Dickens' Mr. Gridley in 1868. "As true as there is a Heaven above us, this is my case. I am

## LOOK AT THE LAW

one of two brothers, my father (a farmer) made a will and left his farm and stock, and so forth, to my mother, for her life. After my mother's death, all was to come to me, except a legacy of three hundred pounds that I was then to pay to my brother. My mother died. My brother, some time afterwards, claimed his legacy. I, and some of my relations, said that he had had a part of it already, in board and lodging, and some other things. Now mind! That was the question, and nothing else. No one disputed the will; no one disputed anything but whether part of that three hundred pounds had been already paid or not. To settle that question, my brother filing a bill, I was obliged to go into this accursed Chancery; I was forced there, because the law forced me, and would let me go nowhere else. Seventeen people were made defendants to that simple suit! It first came on, after two years. It was then stopped for another two years, while the Master (may his head rot off!) inquired whether I was my father's son—about which there was no dispute at all with any mortal creature. He then found out that there were not defendants enough—remember, there were only seventeen as yet!—but that we must have another who had been left out; and must begin all over again. The costs at that time—before the thing was begun!—were three times the legacy. My brother would have given up the legacy, and joyfully, to escape more costs. My whole estate, left to me in that will of my father's, has gone in costs. The suit, still undecided, has fallen into rack, and ruin, and despair, with everything else—and here I stand, this day!"

This was the English legal system that moved Jeremy Bentham to complain that though the Magna Charta provided that justice should be sold to no man, it was sold, at an unconscionable price, to the one-tenth to whom it was not denied. This was the English legal system that grew naturally out of the practice of having judges and court

# LOOK AT THE LAW

clerks pay for their appointments; to get their money back they charged suitors fees for every administrative and judicial service they performed.

Under the English system, "costs" practically meant direct cost to the suitor. Today "costs" has lost its ancient meaning. The cost of litigation, the maintenance of courthouses and the payment of personnel is now largely borne by the people, rather than by the individual suitor. The theory of a democratic government requires that justice be free to all. Though it be no less expensive, when wasteful, its cost is indirect and is submerged in the other costs of government.

We still retain some vestiges of ancient practices of direct costs; there are still fees for filing papers, or for obtaining juries, for sheriffs' services and for similar privileges, in certain jurisdictions; in others, public officers still charge and retain fees as their compensation.

Where such practices still prevail, the charges not only tend to be excessive, but the desire for fees sometimes breeds graver injustice.

In Allegheny County, Pennsylvania, which includes Pittsburgh, there are, according to the *Journal of the American Judicature Society*, 429 justices and aldermen who are vested with minor criminal jurisdiction, of whom only eighty-five are on full time. The Allegheny County Grand Jurors Association reported that not only does "an unsuspecting public pay an enormous tax," but that these minor officials "are daily . . . holding persons . . . for crimes . . . on evidence that discloses not even civil liability, for the mere purpose of collecting fees and costs."

In New York City, the New York *World-Telegram* proudly stated that the Magistrates Court has become almost self-sustaining, through the large amount of fines collected. While the cessation of "fixes," which freed offenders under the previous administration, is commendable, as found by the newspaper, its editorial writer failed to realize the converse danger of having judges try to make a "record" in the collection of fines, an evil akin to that where prosecuting attorneys seek a record of convictions.

Usually, however, the cost of administration of the courts is borne by the public purse. And this cost is excessive and wasteful. Said the late Elihu Root, a most conservative member of the bar, over twenty years ago:

"We spend vast sums in building and maintaining courthouses and public offices and in paying judges, clerks, criers, marshals, sheriffs, messengers, jurors, and all the great army of men whose service is necessary for the machinery of justice, and the product is disproportionate to the plant and the working force. There is no country in the world in which the doing of justice is burdened by such heavy overhead charges or in which so great a force is maintained for a given amount of litigation."

We cannot consider or analyze in this work the waste in these indirect charges. They are not trifling. A single courthouse in the City of New York, built to replace one that had been erected by "Boss" Tweed at a theft of some nine million dollars, cost thirty million. By the time it was finished, the increase in litigation had been such as to threaten its adequacy.

A New York municipal investigation disclosed that, in some cases, court clerks on the payroll had not reported, except to receive their pay checks, for months at a time. Recently, a court attache who drew his pay regularly was found to have been holding down a second public job.

It is not unusual to reward political hangers-on of little or no education with clerical court jobs, or to designate as judges' secretaries men without legal training or experience and to pay them in excess of what legally trained and experienced men could be hired for. It is not possible

# LOOK AT THE LAW

to estimate accurately the loss in time or money to suitors, witnesses or jurors resulting from wasteful, costly and inefficient operation of courts. At best, judicial administration is expensive; the New York Commission on the Administration of Justice recently estimated the cost of a Supreme Court jury trial in New York County at $1,125 per day.

It is no rare occurrence to have a personal injury action tried before a jury for two or three days, with a verdict for the defendant proving the action unfounded, or a verdict for the plaintiff for a thousand dollars or less. At a cost of over a thousand dollars a day for the immediate judicial machinery, it would be cheaper for the county to buy off the plaintiff in these cases.

Errors that result in mistrials or reversals tend to pile up extravagant public and private costs. The Hines mistrial was estimated to have cost the State fifty thousand dollars, ignoring the useless expense to the defendant and the loss of time and money of the many witnesses and the jurymen. A newspaper report told of the tribulations of one of the jurymen in that case, whose wife was trying to carry on and save his business during his enforced absence.

Judicial errors that result in appeals are costly. Appeals are unjustifiably complicated and expensive, because the stenographer's record of what occurred at a trial must be ordered and its cost paid. This record of a long trial will frequently cost many thousands of dollars; for a short trial its cost is invariably in the hundreds. Moreover, the stenographer produces only one or two typewritten copies and the appeal court, for its judges, its clerks and its records, requires twelve, fifteen or twenty copies. The result is that the litigant who would appeal must have the stenographer's record printed (unless he gets special permission from the court for good cause shown), and these printing bills are sometimes staggering in amount. For not only must the stenographer's

## LOOK AT THE LAW

record of the trial testimony be printed, but every document offered in evidence that bears on the question before the court must be included in the "record on appeal" — contracts, photographs, maps, diagrams, the thousand and one papers that lawyers, necessarily or needlessly, submit to court and jury.

Consequently, records on appeal are cumbersome and expensive. For example, one case involved a record of about 7,000 pages, and cost $10,000 to print. Another case had a record of about 4,000 pages, which cost about $6,000. And such records are by no means unusual.

Following the printed record, each side must also print its brief, a condensed statement of the facts in the record and its legal argument to the appellate court. These papers must be submitted on each appeal, and well-litigated controversy often involves a number of appeals (half a dozen is not unusual).

The inordinate cost of appeal frequently means that the losing side is denied the opportunity to appeal since the cost of such proceedings, if taken, may readily consume all of its substance, as in Mr. Jarndyce's case. And here is a more modern example:

The United Press reported:

"The city of Cleveland paid off a $51,498.50 debt today to Miss Viola Nichols, who won a forty-three year court fight to collect for land which had been appropriated by the city as part of Rockefeller Park.

"Miss Nichols started the legal battle in 1895, went to law school to learn what actions to take, and even moved to Buffalo to file Federal suits when she lost in Ohio courts. Federal Judge Paul Jones directed the present settlement last December.

"But Miss Nichols actually received only $5,229.56 of the $51,498.50, for which the city had to float a loan. Her attorney's fee, $24,317.75 — and expenses, $2,863, — and several other costs left her only about one-tenth of the amount awarded."

# LOOK AT THE LAW

In litigation, the principal item of cost to a litigant is the fee of his attorney. Under our rules, each litigant pays his own lawyer, win or lose. The cost of a lawyer is not a charge which is recoverable from the losing side. Though this rule works injustice, particularly in criminal cases where a defendant unjustly accused may be impoverished by the cost of defending himself, we can hardly put a further premium on the chicanery that too often marks the defense of persons accused in our criminal courts by charging the State with the cost of a defense designed to cheat the law. Nor, since result in our courts is not always consonant with justice, could we dare tax an unsuccessful plaintiff with the cost of a successful defense. That would amount to a denial of the courts to too many legitimate litigants and would unduly increase the advantages already enjoyed in our courts by the rich.

Ordinarily, a litigant can get a lawyer to fit his purse. The cost, where the litigation is private and the client has the selection of his own lawyer, is dependent upon his own taste and inclinations. In this, the law is like any other commodity. One may buy crackers out of a barrel and pay for crackers. Or one may buy an imported English crock tied with a ribbon and get the crackers free (upon paying for the accessories, visible and intangible, including the superior feeling that the higher price induces). So with the law. One may hire an unpretentious lawyer out of a dingy office or one may pick a more fashionable one who may be a mere business-getter for a large and expensive legal "shop." And, to complete the analogy, the first lawyer frequently carries more nourishment, at less cost, than his more expensive brother, for the amount of the fee a lawyer charges is not necessarily a mark of his ability.

"Big" lawyers get "big" fees; "little" lawyers must take "little" fees. But as "big" in our civilization does not neces-

# LOOK AT THE LAW

sarily mean "able," so "little" does not necessarily mean "incompetent." Success, under our system, is no mark of virtue; the law is no exception to the rule.

The excessive cost of legal services, the swollen legal fee, is the creation and almost the monopoly of "big" lawyers. Most lawyers go through life earning little more than bookkeeper's pay.

In New York City, the habitat of large fees, one per cent of the lawyers earned $50,000 in the year 1933; fourteen per cent, $10,000 and over; as against fifty per cent who earned less than $3,000, and fifteen per cent who earned less than $1,000. The average income of New York City lawyers in that year was $6,000. Of 3,200 lawyers, (twenty-one per cent of the total number) seven earned almost $1,000,000 (five per cent), as against total earnings of the entire 3,200 of $20,000,000.

In the year 1935, one out of every ten lawyers in New York City qualified for relief under a pauper's oath. But a few lawyers, a small percentage of the whole, command large fees that receive publicity and create the public impression that all lawyers are overpaid.

Thaw's legal fights in the White killing were said to have cost him almost $900,000. They included:

| | |
|---|---:|
| Expenses of first trial, 1907 | $200,000 |
| Expenses of second trial, 1908 | 150,000 |
| Expenses of first insanity hearing, 1908 | 65,000 |
| Expenses of second insanity hearing, 1909 | 50,000 |
| Expenses of third insanity hearing, 1912 | 75,000 |
| Incidentals | 100,000 |
| C. W. Hartridge, attorney of record, who called in many others of counsel (disbursements) | 103,000 |
| Paid detectives | 50,000 |

# LOOK AT THE LAW

In the public service field, where regulation of rates is a constant source of litigation, the companies spend munificently. In New York State, lawyers for the public utilities, according to an official record of the Public Service Commission, received $14,498,020 in the five-year period from 1931 to 1936, excluding the cost of engineers, accountants and other experts; of this total, $9,500,000, or sixty-five per cent, was paid by three or four systems in the metropolitan area of New York City. This included payments to a former president of the American Bar Association, whose firm received $2,437,085 in the five-year period; counsel for the New York Telephone Company and his associates received an aggregate of $1,000,000; while a large Brooklyn law firm received almost half a million dollars from one gas company.

For representing him in creditors' litigation, William Fox, movie magnate, is reported to have paid Samuel Untermeyer, New York lawyer, $1,000,000. Max D. Steuer, leading New York trial lawyer, reported that he had had a net income from professional services from 1935 to 1938, inclusive, of $500,000 per year.

These large fees are not always borne by the rich. The poor and the middle class bear their share of excessive tolls. Large corporations pay swollen fees and charge their cost back to their multitudinous middle-class stockholders. The public utilities that disburse large sums to counsel charge the cost back to the poor in the form of increased gas, electric light and water rates. Judges allow "big" law firms large fees in reorganization proceedings and the cost is borne by thousands of small creditors and stockholders. At the same time, the standards so set by "big" lawyers become the standards that lesser lawyers seek to attain. The client's financial standing is one element that the law recognizes in determining the reasonableness of a lawyer's fee, which is

# LOOK AT THE LAW

another way of saying that the lawyer is entitled to charge all the traffic will bear. The cost to the middle-class client is correspondingly high, and the average middle-class client finds even the average lawyer unduly expensive. The lawyer's cost of doing business is high, for his way of doing business is inefficient. His cost of living is high because he must try to maintain an appearance of prosperity; he must advertise himself by his mode of living, his social and fraternal connections. His fee requirements are therefore disproportionate to the average client's pecuniary abilities.

The client who cannot conveniently pay a lawyer therefore seeks refuge in the contingent fee.

The best example of the contingent fee is the one most widely known and least respected — the one usually associated with "ambulance-chasing."

When a man is struck and injured by an automobile, to recover damages he must hire a lawyer to start a suit. Usually the injured person has no money with which to pay a lawyer, or if he has, he needs it to pay doctors' bills and to support his family during his disability. The driver of the car, on the other hand, is usually insured and the insurance company has a staff of lawyers in its employ and at its command. Under these circumstances, unless the injured person can find a lawyer who will make no immediate charge, but who will take for his services a percentage of what he may recover, the injured man may be deprived of his opportunity to recoup his losses.

If there be no recovery for the client, there can be no pay for the lawyer. The lawyer's fee, therefore, is called a "contingent" fee—it is contingent upon recovery. The law now permits a lawyer to make such an arrangement—though once it was illegal—and not only in a personal injury suit, but in any kind of suit.

Nor is such an arrangement restricted to cases where the

# LOOK AT THE LAW

client cannot pay. It may be made in cases where the client does not have sufficient faith in the outcome of the suit to risk paying a lawyer a fixed fee for bringing it and prefers to have the lawyer gamble with him on the result.

Because of the risks of recovery, it has become the custom in personal injury suits for the lawyer to charge one-third or even as much as one-half of the ultimate recovery (a recent survey made in New York indicates that more reputable lawyers who are not regularly engaged in the personal injury "business" do not subscribe to such rates). The result is that a successful plaintiff may not only find himself minus a leg but also minus half or more of the damages awarded him for his injury. And he complains accordingly.

The contingent fee lawyer is often the most expensive, for he is too frequently contemptuous and independent of his client, and correspondingly neglectful or indifferent. Many times he has no ability to try a case but takes it in hope of a settlement. When he gets one, he bases his fee on the amount of the settlement, regardless of whether it is adequate or whether his services increased the amount. One of the bad effects of this practice is that an incompetent lawyer may claim as much for writing a claim letter as an intelligent and hard-working lawyer would receive for trying the case. Also, since the amount received is the sole criterion, a premium is placed upon quick settlements in large numbers, without work, regardless of the result to the client.

The contingent fee arrangement has been attacked, and with justification. It makes the lawyer not only a partisan but a partner in the case, and in its conduct he is tempted to suborn perjury and to connive at fraud and trickery. It puts a premium on bringing suits to collect their nuisance values, for the plaintiff knows that defending a suit is bound to cost money and to involve risk, and that a defendant will

# LOOK AT THE LAW

usually figure it cheaper to settle for a small sum than go to the trouble, expense and hazard of a trial, however unfounded the suit may be.

Most of the blackmailing suits that are brought result from the contingent fee; only a modicum of unfounded and nuisance breach of promise, assault, and personal injury cases would be brought if the contingent fee were abolished. A boom in the real estate market invariably brings a host of contingent fee actions by brokers for commissions on sales or what, it is claimed, might have been sales; more than a fair percentage of such actions never would have been brought were it not for the contingent fee. Almost every businessman in New York has had some experience with false claims by discharged employees who asserted that they had been employed upon verbal contracts for a year. These cases are almost entirely handled upon contingent bases, especially the simulated ones, because a client is much less willing to give a lawyer a substantial part of a good and honest claim than to share a dishonest one. Personal injury suits are invariably handled on a contingent basis, and the percentage of dishonest claims in that field is anybody's guess. The result is unnecessary expense to honest litigants and to the community in cost of litigation, to say nothing of the result in congested calendars, to which previous reference has been made.

### 3.

Abroad, it is proverbial that each peasant carries a soldier on his back. Here, each citizen is burdened with a politician. Our political entrepreneurs tender the wares of democracy freely, but the organization they create and maintain insists upon its toll. And the administration of justice has no exemption.

# LOOK AT THE LAW

To the extent that political levies are made through the tax rolls, the excessive cost of justice merges in other excessive costs and meets with no specific criticism from the taxpayer.

But at times, as at the present, in New York City, where mandatory judicial and administrative legal costs threaten the municipal financial policy, official criticism of judicial waste and patronage is voiced. The city officials are now seeking to take control of judicial administrative pay rolls from the judges, claiming that the courts have been unnecessarily and politically overmanned. This is unusual, since ordinarily the political party in power, whatever its denomination, makes no attack on jobs and salaries. Ordinarily the taxpayer, being unorganized and unrepresented, remains mute and fatalistic concerning this and other excessive tax burdens.

When however, direct levies, not assimilated in general taxes, are charged to organized groups, businessmen, real estate interests and others, resentment is voiced and action demanded. That is why we hear little or nothing of the unnecessary and excessive cost of trials and appeals, while fervent protest is made concerning the excessive cost of bankruptcy and reorganization machinery and of real estate conveyancing and foreclosure. And that is why we are beginning to read statements such as this one which appeared recently in the New York *Evening Post:* "The average cost of defense against a complaint of the NLRB is $20,572. That figure was obtained by Hartley Barclay, editor of *Mill and Factory*, based on a study of seventy-six companies in twenty-eight States. The big automobile companies were not included.

"Barclay points out that fifty-four per cent of the United States corporations have assets of less than $50,000—how can they afford to spend $20,572 fighting the National

## LOOK AT THE LAW

Labor Relations Board for justice in the courts? The answer is, they can't.

"For the 'little fellar,' there is no 'equality of law' before the N L R B."

Because banks and trust companies profit by the high cost of administration of dead men's estates, we hear little or no complaint of the high cost of those matters.

The expense of bankruptcy and insolvency proceedings has been criticized by organized business and credit agencies. They have stimulated the publicity needed to interest and convince legislators and judges of the necessity for overhauling wasteful and overexpensive legal machinery and have obtained amendments to the laws which, with the cooperation of judicial and administrative agencies, may be expected to effect a measure of change.

The cost of railroad reorganization, in the past, has been a glaring abuse, particularly since such cost has been added to the over-top-heavy debt structures of the railroads and has invited and contributed to the recurrence of catastrophe. The situation of the railroads is at present so precarious that major operations must and will be performed and, with the spotlight of publicity and an amended railroad reorganization act, depredations of the past should not find repetition.

Likewise, in other fields of reorganization, it is a reasonable hope and assumption that the ills of friendly and collusive receiverships having been so glaringly exposed, independent judges, who constitute a majority of our judiciary, will guard against their repetition and will limit compensation to those who have fairly earned it.

Caution is needed in all matters of judicial patronage. There must be fair compensation for the honest services required to permit the legal machine to function. A problem

# LOOK AT THE LAW

is presented, however, when political or financial control undertakes to profit unduly either by rendering unnecessary or incompetent services, or by rendering competent services for excessive compensation.

Politically or financially controlled patronage in the courts creates local problems that increase the cost of administration of the law. Here the remedy is basically political and lies with the people themselves. They cannot sit back and expect those who profit by the system to desist; nor can they expect judges dependent upon a party organization for their posts to take up arms against practices which supply the lifeblood of the organization.

So long as legislatures invite judges to appoint "lunacy" commissions (which was the practice in New York prior to the passage by the 1939 Legislature of a measure which properly allotted the task of determining sanity of defendants to institutional psychiatrists), so long will some judges be tempted to appoint friends, relatives and even persons who would accommodate the judges with loans.

While lawyers should take the lead in fighting these practices, the link between political and financial forces, bar associations and influential lawyers is often too close to expect independent and aggressive action from that source. Besides, lawyers live in deadly and understandable fear of antagonizing judges, politicians or financiers, who therefore have no difficulty, upon occasion, in controlling local bar associations and neutralizing the efforts of fearless and independent lawyers.

There was a striking example of this recently, when an attempt to have the Jersey City Bar Association take a stand on the question of civil liberties in Jersey City was turned back by a wave of Hague-machine-controlled votes and when the Essex County, New Jersey, Bar Association promptly approved the judicial nomination of Hague's un-

## LOOK AT THE LAW

trained son, in an effort to stem a rising tide of public indignation. The New York City Bar Association has had a number of similar experiences when efforts were made to refuse endorsement to machine-controlled judicial nominees.

However, in the past few years, there have been organized movements by younger and more liberal members of the bar which have not only resulted in the organization of new associations, but have compelled liberalization of the attitudes of the existing ones. And older lawyers are beginning to take courage and assert themselves. The intervention of the Civil Liberties Committee of the American Bar Association in the Hague C. I. O. contest over the exercise of civil rights in Jersey City on the side of the C. I. O., represented by the New York liberal lawyer, Morris Ernst, is tangible evidence of this changing attitude on the part even of reactionary lawyers.

But lawyers generally are, and may be expected to remain, timorous until increasing public education through magazines and newspapers, through the lead of intelligent and aggressive public officials and liberal and progressive lawyers, causes laymen to take the initiative in combatting these improper practices, of which the great majority of judges would gladly be rid.

Once the political obstructions are penetrated, the problems of judicial patronage require for their cure only adherence to Canon 12 of the Canons of Judicial Ethics, adopted by the American Bar Association:

"Trustees, receivers, masters, referees, guardians and other persons appointed by a judge to aid in the administration of justice should have the strictest probity and impartiality and should be selected with a view solely to their character and fitness. The power of making such appointments should not be exercised by him for personal or partisan advantage. He should not permit his appointments to

# LOOK AT THE LAW

be controlled by others than himself. He should also avoid nepotism and undue favoritism in his appointments. While not hesitating to fix or approve just amounts, he should be most scrupulous in granting or approving compensation for the services or charges of such appointees to avoid excessive allowances, whether or not excepted to or complained of. He cannot rid himself of this responsibility by the consent of counsel."

Here again we are back in the laps of our judges, our journey's end in the consideration of so many of these problems. Improve their personnel and character, the manner of their selection, and these abuses will automatically end.

The remedies suggested in the previous chapter to end judicial delay will strike at its twin, undue legal expense. Both are to be found in the same places, springing from the same causes. Both will yield to a greater administrative efficiency. And often without great effort.

For example, the cost of appeals could be radically cut by subscribing to the English system of submitting a case to the appellate court upon the original typewritten record and papers. This would save not only money, but time, as it does in England. However, improvement in recording will soon dispense with the stenographer; the record of trials will be available for reproduction upon phonographic discs and the appellate judges will be able to get their information at first hand from reproducing machines. This will make the present system archaic.

Manifestly, greater efficiency in administration would cut court costs. In any event, there is no logical justification for the present outmoded system of charging such costs directly to litigants. How can we justify charging an impecunious litigant a sum of money he cannot afford to pay if he wants to exercise his constitutional right of trial by jury? Or to use his inability to pay such a charge to compel him

# LOOK AT THE LAW

to forego that right? Yet we adopt such expedients—indeed, we increase such charges—in an effort to eliminate jury trials with their attendant delays and expense. Would it not be more in keeping with our pretensions of even-handed justice to allow each litigant who acts in good faith one trial and one appeal on the facts and law, at no direct cost, with necessary precautions to insure the good faith of the litigant?

But the major private cost of legal procedure, as we have seen, comes from the need for privately paying lawyers.

Curiously enough, though the State assumes the entire cost of punishing the man who steals our money, it assumes only a portion of the cost when we sue him to obtain its return. There was a time when the State felt no obligation to redress private wrongs that are now considered public offenses; but it has not yet extended its complete aid to effect civil recoveries. It supplies judicial machinery, but leaves it to the litigants to employ and pay their own lawyers, charges them certain arbitrary fees and, in addition, makes them bear the expense of fees paid to witnesses, experts, stenographers, and the like.

This is an anomalous practice which sometimes decries the equality of the law promises; it becomes a reprehensible one when the costs are unnecessarily and unfairly made excessive.

Our present race of lawyers, privately retained and paid, finds its forebears in the ancient Attican orators, the Roman juris-consults and advocates. But the Attican orator was forbidden to appear an advocate for pay, and the Cincian law of the Romans forbade the Roman advocate from taking pecuniary compensation. Even in England a barrister has no legal right to a fee; he cannot sue for it in a court of law.

Though lawyers' fees have been restricted and regulated from age to age (in Maryland in 1725, for example, the

# LOOK AT THE LAW

legislature not only regulated lawyers' fees but made them payable in tobacco or currency at the option of the client), we have, within recent years, lost sight of the substantial reasons which caused such regulations and restrictions. The result is that legal advice and advocacy have become commodities, for sale like other commodities, regulated by no law save that of demand and supply.

The consequences are many and varied. Here we are concerned with the effect upon those who purchase these commodities. Only the rich can buy from those whose services are in much demand. This, of course, gives them a double advantage when merit and repute are found in the same repositories.

The middle, the so-called white-collar, class, as we have seen, are subjected to costs out of keeping with their financial status; legal fees are so disproportionate as to be prohibitive, and drive people to the contingent fee. The poor have little choice. If they have a claim, they can agree to sacrifice a substantial portion of it to a lawyer who will handle it on a contingent basis, or they can seek free legal aid. If a claim is being made against a poor man, his refuge is his poverty, unless his life or liberty is affected. In that case he must content himself with assigned counsel, with usually dire results, or look to a public defender.

The ancient Roman theory that the strong were obligated to help the weak was the basis for the rule that advocates should not be paid. The democratic notion that the State owes an obligation to its citizens to see that they receive justice springs from similar sources. Such a theory cannot be reconciled with the failure of the State to provide needed counsel and aid to that portion of its citizens who cannot afford to pay fees to lawyers, or to the white-collar class to whose financial abilities legal and medical charges are disproportionate. Nevertheless, the theory of free legal and

## LOOK AT THE LAW

medical aid by volunteers who charitably offer services or money persists, though tendencies are being manifested, particularly in medicine, toward fairer and more permanent expedients.

Legislatures have offered lip service by permitting poor persons to sue or defend *in forma pauperis*. As a practical matter, this merely waives formal court costs and accomplishes little, if anything. The cost of the lawyer is and still remains the major obstacle, and experts and witnesses are not available gratis.

Provision for assigned counsel in criminal cases, as we have seen, is largely ineffectual. Public defenders, when supported by private charity, do not meet the problem adequately. The approach is wrong. The right to be defended must not rest upon charity; the public defender system, to be successful, should be adequately staffed and financed by public funds. The growing recognition of this principle is attested by Attorney General Murphy's recommendations for a public defender system in the Federal courts, and the approval thereof by the American Bar Association and other bar associations.

In civil cases, legal aid societies and free individual legal aid have, over a period of fifty years, run the gamut from charitable societies of limited scope to semi-public agencies recognizing and assuming the governmental obligation, working in conjunction with lawyers, bar associations and others interested in social service work. These functions should not be left to private initiative, but should be assumed by the State. In a limited sense, this is gradually being accomplished; compensation and labor boards, small claims courts and conciliation tribunals are being provided, from time to time, in an effort to supply the poor man's needs without the intervention of privately paid lawyers. Recently, the Committee on Legal Service of the Philadelphia

# LOOK AT THE LAW

Chapter of the National Lawyers Guild promulgated a plan calling for the opening of subsidized neighborhood law offices, staffed with younger members of the bar serving on a part-time basis at modest fees. But the problems are tackled piecemeal, and not upon a thesis of obligation of the State to provide a system of justice within the means of the poorest citizen. The subject requires broader consideration. We discuss it further in the following chapter.

The undue expense of litigation is by no means unavoidable. Basically, it merges in the greater problem of governmental waste as reflected by our tax burdens and in the underlying questions of whether the cost of administration of civil justice and of criminal defense should not be borne by the State.

# CHAPTER IX

## *The Layman Says:*
## LAWYERS ARE DISHONEST

*1.*

ONE BARTLETT, who died in New York in 1912, in his last will and testament had this to say regarding lawyers: "I hereby particularly warn you against Probate Judges and Attorneys at law and sincerely trust you will not have occasion to consult or employ the latter in regard to this instrument. My personal experience in dealings, social and otherwise, with lawyers has been extensive and careful observation in other instances has convinced me that they are all dangerous crooks, only disguised, and expressly educated and trained to obtain one's confidence in order that they may defraud and rob with impunity."

Such denunciation of lawyers is not unusual. It expresses the opinions of a considerable number of people, and the number runs higher in the ranks of the illiterate and the ignorant. It finds some substantiation in periodic occurrences.

In New York City, within recent years, lawyers have been convicted and sent to jail for forging bogus divorce decrees; for organizing "rings" of doctors, witnesses, and participants, who concocted fake accidents and injuries and made false claims based thereon; for organizing and participating in associations which operated blackmailing labor rackets; for operating policy rackets; for organizing and pressing fraudulent claims to collect on policies of health insurance; for suborning perjury in connection with per-

## LOOK AT THE LAW

sonal injury cases; and for embezzlement of clients' funds. Even more recently, the entire nation was astounded at revelations of the criminal practices of Federal Circuit Court Judge Manton, who received loans and favors from lawyers and litigants interested in cases pending in his court. These are undeniable criminal practices that brook no defense.

But, lawyers point out, while crooks are to be found in the legal profession, as they are in other businesses and professions, the ratio is smaller than in other callings. As proof of this, they rely on "crime statistics."

Yet statistics are not of themselves sufficient, since the complaining laymen may claim, first, that lawyers, being skilled in the law, are skilled in evading it; and second, that the law is made by and for lawyers in such manner as to enable them to claim professional immunity for practices which, committed by laymen, would be punishable as crimes.

The truth of these two contentions is indisputable. For example, a layman who is guilty of harboring a criminal is himself guilty of a crime. Yet criminal lawyers not only harbor criminals but advise them where to go to avoid detection or extradition until the lawyers are ready to negotiate with the authorities for their clients' production.

An intermediary who aids a kidnaper in seeking ransom is charged with being an accessory to the crime; a lawyer who acts in such a capacity claims a professional privilege.

Louis Piquett, a Chicago lawyer who had worked with the underworld throughout his professional career, was finally brought to book for conspiring to help the criminal Van Meter change his physical characteristics, including his fingerprints, and for harboring him while a fugitive from justice. Piquett had previously been charged with the same offense in the case of the notorious criminal Dillinger, but

# LOOK AT THE LAW

had pleaded that he was Dillinger's regularly retained attorney and that the "services" he had rendered Dillinger were legal, not criminal, services. On this plea he was acquitted. But in the Van Meter case, it appeared that he had not been Van Meter's regularly retained attorney. Therefore, he could not claim the "privileges" of an attorney and, as a result, was convicted.

The lay recipient of the proceeds of a crime is charged with receiving stolen goods; the lawyer takes a part of the loot as his fee. The story is told of Howe, a noted jury lawyer, who defending his client charged with having stolen a pair of diamond earrings, assured the jury that his client was no more guilty than he (Howe) was. Howe was brazen but truthful; he was wearing a stickpin in which reposed one of the diamonds his client had stolen.

A Philadelphia newspaper reported that five men entered the branch office of an electric company in the heart of the city, cowed the sixty employees, slugged three men who got in their way and escaped with a payroll of $48,000. According to the newspaper account, it was believed that the five men who carried out the holdup were members of a larger gang and that they committed the crime in order to set up an "attorneys' fees financial reserve."

And, as we have seen, the recent Hines trial in New York City disclosed that the Dutch Schultz mob allocated a portion of their "take" in the policy racket for legal fees.

When the layman charges the lawyer with being dishonest, the lawyer does not make adequate answer by pleading that he keeps within the law. The layman isn't technical in his definition of "crooked" when he uses the term. He doesn't limit his charges to acts and practices that are punishable by the criminal law. He includes and refers more particularly to sharp rather than criminal practices. Lawyers' craft and lawyers' greed—these are and always

# LOOK AT THE LAW

have comprised the more common charges leveled against the lawyer, from the earliest times to the present.

Sir Thomas More conceived a Utopia "that utterly excludes and banishes all attorneys . . . which craftily handle matters and subtly dispute the laws." The Chinese are said to have had an invincible repugnance to lawyers, as men who prove "that right is wrong and wrong right." The old Latin rhyme read, "A good lawyer, a bad Christian." In Edward III's reign, the House of Lords voted that lawyers should be excluded from Parliament because of the prevailing feeling that lawyers were knaves and promoters of legislative mischief.

Complaints were universal in the seventeenth century regarding the avarice and extortions of lawyers. They were charged with "picking the public pocket," engaging in "knavish tricks," talking unnecessarily in order to protract litigation, injuring their clients by vexatious and bootless delays and unnecessarily increasing work so as to increase fees.

The American colonists also were notoriously suspicious of lawyers. According to James Truslow Adams, in Connecticut, in the seventeenth century, lawyers were legislated against in company with drunkards, keepers of disorderly houses and other people of ill-fame. John Adams wrote that "the mere title of lawyer is sufficient to deprive a man of the public confidence."

The early miners of the Pike's Peak region in Colorado exhibited their aversion in more practical form. They resolved that "no lawyer shall be permitted to practice law in any court in this district, under penalty of not more that fifty, nor less than twenty lashes, and be banished from the district."

The execration of lawyers continues, unabated, in modern tempo: The President of the United States charges

# LOOK AT THE LAW

lawyers with encouraging and abetting law evasions; a prominent inventor charges patent lawyers with practices "close to fraud"; a governor of Pennsylvania brands lawyers as "hairsplitters" guilty of toryism; an Assistant United States Attorney taxes lawyers with "frustrating democracy"; while the annual Congress of the American Prison Association holds lawyers to be accessories to criminals.

Charges such as these, not charges of violation of penal statutes, call insistently for answer by those who labor at the law.

2.

The difference between what a lawyer may do and what he does do is often so slight as to be imperceptible. Ordinarily it is not provable. Yet it marks the distinction between the ethical standard the lawyer preaches and the legal immorality with which the layman charges the lawyer.

If a politician or legislator takes money for influencing or voting for the passage of a bill in the legislature, he may be sent to jail for bribery. If a gangster exacts money as a condition of not intimidating one's workers to strike, he also violates the criminal laws. But if the payment, in either case, is made to a lawyer as compensation for "legal services," ordinarily it is difficult to complain.

All that needs to be done in such cases is to have a lawyer paid a "yearly retaining fee." This enables him to say he received a retainer for such work as he may have been called upon to do. It is immaterial that he was never called upon to do any.

A New York assemblyman, a member of the bar, was convicted recently for taking legal retaining fees from a taxicab company under such extreme circumstances as to constitute bribery. Such a result, however, is unusual,

# LOOK AT THE LAW

though open charges are made constantly, in newspapers and elsewhere that legislative bribery is rampant.

Columnist Westbrook Pegler openly charged that in New York and in Florida, for examples, bookmakers and other race-track followers raised a huge "slush-fund" for legislative purposes. Though these practices may be concealed by the use of cash, income tax report requirements are such that the cover of "legal fees" is a safer disguise.

It is notorious that in isolated cases, at least, legislators and other public officials, administrative and judicial, politicians, labor leaders and others, take "legal retainers," directly or through intermediaries, to influence official operations. In this field, the operations range from low-class retainers to have a convicted criminal housed in a hospital instead of in a cell, or to obtain a pardon from the governor or the parole board, to more respectable endeavors, such as lobbying for legislation or obtaining remission of income and other taxes.

Similarly, in the courts, and particularly in the lower criminal courts, there are politician-lawyers who use their influence with the public prosecutor to avoid or obtain indictments, or to quash prosecutions; with the commissioner of jurors to influence the selection of jurors; with the clerks, the attendants and the judges, to obtain continuances, to influence decisions and sentences.

In a recent labor racket investigation, it was revealed that when crooked labor leaders called a strike, the employer was advised to "retain" a firm of lawyers who, upon payment of the required "legal fees," would undertake to negotiate to have the strike called off. Other disclosures have revealed lawyers who acted directly as conspirators in racketeering labor movements, even to the point of violating criminal statutes.

A system flourishes in the national and in State capitals

## LOOK AT THE LAW

whereby politicians and ex-statesmen, usually lawyers, take retainers to influence legislative and executive action, capitalizing on friendships and contacts, to subordinate the public interest to private purposes. It has recently been charged that many former employees of the Federal Internal Revenue Department are responsible for many income tax evasions; that the number of resignations of men who have improperly capitalized their experience and contacts while in the government service to thwart its purposes thereafter amounts to a public scandal. According to a special dispatch to the New York *Times*, Mayor Thomas J. Spellacy of Hartford, Conn., testified in the criminal trial of former officials of Waterbury, Conn., that he received $1,500 in 1933 for "advisory work on legislative matters and $11,000 in 1935 for lobbying for Waterbury bills in the General Assembly." Under cross-examination, he testified that "he assumed he was employed 'as a lawyer' and not as a politician." Former City Court Judge John F. McGrath testified in the same case that he received "about $40,000 from the city for lobbying services from 1931 through 1937."

The difference between legitimately capitalizing upon one's experience and friendships in a proper way, and improper practices, approaching actual embracery, is a fine one.

Though the practices of these lawyers may violate no law (the Federal Government has a law that prohibits an ex-employee from practicing before his department within two years of his severance from it), no fair standard of ethics will brand many of their acts as proper.

And though it may be impossible to convict the politician-lawyer who takes "fees" for obtaining favors for a convicted criminal, or for having him pardoned or paroled, or for "influencing" legislation, or contracts or favors, he is nevertheless condemned in the public mind.

# LOOK AT THE LAW

Nor does the public mind any longer distinguish between the gangster-lawyer and the banker-lawyer in this respect. It knows that in these instances the racketeer and his lawyer have merely adopted the methods and the practices of our best people for their own. The racketeer who asks a lawyer to set up an alibi for him before he goes out "to knock off a rival gangster" is emulating financiers who retain counsel to advise them how they can sell watered securities or gilded bonds of an insolvent and defaulting South American republic to a gullible public, without liability to themselves. The gangsters are merely stealing the methods of respected, church-going leaders of industry who brag that they hire lawyers to tell them what laws they need not respect. What difference is there, asks John Q. Public, between the lawyer who advises the banker how he can avoid the penalties of a Securities Act, and the lawyer who tells a gangster how he can avoid the provisions of an extortion statute?

At what point a lawyer who advises a client how he can evade the law becomes himself a participant in the crime may be a difficult legal question in the courts, but on the street the average layman, without resort to technicalities, forms his own opinion of the lawyer's guilt.

Adela Rogers St. John tells the following incident concerning her father, Earl Rogers, the famous criminal lawyer of the West, which illustrates the trifling difference between an accomplice and an adviser: "One day I was sitting in my Dad's office when a well-dressed, high-bred old Chinaman entered. This Chinaman wanted to know how much Dad would charge to defend him for murder. Dad told him. He sat down, began pulling little bags out of his voluminous garments and finally counted out the money in gold. Then he arose and with a deep bow started out. 'Hey,' said Dad, 'come back here. What's all this? Where

# LOOK AT THE LAW

are you going?' 'I go kill the man now,' said the Chinaman, 'then I be back.'"

A recent case in New York also illustrates this cogently.

The Bank of United States had a large number of branches in New York City prior to 1930, when it failed with millions of dollars of liabilities. In that year the two principal officers juggled funds of the bank to reduce to the legal limit loans which they had the bank make to three of their other corporations. The entire plan was conceived and carried out by the two officers with the aid of their lawyers. The court found that the minutes of the meetings were "fictitious, written up in the lawyer's office." There was testimony that the principal lawyer for the bank "was consulted in all these transactions and advised as to the papers used in accomplishing the result." A draft of memorandum of the transaction with changes and interlineations in his handwriting was produced "showing that he must have been somewhat familiar with the purpose of the draft and the object of its use" and "indicated his guidance."

The two principal officers of the bank, its principal lawyer and his clerk, who, incidentally, was the son of one of the two officers, were all indicted for violation of the State banking laws.

The officers of the bank and the young lawyer were tried first, the older lawyer later. The jury convicted the two principal officers and the young lawyer. The appellate court affirmed the convictions of the clients, saying, "The fact that these defendants may have been advised by their attorney" and though they had, in reliance upon their counsel's advice, believed "that this application of funds was legal, or the fact that no loss followed, would not constitute a defense...."

The court turned the young lawyer out, saying that while he had aided in the crime by his work as a clerk, he

# LOOK AT THE LAW

had submitted the papers for approval to his employer, the principal lawyer, and had not participated as a criminal.

Later, the older lawyer came on for trial. He, too, was convicted by a jury. On appeal, however, the Court said that though "he was one of the principal actors, both in the planning and in the consummation of the forbidden act, his sole connection with the transaction was as a lawyer. The extent of his offending is that he failed to forbid his clients to proceed. He swore that he believed the plan to be within the law. The court of last resort has since held he was mistaken. A lawyer is not to be held criminally responsible because he honestly gives mistaken advice upon a doubtful question of law." His conviction was reversed and he was freed. Meanwhile the two bank officers were "doing time" and ultimately served their sentences.

Laymen find it difficult to appreciate such distinctions. By their standards, if a layman, unversed in the law and acting on the advice of a lawyer, is found guilty of a crime, how is it possible to excuse the lawyer, versed in the law, who aids and counsels him? How is it possible, asks the layman, if a layman's ignorance of the law is no excuse, for a court to exculpate condemnation lawyers who solicited retainers in the face of a penal statute which clearly prohibited such practices, by saying it was generally supposed that solicitation was all right in condemnation proceedings, as a New York court recently did? The layman cannot justify such distinctions in determining the dishonesty of lawyers. And in their hearts, honest and intelligent lawyers know that lay opinion is correct.

The lawyer who brings an unfounded suit or files objections in a legal proceeding that he may be "bought off," or to enable his client to be "bought off," may keep from being a blackmailer in the eyes of the criminal law, but he is nevertheless dishonest in the public mind. And the lawyer

# LOOK AT THE LAW

who buys him off is a participant in the offense, by proper lay standards.

Similarly, the lawyer who, on a contingent basis, prosecutes "fake" claims, be they for brokerage commissions, or for damages for personal injuries, or for breach of contract, is adjudged dishonest, though he may plead that he has a right to rely on his client's story and that every man is entitled to his "day in court." And the courts are full of such claims skulking behind such lawyer-pleas. At the same time, the lawyer who draws a "perjured" answer to an honest claim is dishonest, though his client is a "reputable" businessman who merely wants delay.

The criminal lawyer who gets his guilty client acquitted by a defense which his client fabricates (with or without his aid or suggestion) is to be considered dishonest, although he may plead that the law entitles him to defend his client to the limit of his ability.

Every lawyer and layman knows that a lawyer wants to win his case and makes every conceivable effort to accomplish his purpose. However, to many lawyers, the justice or injustice of his client's cause means little or nothing except as it may strengthen or weaken his case with the jury. Such a lawyer uses every trick and device he knows to fool the jury, to mislead it, to influence its passions and emotions, to get before it helpful though improper evidence and to keep from it proper but damaging evidence, to lead the judge into error, to avoid the judge's charge on the law where it is harmful, to influence the judge, to induce the clerks and attendants to favor him so that they may drop a hint to some member of the jury, and even to the point, in more isolated cases, of having jurors "seen."

In presenting his case, such a lawyer tolerates and often even suborns perjury; he seeks to distort and unfairly discredit what he knows to be the true testimony of adverse

# LOOK AT THE LAW

witnesses; he suppresses unfavorable testimony. In criminal cases, he often fabricates defenses or presents defenses he knows to be manufactured and false. He cloaks and justifies these trickeries by the specious and sonorous phrases, to which we have referred, that "every client is entitled to his day in court," "that every lawyer is entitled to present the best defense his client has," "that no lawyer has a right to prejudge his client's case," etc., etc.

And judges, primarily concerned with the danger of curbing a lawyer defending his client's constitutional liberties, become so accustomed to these perversions of constitutional rights that they wink at them and, indeed, sustain them.

The lengths to which the law as a choice of evils permits lawyers to go, is readily illustrated.

A former judge in New York was appearing for the defense in a criminal case in which the District Attorney charged that the defendant had spirited away an important and necessary prosecution witness. The charge was true — the fact was that the defendant had kept the witness, a woman, in hiding in the city. He had brought her to his lawyer's house for consultations and the lawyer instructed her to come to court to testify for his client after the prosecution had closed its case. On the afternoon of the second day of the trial, the witness suddenly entered the courtroom, carrying a suitcase. The defense lawyer put her on the stand and she testified that she had read about the case in a newspaper while she was in a small town upstate and, thereby learning that her testimony was important, she had taken the train to the city. She said she had just arrived on the train that morning, and had hurried to the courthouse.

When she was cross-examined, she gave an account of her actions between the time that she was supposed to have gotten off the train and the time she got to court. She not only lied about having come down on the train the night before, but concealed the fact that she had seen the defendant's counsel at his home that very morning. She also concealed the fact that she had come to court pursuant to his instructions.

However, when he summed up to the jury, defendant's counsel said: "We have got her here, and thank God, gentlemen of the jury, that Divine Providence has brought that woman here. If it was the *Evening Journal*, I thank the *Evening Journal*. If it was anybody else — she said it was the *Evening Journal* that she read it in, and by the way, she produced a clipping to the Judge, if I am not mistaken; isn't that right, Judge?" The Court: "Yes." Counsel: "Thank God, I say to the press."

The bar association brought the matter to the attention of the Court and asked that the defendant's counsel be disbarred for knowingly presenting false testimony. The counsel urged upon the Court that no one had ever attempted to disbar a lawyer for such actions in a criminal case; that wherever a lawyer was reprimanded for such an act, it was in a civil case. He claimed that the obligations of an attorney to the law and to his client were very different in a civil and in a criminal action. He admitted that in a civil case, if his client were not in the right and had wilfully deceived him, counsel was under an obligation to inform the Court of the facts and to withdraw from the case. He contended, however, that in a criminal case, having accepted a retainer to defend the accused, counsel may not withdraw even if his client confesses his guilt, so long as his client insists upon his continuing. He pointed out that these differences were recognized in the Canon of Ethics, which, applying to a criminal case, says:

"It is the right of a lawyer to undertake the defense of a person accused of crime regardless of his personal opinion

# LOOK AT THE LAW

as to the guilt of the accused, otherwise innocent persons, victims only of suspicious circumstances, might be denied proper defense. Having undertaken such defense, the lawyer is bound by fair and honorable means, to present every defense that the law of the land permits, to the end that no person may be deprived of life or liberty, but by due process of law."

He further pointed out that the rules of professional ethics said:

"It is not to be termed screening the guilty from punishment for the advocate to assert all his ability, learning and ingenuity in a defense, even if he should be perfectly sure in his own mind of the actual guilt of the prisoner."

The defendant's counsel admitted all the facts claimed by the bar association and contended that he had done nothing more than his duty. The first court to which the question was submitted divided in its views. A majority of the judges agreed that he should be disbarred; but the dissenting judge said:

"In my opinion there was nothing in the conduct of the respondent which merits condemnation." This judge argued that the lawyer faced a question which no lawyer should be charged with answering: "Shall I betray my client or shall I take the risk of disbarment?" The dissenter contended that his brethren had adopted a stricter rule than had ever before been applied by the courts or the profession at large.

After the lawyer was disbarred, he appealed to the highest court of the State and there, by a vote of five to two, the disbarment was set aside and he was reinstated to practice. The higher court wrote no opinion. It apparently agreed with the views of the dissenting judge below.

Just what the result of this case was, except to the lawyer involved, is difficult to say. Mathematical computation

# LOOK AT THE LAW

shows that the ultimate vote was six judges one way and six another, thus leaving the question pretty much unsettled in the law. But lay opinion has no difficulty in branding the tender of knowingly false testimony by a lawyer as improper, regardless of its justification by technical argument.

In a later case, a noted trial lawyer took advantage of this legalistic attitude to influence a jury to acquit his client who was charged with a serious crime. The time of the commission of the crime was fixed as having occurred at a given place, on a given day, at a given hour. The defendant claimed that at that hour and day he was elsewhere. In fact he wasn't, though he produced several witnesses to support his alibi. In summing up the case his lawyer said to the jury:

"Gentlemen, I ask you to acquit my client, not because I believe him to be innocent, but because I know him to be innocent. How do I know him to be innocent, you ask?" The noted trial lawyer hesitated. He let his last words sink into the jury's consciousness by repeating them slowly: "How do I know, *know*, I said, gentlemen? Am I asked that question?"

Again he waited. Then he said slowly: "Because I, too, saw him at the day and hour in question at the place at which he and the witnesses we produced testified he was. So he could not have been at the scene of the crime at that time and, consequently, the prosecution's witnesses testified falsely."

Assume the lawyer's statement was untrue. If it was untrue, he would not take the stand and, like the other false witnesses, commit perjury. For that he would have been criminally liable. But he could take refuge in a lawyer's privilege on summation and thereby keep himself within the law.

# LOOK AT THE LAW

Behind these perversions, a real issue, a choice between real evils, is involved. Shall a lawyer be restricted in presenting the best defense his client has, regardless of his personal opinion of his guilt; or shall the lawyer, not the jury, be the client's judge? Should a lawyer undertake a case which he was satisfied was not a just one?

In the middle of the nineteenth century, there was a good deal of agitation on these questions in England, growing out of the defense of a murderer by a prominent barrister, Charles Phillips. On the second day of the trial, the defendant advised Mr. Phillips that he was guilty. Mr. Phillips offered to plead guilty for him, but the prisoner refused and said that he expected him to defend him to the utmost of his ability. Mr. Phillips consulted with a judge, not sitting in the case, upon whose opinion he relied, and as a result, he continued in the trial, using, in his client's behalf, all fair arguments arising from the evidence. The defendant was convicted and thereafter the story came out. The judge who knew of the situation made it a point to listen to Mr. Phillips' summation, and though Mr. Phillips exerted every possible effort to clear his client, he did not conclude that he had transgressed his duty to the State.

Dr. Samuel Johnson summed up this issue. "Sir, [said Mr. Johnson] a lawyer has no business with the justice or injustice of the cause which he undertakes, unless his client asks his opinion and then he is bound to give it honestly. The justice or injustice of the cause is to be decided by the judge. Consider, sir; what is the purpose of courts of justice? It is, that every man may have his cause fairly tried, by men appointed to try causes. A lawyer is not to tell what he knows to be a lie; he is not to produce what he knows to be a false deed; but he is not to usurp the province of the jury and of the judge, and determine what shall be the effect of the evidence,—what shall be the result of legal argument.

# LOOK AT THE LAW

As it rarely happens that a man is fit to plead his own cause, lawyers are a class of the community who, by study and experience, have acquired the art and power of arranging evidence, and of applying to the points at issue what the law has settled. A lawyer is to do for his client all that his client might fairly do for himself, if he could. If by a superiority of attention, of knowledge, of skill, and a better method of communication, he has the advantage of his adversary, it is an advantage to which he is entitled. There must always be some advantage, on one side or other; and it is better that advantage should be had by talents than by chance. If lawyers were to undertake no causes till they were sure they were just, a man might be precluded altogether from a trial of his claim, though, were it judicially examined, it might be found a very just claim. This was sound practical doctrine, and rationally repressed a too refined scrupulosity of conscience."

Lawyers constantly are influenced in their advice and their actions by the hope of receiving fees. Sometimes the influence is subtle, sometimes even subconscious. With some lawyers it must be, else it will be resisted; with others it is conscious and willful, even to the point of dishonesty. But it is a dishonesty of which the lawyer cannot be convicted, even if it can be discovered or proved.

A lawyer who represents a wife in a matrimonial dispute with a wealthy husband will frequently advise her to go to law instead of going home and forgetting her alleged grievances. One way he has a case and can get a fee; the other way he cannot. Or he may advise a reluctant wife to give her husband the divorce or separation he desires, influenced to do so by the implied promise of the husband's lawyer to be generous in paying him a counsel fee. Lawyers frequently advise clients to settle, or to fight, in accordance with the best fee instincts of the lawyer. They sometimes ad-

# LOOK AT THE LAW

vise clients to adopt a course of action that will produce a result calculated to fee the lawyer, even though the clients' interests might be better served by a different course. Lawyers will organize committees in reorganization cases to represent security holders as against the management, and then offer cooperation to the management or other adverse interests which directly or indirectly control the purse-strings.

These are faults of many lawyers, in a greater or lesser, to a more or less conscious, degree.

### 3.

Here we have some of the bases for the layman's charge that lawyers are dishonest.

Are lawyers dishonest? If dishonesty is taken to mean criminality, crime statistics, for what little they may be worth, say no. The publicity given the criminal lawyer practices through the newspapers, the magazines, the radio, and the movies, creates the public misapprehension that many lawyers share the criminal vices of the few.

Disbarment statistics show only a small proportion of complaints and an infinitesimal percentage of prosecutions and convictions, compared with the number of lawyers. Such statistics, of course, offer no clue to the extent of similar practices never complained about; lawyers are loath to advise complaint about other lawyers; "there but for the grace of God go I" is the generally prevailing attitude among most lawyers.

A recent study of these matters proves chiefly how little definite factual information is to be found, and leaves it for individual experience to draw individual conclusion.

If dishonesty is taken to mean that lawyers are untrustworthy, again we believe the answer should be no. In the

# LOOK AT THE LAW

main, lawyers as a class justify the confidence that their clients, even their professional opponents, repose in them.

If, however, the lawyer when charged with dishonesty is being charged with dishonesty in his pretensions, that is another matter. Here, the record we have cited would say: "Guilty—guilty of false pretensions that he acts as an officer of the court should; guilty of false pretensions that he is more concerned with the promotion of justice than he is with the furtherance of his own pecuniary interests."

Like everyone else, the lawyer's primary effort is devoted to making money; initially, to make a living; later, to obtain security for reasons of vanity and power or for no reason at all. To make money, the lawyer (to paraphrase Dean Andrews) must transmit the high function of public service "into a scramble for money"; he must adopt business methods to obtain business and to hold it against the efforts of his fellow lawyers to wrest it away. While competition may be the life of a trade, it tolls the death of a profession. This is particularly true of the law.

Upon analysis, the practices which lay the bases for the founded charge that lawyers are dishonest are practices which are honored in trade but repugnant to a profession. The charge of dishonesty comes to one of hypocrisy to which lawyers and laymen alike should plead guilty. The lawyer who claims to be a member of a profession dedicated to public service is hypocritical; the layman who criticizes the lawyer for not holding strictly to his professional tenets while he wants him to serve his venal private ends is equally hypocritical.

Clients demand lawyers who are willing to compromise the standards of their profession. Lawyers are not hired for their integrity; they are selected for their ability to get results, and if the results can best be achieved by influence and connections, the lawyer with the best connections and

# LOOK AT THE LAW

greatest influence gets the job. Even when clients have lawyers of ability and integrity, they hire special counsel with special connections for special jobs.

To make money for themselves, lawyers, big and little, advise their clients how they can do things and still keep within the law. The big lawyer tells his corporate clients how to evade the banking laws; the little lawyer tells his gangster clients how to avoid anti-racketeering statutes. Big lawyers devise sharp stock and corporate practices whereby our best people seek to make money in violation of equitable and legal standards, as investigations by the S. E. C. and Senate Committees on Railroads, Banking and Currency and Federal Receiverships have revealed. Little lawyers advise installment dealers, fake jewelry concerns, mock auctioneers and preying labor leaders how they can indulge in similar but smaller practices without going to jail. Lawyers, big and little, not only advise but devise such practices, for if it is proper that the layman indulge in them, it is equally proper, by trade and by current legal standards, that lawyers devise them, so long as the lawyer does not know them to be a violation of some criminal statute.

The big lawyer solicits a fellow club member judge to appoint a mutual friend as a receiver for his corporate client in need of reorganization, while the little lawyer drops into the neighboring political club to say "good evening" to the magistrate before whom he must appear the next day. So long as neither seeks anything legally "improper" in any legally "improper" way, he can defend his act. Needless to say, his layman client approves it if, in truth, the client did not retain him because he knew the judge.

The little lawyer brings a minority stockholder's suit hoping the defendants will buy his client's stock (as they have a "legal" right to do); the big lawyer advises the defendants to buy the plaintiff off to avoid a trial of the suit

# LOOK AT THE LAW

and a possible judgment, on the plea that the pendency of the action affects the corporation's good will.

Again, these acts can be justified by lawyer and by client as "legal." But keeping within the law is not the mark of the practice of a profession. That may be a tradesman's duty, but it is not the standard of a lawyer, an officer of the court, a member of a profession dedicated to the furtherance of justice and the promotion of good government.

The lawyer's professional standards prohibit the solicitation of business upon the theory that such solicitation is incompatible with the dignity of a profession. Yet, while decrying encroachment by lay agencies upon legal fields because they solicit business, the lawyer himself solicits business.

The big lawyer solicits legal business by participating in the acquisition of business enterprises, utilities, investment trusts; by seeking directorates in banks, trust companies, title companies and other business corporations; by employing or engaging in partnership with influential lawyers, public officials or ex-public officials, who act solely as business-getters. The little lawyer solicits negligence and divorce business, joins clubs and lodges and seeks publicity, for similar purposes.

The little lawyer advertises for divorce business; the big lawyer has his client, a trust company, advertise to induce prospective decedents to let its lawyer draw their wills. The little lawyer sends out runners to get him negligence business; the big lawyer's trust company client sends out solicitors to get trust business for him and for itself. The little lawyer buys a bond or a share of stock so he can appear and try to get a fee in a corporate reorganization proceeding. The big lawyer's clients buy a block of bonds or stock so they can organize a committee which he will represent in the same proceeding.

# LOOK AT THE LAW

In his quest for business, the big lawyer organizes huge "shops" that are mere branches of the giant commercial organizations his corporate clients maintain. A big New York City lawyer once said in justification of his seeking a guaranty of $1,000 a day for a court appearance that the sum represented only his cost to his firm, that he had to produce more than that if there was to be any profit beyond his share of the cost of the organizations he maintained. One large law office in New York City had a single department devoted to corporate work for its clients, employing over one hundred lawyers, clerks and stenographers at an annual overhead cost of over half a million dollars. That huge cost had to be absorbed by the business brought in by the partners, and in off years succeeding the depression, when there was little corporate business, failure to produce the necessary business meant a staggering loss of overhead.

Another large law office has some thirty resident and a half-dozen foreign partners, a staff of managing attorneys, lawyers, law clerks, secretaries, stenographers, cashiers, bookkeepers, diary clerks, file clerks, receptionists, librarians, clipping clerks, telephone operators, mail clerks, messengers, comprising day and night forces, running into the hundreds.

The need for maintaining such organizations makes it as imperative for big lawyers to get business to survive as it is for little lawyers to get business to live. The result is competition for business, which starts with solicitation and ends in yielding any barrier of restraining professional standards to clients who seek results only and are not concerned with methods. Whether the cycle is initiated and maintained by the client's suggestion or demand, or by the lawyer's prompting, whether it springs from the client's initiative and the lawyer's advice, or the lawyer's device and the client's concurrence, the result is the sale by the lawyer of

# LOOK AT THE LAW

his professional standards, a yielding of his professional independence, for money. Nowhere is this more pronounced than in the case of the lawyer who is under a general retainer from an important client, the so-called "kept" lawyer.

By heritage, the general retainer lawyer is the aristocrat of the profession. When the lord of the manor was charged with the duty of administering justice to and between his tenants and retainers, he required the constant aid and assistance of someone versed in the law. It became the practice to attach to his person a legal adviser, as well as a spiritual and medical one. For their services the latter had a living, while the legal adviser had a general retainer. By the seventeenth century, general retainers were so common in England that lawyers had no scruples about taking them from anybody. It became the pretentious practice for upstarts at court to equip themselves with a staff consisting of a doctor, a curate and a barrister under general retainer.

Today, every large corporation has its army of legal mercenaries. Every release by the Securities and Exchange Commission of salaries paid by large corporations shows legal Abou Ben Adhems leading all the rest. Sometimes a firm of lawyers is paid a yearly "retainer"; sometimes individual lawyers are "retained" and paid weekly salaries. Many of these lawyers become mere employees; they have no other clients and no other business; their retainers take all their working time. Some of them ultimately become the principals; a number of large corporations are headed by their former counsel. Even large firms become wedded to single clients in this fashion.

These lawyers, no matter how big, are often compelled by this system to sell their independence for money. The clients become the bosses; they dictate policies and they frame them according to a businessman's conception of propriety, not according to the lawyer's code of ethics. The latter is not only unknown but would be incomprehensible to the average businessman.

When, for example, it was recently charged that litigants had made loans to Federal Judge Manton, while they had litigation pending before his court, one of the litigants was quoted as saying the loan was a "straight business transaction."

At a recent hearing before the Federal Power Commission, the Commission's attorney, according to an Associated Press dispatch, "placed in evidence the names of sixteen Eastern law firms which, he said, acted as holding companies or performed other interlocking services for industrial clients. By this means, he charged, the concerns attempted to thwart investigation by government regulatory bodies."

Obviously, under the present system, the trade standards of the client and the professional standards of the lawyer must find a common level; the client who seeks to evade a just contract must find no advocate, or a frank one. If the dishonest client could find no lawyer to serve his dishonest purposes, the standard of morals of the market place would be automatically raised. If a lawyer is merely to serve the client's purpose, "legality," not ethics, must become the standard of all lawyers who will then confessedly work at a trade instead of claiming to practice a profession.

*4.*

In demonstrating that lawyers are as other men, that they are influenced, as are other men under the present capitalistic system, in working overmuch for money, we are seeking to establish facts, not to assess faults. Why should one expect a man, simply because he is a lawyer, to put at rest individual biologic fears that induce a desire for money as a means of security when his physical vigor wanes? Or to still the selfishness and greed that grasping nature and a struggling heritage have implanted in him? Is a lawyer to be expected to deny the faults of a system born of centuries of inexorable economic and habitual trends, from which all the rest of us suffer?

In a commercial age, a lawyer will share in the commercialism rampant about him. Lawyers alone will not and cannot be expected to stem the flood, even though it wash away the emblements of civilization and progress, as it did in ancient Athens, in Egypt and in Rome. The inroads of our present capitalistic system upon the ethics of our lawyers and upon our legal system will not be stopped by appeal to the lawyers. They alone cannot be expected to live lives of rigid, monkish asceticism.

On the contrary, to drum up trade, the lawyer must make a show of wealth and prosperity, he must be a conformist to the existing social order. Lawyers must live well, even though they may die poor. As Juvenal said, "It is the purple robe that gets the lawyer custom—his violet cloaks that attract clients. It suits their interest to live with all the bustle and outward show of an income greater than they really have."

Nor can lawyers, as a class, be expected to stem the individual tide that sweeps them into money-making currents. Whether practice of the law is a profession or a trade depends not upon the lawyers but upon the public mores. Lawyers can be regarded as a class apart, the servants of the government. Subsidized by the State, preferred in the service of the government, as were the Romans, constituted a lesser order of nobles, as were the French, they might forego money-making to adhere to the tenets and ethics of a profession. But left to their own devices, as at present, they will be driven to adopt the rules and customs of a trade.

# LOOK AT THE LAW

Clearly, lawyers should be one thing or another. Subjected to the play of free competition, largely unregulated and unrestricted, they cannot fulfill their obligations to the State. Under present conditions, they are bound to be guilty of the faults with which the public mind justly assesses them. They are expected to be partisan, yet they are supposed to administer and promote justice. They are expected to work for money; yet they are supposed to be "officers of the court" and to subordinate their needs and desires for fees. They are supposed to have social responsibilities; yet they are left to perform these without incentive of reward in dignity, public faith and confidence. In consequence, they make virtues of necessities—they profess to run with the hares while they actually hunt with the hounds.

This condition is the result, not of a deliberate, but of a Topsy-like, unregulated growth. Originally, lawyers in the American colonies, like their English progenitors of the seventeenth and eighteenth centuries, were a despised class. They were legislated against and regulated. Later, beginning with the Revolutionary period in this country, they became a paramount social and political force. The Jacksons, Clays, Websters and Lincolns were dominant in shaping the social and political philosophy of our experiment in democratic government.

Later, with the passage of the Civil War, a growing population, a changing frontier, and scientific invention and development offered unparalleled opportunity for financial gain. Rapacious and unscrupulous financial barons called lawyers to their aid, and the overwhelming opportunity for profit converted the flower of the American Bar from advocates to advisers, from counsellors to initiators. The practices and precedents thus fashioned and the inordinate rewards which they produced, attracted to the law a large and constantly increasing number of novitiates, who came not

# LOOK AT THE LAW

for distinction but as a step toward money-making. Six decades of practices originated and approved by the big lawyer and followed by a large, unregulated, and unrestricted number of little lawyers developed into a system which now holds the members of the profession, however social-minded they may tend to be individually, in an unbreakable grip.

At present, competition within and without the profession drives lawyers to employ business methods to obtain and to hold business. The widened scope of the specialized competition of trust companies, banks, real estate title companies, credit associations, collection agencies, notaries public, accountants, tax experts, and the like, have reduced the field of the general legal practitioner. While this may appear to be competition without the profession, it is, in reality, one class of lawyers, masking behind or acting in cooperation with businessmen to take portions of the law business from other lawyers. Legal innovations, compensation, labor, securities, public service boards and commissions have diverted other classes of legal business to legal and lay specialists outside the profession. Specialization within the profession has further reduced the sphere of the general practitioner and, running along efficient business lines, makes the legal specialist more businessman than lawyer.

Within the profession, overcrowding puts severe economic pressure on the lawyer and drives him to practices he might otherwise scorn.

That there are too many lawyers in large urban centers seems generally conceded, although there seems a lack of authoritative agreement on the elements that determine the number of lawyers needed and a lack of sufficient surveys to justify general conclusions.

Where there is overcrowding, the consequences are far-reaching. Primarily, it puts lawyers into undue competition

# LOOK AT THE LAW

for clients and that, in turn, puts the client into the ascendancy.

Overcrowding—too many lawyers—causes unethical and even dishonest practices by those who lag behind. Failure means not only yielding to the dishonest importunities of the client, but it results in the overexercise of the lawyer's initiative in his times of economic need. It leads the lawyer to make himself overimportant in fields of endeavor into which he should never have strayed and which he should never have corrupted. It causes lawyers to oppose legal and civic reforms that may further diminish their business and perquisites. It leads lawyers to mold public policies in their self interest and in denial of the public interest.

The lawyer is torn between his desire to be a member of a profession and his need for money. He is squeezed between economic and social pressures. He should be a member of a class serving the State; instead, he is left as an individual to make a living. He is asked to profess adherence to class traditions, while he is required to violate them in order to live. He is expected to be an idealist in a world of realities. The State and the lay public does nothing to make it possible for him to fulfill his class obligations; it lets him sink or swim by individual efforts while the leaders of the bar, assured of their positions by superiority in the individual tactics they professionally decry, give lip service to tenets many of them have long since abandoned.

The consequences to the layman, as we have seen in a previous chapter, are a denial of justice to the poor; a disproportionate burden of expense to the middle class and undue advantage to the rich.

5.

The problem of making the lawyer honest, if our analysis of the problem has been a true one, is simple in statement.

# LOOK AT THE LAW

One need only to make his conduct conform with his code, or to revise his code to conform with his conduct. Or, to put it differently, agree with the lawyer on whether he is to be a professional man or a businessman. Shall he commit himself and adhere to the ancient Code of the Romans, not to undertake unjust causes nor to maintain them with trickery, not to exhibit a sordid avidity of gain by putting too high a price on his services and not to refuse his services to the indigent and oppressed? Or shall he, as an individual under a capitalistic system, sell what purchasers seek for the highest price attainable, employing any means not forbidden by the criminal law?

If he selects the former, means must be found to enable lawyers to live in manner compatible with the standing and distinction that would accrue to them by such service to the State; if he selects the latter, means must be found to limit the ability of lawyers to injure the State.

While there is an apparent choice, in fact there is none unless we so restrict the activities of lawyers as, in effect, to destroy them. So long as lawyers retain the importance they have achieved under our present system, they cannot be allowed to run loose to ravish and prey, subject to no code except the criminal code which regulates the activities of laymen.

The lawyer's importance in our present system is so great, his influence is so far-reaching, that so long as he works for money he is a source of danger to democracy. The lawyer is not a mere private citizen; he is as much an officer of the law as if he wore a blue coat and brass buttons. He is an essential part of our system of law and order, as much a cog in the machinery of law enforcement and law administration as a public prosecutor or a judge. And with the increase of administrative agencies in government, with the increase of government responsibility in social and economic

# LOOK AT THE LAW

fields, the lawyer's public importance is increasing in greater proportion than his private importance. Without men trained in the law we cannot maintain our present democratic form of government. We need them in the formulation of our laws, in their execution and enforcement. We need them to prosecute infringers, to construe the law, to sit in judgment upon offenders and to protect citizens from unjust enforcement. We need them to shape and to guide the destinies of our democracy.

In these capacities, lawyers are arms of the State in serving the cause of law, order and democratic government. Not only is their presence necessary but their active cooperation is essential that the law may function. If lawyers went on strike, if they ceased functioning, however we might enjoy jokes to the contrary, the ministrations of community living would slow up and perhaps stop until we readjusted the mechanics of our government. When they go through the forms of functioning, and instead of performing their jobs, undermine them, and instead of doing their duty to the State, sell it out, then democratic government, not guarded against their depredations, is seriously endangered. The layman who selfishly and ruthlessly works for his own pocket all the time is ordinarily in no position to harm anyone but himself. The lawyer, no matter how humble, who avoids his obligations to the State and devotes himself to self-interest is actively doing a public harm.

It is the State's business to see that its citizens have fire, police, health and legal protection. It can furnish the latter only through lawyers committed to public service and fulfilling their commitments. At the same time, it is becoming generally accepted that the functions which the State has entrusted to the lawyer are not matters for exercise as a matter of right by any citizen, as was once thought, but are special privileges the State has conferred, distinctions and

# LOOK AT THE LAW

opportunities which carry with them corresponding responsibilities. These include the obligation to enact and conform to a code of conduct, a standard of living and acting that will make and keep the lawyer a true servant of the people, enjoying their confidence and faithful to his trust. The lawyer's oath of office is the basis of this code, which is as much a part of the structure of democratic government as any other part of its body of law.

The primary professions of the lawyer make him an instrument, an officer, a servant of the State. This is no Fascist credo, for here the lawyer serves a constitutional State that guarantees liberty. When, in defense of such guarantees, he opposes other officers of the State who seek to infringe upon these rights, he is still serving the State.

If the legal profession is treated as an arm of the State, then the profession will not be overcrowded. On the contrary, there will be an immediate increase of clientele in the great mass of the people who are now neglected.

Under the present confusion, all the available lawyers are competing to serve the small portion of the population that can afford to pay them. There are more lawyers than there is need for them by that small portion of the population. As a result, the profession appears overcrowded. But it appears overcrowded only because the lawyers are not available for service to the large majority of the people who cannot afford to pay what the lawyer must charge in order to live under the present system. While there is a lack of data, the only available survey—one made in Connecticut—indicates a considerable amount of latent legal business. As with medicine, as in agriculture, the lawyer cannot afford to produce and supply what the submerged portion of our population could use, because the latter, under present methods, does not have the means to pay at rates compatible with the cost of production. All the crops the farmer

# LOOK AT THE LAW

could raise could be consumed if the underfed and underclothed could afford to buy all the food and clothing they could consume. Just as crops would not have to be plowed under, so ambitious law students would not have to be discouraged from their profession.

The present method is inept, as inefficient in the field of law as it is in the fields of medicine and dentistry. Lawyers cannot afford to recognize their obligations to the mass of the population which lacks the money to hire them. And voluntary and charitable legal aid societies and charitable services by members of the bar have been wholly insufficient to provide for the needy. They can be provided for only by recognition of the obligation of government to provide adequate legal aid to those who cannot purchase it. And this should not be withheld until the gates of a jail yawn for the indigent.

Lawyers should be licensed, like those in the reign of Edward I, from among those "best and most apt for the learning and skill who might do service 'to the Court and the people.'" The ranks should not be thrown open to the unlettered or the unskilled. This need is recognized by lawyers themselves who have been working through their bar associations to have admission standards raised by law schools and by the courts, and who have been promoting the growth of legal institutes designed to promote post-admission education of lawyers.

There should be limitation of lawyers by character. Education is important; morals are of even greater importance. There must, of course, be freedom of action for the lawyer, not so much in the interests of the lawyer but because the freedom granted a lawyer to represent his client fully is a grant which a free and representative government confers upon its citizens. We point out elsewhere that the first act of a tyrant is to suppress the right of lawyers freely to de-

## LOOK AT THE LAW

fend their clients' causes in the courts. The suppression of free speech in the market-place and on the commons and the muffling of the press must be followed by gags upon the lawyers. If the lawyer is to be denied the right to fight for the cause the majority believes wrong, then the minority is going to be denied its right to fight for what it believes to be right.

In times of stress, there are always lawyers who are willing bravely to champion minority causes. And no one can do so more ably than lawyers. Today, for example, a Civil Rights Committee of the American Bar Association, charged by many with being reactionary, offers its services to indigent persons whose civil rights have been violated and intervenes in opposition to Mayor Hague's attempt to suppress free speech in Jersey City. Similarly, the New York City Bar Association protests Nazi racial and religious persecutions abroad.

But the lawyer, who must have freedom of action, should have no incentive under cover of this necessary lack of censorship for using every trick and device which art and strategy can conceive for freeing Dillingers and Capones. He should have every incentive to follow the French injunction: "Combat for truth and not for victory."

We must restrict the rewards for which, to quote Mr. Dooley, corporation lawyers build "triumphal arches out of stone walls." We must put our practical practicing lawyers in somewhat the same category as our law school professors who, by virtue of undivided allegiance, are fast becoming the true leaders of the bar. We must not be diverted by the "restraints upon initiative" cry which such suggestions will raise. The policeman has his private initiative restrained—he goes to jail if he is found taking money from the gambling house he allows to run. The judge on the bench, the public prosecutor, find their initiatives restrained

# LOOK AT THE LAW

and are confined to moderate earnings. Why not these other officers of the law, the lawyers? If a policeman or a prosecutor cannot take money for turning a defendant out, why should a lawyer be allowed to take extraordinary sums for extraordinary services in freeing a guilty criminal ? Or for defeating a just claim?

There is no good reason why contingent fees as well as the fixed fee should not be regulated to reasonable amounts in the light of all the existing circumstances. There is no more reason why the big lawyer should be incited to improper practices by inordinate fees than the little lawyer should be spurred to unethical acts in a contingent case in order to get any kind of fee.

Let the lawyer of tomorrow take a form of Hippocratic oath, such an oath as has been recommended by the American Bar Association, and put him in a position where a reasonably honest man can subscribe to it though the world about him sacrifice manhood to Mammon:

"I Do Solemnly Swear:

"I will support the Constitution of the United States and the Constitution of the State of ——;

"I will maintain the respect due to courts of justice and judicial officers;

"I will not counsel or maintain any suit or proceeding which shall appear to me to be unjust, nor any defense except such as I believe to be honestly debatable under the law of the land;

"I will employ for the purpose of maintaining the causes confided to me such means only as are consistent with truth and honor, and will never seek to mislead the judge or jury by any artifice or false statement of fact or law;

"I will maintain the confidence and preserve inviolate the secrets of my client, and will accept no compensation

# LOOK AT THE LAW

in connection with his business except from him or with his knowledge and approval;

"I will abstain from all offensive personality, and advance no fact prejudicial to the honor or reputation of a party or witness, unless required by the justice of the cause with which I am charged;

"I will never reject, from any consideration personal to myself, the cause of the defenseless or oppressed, or delay any man's cause for lucre or malice.

"SO HELP ME GOD."

# CHAPTER X

## *The Layman Says:*
## JUDGES ARE CORRUPT

*1.*

MARTIN T. MANTON, the tenth highest ranking Federal judge in the United States, was charged with the wholesale sale of justice in his high court. He was indicted, convicted and sentenced to a prison term.

On the day his trial started, in an adjoining county a County Court judge went to trial in his own courtroom on charges that he had taken a sum of money to influence his dismissal of a criminal abortion charge against a doctor. This judge, however, was acquitted by a jury.

These prosecutions were concurrent with proceedings in the same counties to remove magistrates of the inferior criminal courts, one upon a charge that he had taken a small sum of money to intercede on behalf of a prostitute with a fellow magistrate, another upon a charge that he had misconducted himself in connection with the dismissal of a gambling charge, at the intercession of a district leader.

While these matters were brewing, it was openly charged that just across the Hudson River, judges who owe their nominations to Mayor Hague, political boss of Hudson County, New Jersey, had been sentencing his political enemies to jail for doubtful criminal offenses. Meanwhile, newspaper columnists charge that liaisons between judicial officers, political organizations and criminals make a mockery of justice.

Sifted, the charge of judicial corruption which these incidents bring to the surface is found to vary. Generally, it

## LOOK AT THE LAW

is not believed that our upper court judges are guilty of personal dishonesty, that they take money to influence their decisions. On the contrary, it is believed that these judges are personally honest, that while they may be swayed in their actions by their friends, including those who influenced their selection, a real malfeasance is a rarity. This feeling is born of long experience during which few cases of actual judicial corruption have come to light.

The judge who sentenced Manton said that he knew of no comparable case since that of Lord Bacon. Research discloses no high ranking judicial officer guilty of such offenses with so little excuse since the ancient days when magistrates took gifts and bribes as a matter of course.

Recognizing that "a gift perverteth the ways of judgment," the Scriptures tell us that the sons of Samuel, as judges, took gifts. In Athens the only real check on bribery, which was an acknowledged factor in every important trial, was the number of judges who sat at the trial and who had to be bribed to get a result. The Greek historian, Xenophon, said: "I must admit that many things are transacted at Athens by means of bribery and that much more would be done if more were ready to give bribes."

The Roman jurist was no exception in the prevalent practices of bribery; no class or condition was exempt from Roman corruption.

But we have been singularly free from this abuse. Compared with the large number of our judges who conscientiously perform their duties, corrupt judges are the rare exception.

Only half a dozen Federal judges have been impeached for misconduct over our 150 years of government. While this small number is due in part to the statement in the Constitution that a judge may be impeached only for "treason, bribery or other high crimes and misdemeanors," it is also

# LOOK AT THE LAW

true largely because the misconduct of our judges is not generally corruption in the criminal sense. For example, poor old Federal Judge Pickering of New Hampshire was charged with crimes and impeached solely to get him off the bench because he was insane. Judge Bradbury of Massachusetts was impeached a few months before his death because he was afflicted with paralysis.

Federal Judge Archibald was removed in 1913 upon charges of moral delinquency which fell short of actual corruption, while Federal Judge Winslow resigned while charges of "serious indiscretions" in connection with bankruptcy appointments were pending against him.

Recently Federal Judge Halsted L. Ritter was impeached by Congress. It was charged that he had appointed his former partner as a receiver of a large hotel, that he had allowed him an exorbitant fee as receiver and that the judge had taken a portion of the fee in cash, without witnesses or receipt.

A New York civil court judge recently resigned upon disclosure of deposits of $150,000 in his bank account during a time when his salary had aggregated only $44,000.

Corruption of judges in the criminal courts and particularly the lower criminal courts is more common. The Seabury investigation in New York City in 1931-1932 disclosed an undeniable link between members of a ring which preyed on prostitutes—a ring consisting of lawyers, bondsmen and some of the city magistrates. Prostitutes who paid for protection received it; their cases would be jockeyed before a friendly judge and they would be released. Those who refused to pay tribute found themselves haled before a magistrate who, now unfriendly, would jail them, regardless of the evidence, under a statute empowering magistrates, upon a proper complaint, to adjudge girls between sixteen and twenty-one to be "wayward minors." Though

# LOOK AT THE LAW

the law required that the charge be established upon competent evidence at a hearing, certain magistrates were found to have incarcerated some twenty-seven of these girls without any real trial whatsoever.

As a result of the same investigation, a New York magistrate was removed from office for accepting a loan of $19,000 from one Arnold Rothstein, a notorious gambler. This judge was shown to have deposited large sums in his bank account in addition to his salary.

A member of the Chicago Crime Commission said a few years ago that a certain Chicago Municipal Court judge was so purchasable that he was known to the criminals as the "cash register."

Even a Communist judge is not necessarily immune from temptation. A Superior Judge of the U.S.S.R. was shot and members of his staff imprisoned after burning the courthouse to destroy records which indicated that he had handed out light sentences to those who could and did pay for the consideration. In successfully destroying the courthouse, the conspirators were charged with having burned the janitress to death in the fire because she knew too much about the judge and his affairs.

Where we find a judge taking money, the reason is often similar to those that caused the widespread, notorious corruption which marked the administration of justice in England from the fourteenth to the eighteenth centuries. During the reigns of the first Edward, a popular ballad read:

> "Judges there are whom gifts and favorites control,
>   Content to serve the devil alone and take from a toll,
> Such judges have accomplices whom frequently they send
> To get at those who claim some land, and whisper as a friend,

# LOOK AT THE LAW

' 'Tis I can help you with the judge, if you would
  wish to plead,
  Give me but half, I'll undertake before him you'll
  succeed.' "

The chief reasons for English judicial corruption were the practice of selling judgeships and the meager salaries paid, the Lord Chief Justice at one time receiving less than £250 per annum while the Barons of the Exchequer received less than £100. To recoup the moneys paid for their appointments and to augment their salaries, the judges, clerks and minor court officers depended upon fees and gifts and ofttimes upon the sale of judicial decisions.

Court attaches invented excuses to demand gratuities, and ultimately this settled into a practice of charging a fee for every service. No suitor could obtain a hearing from a judge until he had paid into court certain fees, of which the greatest part was for the judge's personal use.

It was also customary for wealthy men and great corporations to show their respect for the judges and chief officers of the courts by offering them valuable presents.

Today, periodically, we hear rumors that a judicial nominee has "contributed" a substantial sum to his political organization or to his political boss in consideration of the nomination. Sometimes the facts are disclosed. Some years ago in New York, a prominent lawyer named Willets was convicted of paying $50,000 to Cassidy, the political boss of the county, for a Supreme Court nomination. Just before the 1938 election in Kings County, New York, there was an investigation concerning rumors that a similar sum, $50,000, had been paid for a Supreme Court nomination, but no corroboration was discovered.

A New York magistrate testified that he "lent" $10,000 to his political leader at a time when his leader was successfully recommending him for a magistracy at $12,000 a year.

# LOOK AT THE LAW

Edward M. Martin, in a recent study of judicial elections in Chicago, said that "for at least forty years both the Republican and Democratic organizations in Cook County have assessed judicial candidates. In the nineties the assessment ranged from $2,000 to $5,000 per candidate."

Impecunious judges sometimes give their notes, says Martin, and, according to a story current in Chicago, sometimes fail to pay them, with the result that judicial nominations now are given only upon a C.O.D. basis. As one politician complained, "It's getting so you can't trust nobody, not even a judge."

Some years ago, Joseph H. Choate, leader of the American Bar, said: "There is one other abuse against which we can at least utter an indignant protest. I mean the toleration of judicial candidates who are willing or are permitted to pay for their nomination or to pay their party for their election. No matter what their personal or professional qualifications in other respects may be, such a means of reaching office cannot but degrade the Bench."

Even after a judge has been elected, he is expected to help finance the political organization that has elected him.

According to Martin, a judicial candidate claimed that the Cook County organization has assessed judges in one year when there was no campaign at all. One sitting Chicago judge complained that he was denied a renomination because he had been a little slow in coming through with his contribution. Another judge who was short of cash borrowed the money as a "loan" from one of the men to whom he frequently gave receiverships. Still another judge openly grumbled about a proposed economy reduction in his salary on the ground that he had too little left after paying for the privilege of running for office.

The late Frederic Kernochan, Chief Justice of the Court of Special Sessions in New York City, was told by the

# LOOK AT THE LAW

treasurer of Tammany Hall that other judges were contributing $500 to $1,000, and his own $50 campaign contribution which was returned to him was "too cheap."

Where the custom of taxing a judicial nominee prevails, the candidate frequently finds it necessary to borrow the money to make payment. During his term, with the necessity of repaying his borrowings, making annual political contributions and saving money against the time of his renomination, he may be so hard put to manage that he will relieve his stress by venality.

One judge, newly elected, went into virtual social isolation for five years until the money he had borrowed to be nominated and elected had been repaid, while another undertook a campaign of economy several years before his term expired so that he might be in funds when the call came for his renomination.

Judges who continue active in business affairs while on the bench, like ex-Judge Manton, or who live beyond their means, are constantly subject to the temptation of getting extra money by some of the many means available to them.

During the Seabury Magistrates Court investigation in New York City, according to Northrop, Magistrate Francis X. McQuade resigned on the morning of his examination in public "to devote time to the protection of his business interests." While a magistrate, he was active in sponsoring the stock of a new and speculative company. This "speculative venture of questionable merit is no longer in existence, and apparently those who invested in its securities have suffered a complete loss," reads a report on this case. While he was a magistrate, Mr. Northrop said, the judge had a financial interest in the gambling room of the Havana Casino.

Magistrate Jean Norris, according to Northrop, was removed as a result of the same inquiry because she "pur-

# LOOK AT THE LAW

chased and held stock in a bonding company with whose representative in the Magistrates Court she was in close contact and as to whose bonds she was frequently called upon and did act in her judicial capacity," and also because she endorsed, for money, the advertisement of a commercial product, namely, yeast, and thus "sanctioned the exploiting of her judicial position in the advertising of a commercial product contrary to the essential dignity of judicial office."

The principal cause of dishonesty in judges is the political influence in their selection. While most political leaders do not demand dishonesty in their judges, and while, astonishingly enough, most judges, though politically selected, are not dishonest, the selection of judges by standards of political merit too often results in the selection of men who by character and training lack the understanding and fortitude required to withstand the temptations to which they are subject.

The political basis of selection of judges has been frequently and frankly revealed. In the course of the Seabury investigation of the New York Magistrates Courts, Magistrate Brodsky testified that he had spoken to his leader, James J. Hagan, who presented his name for the appointment to the leader of Tammany Hall, while Magistrates Silberman, Dreyer and Gottlieb frankly cited their activity in the party as bases for their claims upon their district leaders for appointment.

A judge on the bench is a valuable possession for any political leader. A judgeship carries much patronage with it. The judge often lets the political organization designate his secretary and his attendant. Where the judges have the appointment of court clerks and court officers, stenographers and bailiffs, these jobs are also available to the organization.

A judge can excuse jurors at the behest of the boss and of

# LOOK AT THE LAW

his henchman; he can kill a summons in a speeding case where it will help the organization. He can release prisoners, fix bail high or low as occasion demands, grant continuances and stays and otherwise perform or refuse innumerable favors, as the organization urges. A judge who will remain grateful to the organization can aid it in a thousand and one ways; gratitude in a judge is more important to his nominators than judicial qualifications.

The average judge nominated by a political organization is ordinarily no ingrate. Nor is the average political leader an illusionist. The judge expects to be called upon and the political leader expects the judge to grant favors to the organization—ordinary favors at least. The halfway decent political leader — and there are many such — wants nothing more. He permits his judges to be honest in performing their judicial functions.

However, some political leaders also expect their judges to continue to render political service at the clubhouse. Some judges do. This is a vicious practice that degrades the judicial office.

The New York City Police Commissioner recently called a sitting Kings County Court judge a "peanut politician" and charged him with hanging around the political clubhouse nights, making "political contracts."

In 1936 the Chicago Bar Association expelled four judges on the ground that they had engaged too actively in Illinois primary politics in violation of Canon 28 of the Canons of Ethics of the American Bar Association, which says a judge should not engage generally in partisan activities to avoid any suspicion of being warped by political bias. Seven other judges were censored and thirty-seven other judges resigned from the Association after it began its investigation.

Some political leaders exercise control of their appointees

# LOOK AT THE LAW

by the need for renomination or reappointment. Others are less subtle and patient.

On July 15, 1936, Governor Hoffman of New Jersey announced that he accepted the resignation of Judge Umansky. The latter thereupon wrote the Governor insisting that he had not resigned. The ensuing controversy disclosed that the Governor claimed to have found Judge Umansky's undated resignation on his desk (the Governor's aide said that the Governor was not clear as to how the resignation got there) and the Judge confessed that he had given his political leaders his undated resignation prior to his appointment.

The New York *Times* said, on July 16, 1936, that political observers in New Jersey claimed it was not uncommon for political leaders to exact undated resignations from bench nominees or appointees.

In Chicago in 1921, Martin said, judges of the Circuit Court were denied renomination because of their unwillingness to give pre-election pledges to the political organization; and three sitting judges were dropped in 1927, one charging that his omission was due to his opposition "to the County Treasurer's demand for 135 more jobs in his office and to an opinion he had written . . . declaring city officials guilty of a breach of trust in failing to turn profits . . . into the city treasury."

In New York City, Municipal Court Judge Lewis charged he was denied renomination for refusal to grant political favors, and the late Judge Kernochan publicly told of the political leader who threatened him with reprisals when the judge refused to rescind a convicted criminal's sentence.

For one such reason or another, judges will be found who succumb to the demands made upon them by their political friends and sponsors, judges who are too weak to resist the

# LOOK AT THE LAW

demands of friendship and gratitude and judges who have become too blunted by political standards to uphold the necessary judicial niceties. However honest the intentions of such a judge may be at the outset, the taint of political influence and obligation demands his future service. What starts with political patronage may readily become nepotism; what is initiated in the name of favors is easily translated into a "contract," a "fix" or a "consideration." A weak judge parcels out lucrative receiverships to his political cronies. It becomes a temptation to center the most profitable ones in a few friends who will "treat" the judge to week-end sojourns, to European trips, to flyers in the stock market, and finally, who will split the fee with the judge. Deciding a case the right way at the instance of a political leader is only next door to deciding a case the wrong way for a friend. The transition is gradual as habit strengthens and conscience weakens.

*2.*

Though personal dishonesty is uncommon among our judges, we have become habituated to practices that are of themselves improper and which contain the seeds of future and more widespread corruption. Some of such abuses and evils, the spawn of the political selection and control of judges, are summarized thus by the New York *World-Telegram:*

"Fat receiverships, lunacy commissions and the like showing rank political favoritism in judicial appointments; overstaffed courts and oversalaried court employees maintained for political patronage on the plea of judicial 'independence'; lax supervision of jury panel selection; court probation departments revealed as mere 'happy families' of incompetents; not to speak of magis-

# LOOK AT THE LAW

trates accused of favoring bail bond fakers or of lying on the witness stand to shield powerful political protectors. And the end is not yet."

Manifestly, it is not enough that a judge be personally honest. That is not the measure of his obligation. He must conduct himself so as not to bring reproach upon himself or to reflect upon his high office. When a judge does not so conduct himself, he shakes public confidence in the Bench and is as false to his trust as though he were corrupt.

Supreme Court Justice Lauer in New York City recently resigned when his wife was convicted of smuggling. Other judges have been asked or forced to resign because they were insolvent, because there were unpaid judgments against them, because their salaries were garnisheed, because they were habitués of race tracks, and because they associated with gamblers. The New York City Police Commissioner recently stated that he had refused to recommend the appointment of a lawyer to a judgeship because he had been counsel for a notorious gangster.

The practice of putting nominees of large corporations on the Bench in counties where the dominion of such corporations is absolute has been a common practice for years. The appointment of corporate-minded judges marked the pre-depression era and the biased rulings of such judges lent nothing to the prestige of the courts.

Entertainment of suits involving General Motors by a Detroit judge owning General Motors stock; participation by a Harlan County judge owning an interest in coal mines in labor troubles—acts such as these shake public confidence in the integrity of judges although there may be no element of corruption or personal dishonesty involved.

Independence is a paramount requirement for a judge; political, corporate, or labor subservience breeds corruption

# LOOK AT THE LAW

and seriously jeopardizes the maintenance of our democratic system of government.

We discuss elsewhere the methods of selection of judges designed to free them from political control. Here we need but repeat Sir Matthew Hale's

### Rules for Judicial Conduct

#### Things Necessary to be Continually Had in Remembrance

i. That in the administration of justice, I am entrusted for God, the King and Country; and therefore,

ii. That it be done, 1. Uprightly, 2. Deliberately, 3. Resolutely.

iii. That I rest not upon my own understanding, or strength, but implore and rest upon the direction and strength of God.

iv. That in the execution of justice I carefully lay aside my own passions, and not give way to them, however provoked.

v. That I be wholly intent upon the business I am about, remitting all other cares and thoughts, as unseasonable and interruptions.

vi. That I suffer not myself to be prepossessed with any judgment at all, till the whole business and both parties be heard.

vii. That I never engage myself in the beginning of any cause, but reserve myself unprejudiced till the whole be heard.

viii. That in business capital, though my nature prompt me to pity; yet to consider, that there is also a pity due to the country.

ix. That I be not too rigid in matters conscientious, where all the harm is diversity of judgment.

# LOOK AT THE LAW

x. That I be not biased with compassion to the poor, or favour to the rich, in point of justice.

xi. That popular, or court applause, or distaste, have no influence into anything I do in point of distribution of justice.

xii. Not to be solicitous what men will say or think, so long as I keep myself exactly according to the rule of justice.

xiii. If in criminals it be a measuring cast, to incline to mercy and acquittal.

xiv. In criminals that consist merely in words, where no more harm ensues, moderation is no injustice.

xv. In criminals of blood, if the fact be evident, severity is justice.

xvi. To abhor all private solicitations, of what kind soever, and by whom soever, in matters depending.

xvii. To charge my servants, 1. Not to interpose in any business whatsoever, 2. Not to take more than their known fees, 3. Not to give any undue precedence to causes, 4. Not to recommend councill.

xviii. To be short and sparing at meals, that I may be the fitter for business.

# CHAPTER XI

## *The Layman Says:*
## WITNESSES ARE LIARS

*1.*

THE ROAD to justice is marked by obstacles. Some the law puts in its own path; some lawyers and judges impose. But the greatest obstacle is the one litigants and their witnesses themselves create—the barrier to reaching the truth because of the tendency of litigants and their witnesses to lie.

One of the most difficult tasks of those who administer the law is to detect and to overcome liars, to segregate out of the welter of their lies an approximation of truth and to forge from it a measure of justice. The smithy in which this Herculean task is attempted is the courtroom; the smiths are the judges, the lawyers and the jurors.

The tendency of early man to lie is attested by the scriptural injunction against bearing false witness; by King David's plaint that "all men are liars."

No method that any legal system has been able to devise has succeeded in completely deterring the false witness. The Athenian system of justice was wrecked by liars; the Egyptians feared liars so much they made perjury a capital crime and the Romans threw perjurers from the Tarpeian rock.

Various means have been employed to adduce the truth and expose the false. The ancients resorted to trial by ordeal. The defendant was thrown into the river. If he sank, he was guilty; if he floated, God had furnished proof of his innocence. Other similar tests were resorted to; from their effects was read the judgment of the Divinity. The de-

# LOOK AT THE LAW

fendant was required to walk through fire, to carry a hot iron, to plunge his hand in boiling water. These were the origins of the modern phrase "going through fire and water."

Trial by "battel" was another method, wherein the contestants fought and the result determined upon whose side God rested, the accuser or accused.

At present we use the oath as a means of inducing a witness to testify truthfully.

The ancient theory of the oath was to call the attention of God to the witness so that if he lied, God would punish him. The oath is a relic of a day when it was believed that there was a supernatural supervision of earthly judgments. It was the basis of the ancient trial by compurgation, where the taking of an oath was so honored that cases would be decided by an *ex parte* oath upon which the dispute would be concluded without going into the evidence and sometimes without hearing the other side. At present, the oath is administered on the theory that if God fails to punish the perjurer, an avenging district attorney will; but most people have proved, by empiric methods, that neither the Deity nor the prosecutor is to be feared in this connection. One unintended consequence of the oath is to prevent persons such as Quakers, atheists or other conscientious objectors, who would testify truthfully without an oath, from testifying.

The present method of administering the oath indicates little reliance on its efficacy. When an adult witness takes the stand a clerk whose voice is indistinguishable in the hustle and bustle of the courtroom, mumbles the following:

"Raise y'right han'. The testimony y'ar about t'give will be th' trut', th' whole trut' and nothin' but th' trut' s'help y'God kiss th' book."

When a child takes the stand, the following occurs:

Judge: "What is your name, sonny?"

# LOOK AT THE LAW

Witness: "Bobby."

Judge: "Now, Bobby, do you know why you're here?"

Witness (who has been thoroughly coached): "Yes, sir."

Judge: "Why?"

Witness (mechanically): "To tell the truth about what I am asked."

Judge: "Do you know what happens if you lie?"

Witness: "Yes, sir."

Judge: "What happens, Bobby?"

Witness: (brightly remembering his piece and enjoying the opportunity to use forbidden language): "I go to hell."

Judge: "Proceed, counsellor, the witness is qualified."

The oath is notoriously ineffectual to elicit the truth from interested witnesses. At one time the self-interest of the litigant was considered so certain an inducement to perjury that he was not permitted to testify. In England, until a late day, the defendant was not permitted to testify in his own behalf, even when he was charged with a crime. Ultimately, so much injustice resulted from this prohibition, that it was decided to permit guilty parties to perjure themselves in the interests of permitting innocent ones to talk themselves free.

But interested witnesses may include not only the litigant himself but his relations, his friends, the witnesses to whom he promises a share of the reward if he wins, the witnesses whom he hires to testify, so-called alienists, and handwriting, ballistic, medical and a variety of other "experts." This latter class of witnesses is given legal carte blanche to sell their testimony for pay and to lie at will, for they are allowed to testify to their opinions, and no man can be brought to book for saying what he claims he thinks.

It has become the custom to call "expert" witnesses to give "expert" testimony on almost every conceivable sub-

# LOOK AT THE LAW

ject, and many such "experts" make it a practice to sell any believe-it-or-not opinion for which a litigant will pay. Often, even an honest expert indulges in wishful thinking and stretches the probabilities to favor the side that calls him. In consequence, it is never very difficult to get an expert to testify "con" to combat the testimony of an expert who has testified "pro."

Experts, even when honest, are frequently overopinionated. Back in 1859, it was discovered that experts in the English courts had long and confidently been testifying to opinions concerning the presence of arsenic in human organs, without realizing that they had been producing arsenic by using copper in the course of their experiments. Today, experts testify to the truth or falsity of statements made in the presence of mechanical lie detectors, although the New York Court of Appeals recently declared that the infallibility of such devices has not been sufficiently established.

While a later day may accept or reject the scientific conclusions of an earlier one, expert witnesses are usually available to testify to conclusions which no known science can corroborate. Thus, a handwriting expert in the recent Hines trial claimed to be able to tell, from its appearance, whether a memorandum had been written while taking down an overheard telephone conversation, and an expert in the Hauptmann trial claimed to be able to testify that wood in a ladder came from certain boards and none other. In other cases, experts have offered opinions of a mule's disposition based on the "look of his eye," of whether a forger is more particular at the beginning than at the end of his effort, and other similar remote conclusions.

The average witness is ordinarily, at least, a potential liar. Frequently he is an actual one. Some witnesses are conscious, some unconscious, liars. It is difficult for a witness to tell the strict truth, even when he tries to do so; it is a

# LOOK AT THE LAW

practical impossibility when he makes little or no effort.

The honest witness suffers from difficulties of self-expression, which is not surprising. The faculty of accurate self-expression is the mark of the trained speaker or writer and is a gift not given to ordinary men, who are limited in vocabulary and in scope of imagination.

On Boswell telling Doctor Johnson of an earthquake which had been felt in Staffordshire, Dr. Johnson said to him: "Sir, it will be much exaggerated in public talk; for in the first place, the common people do not accurately adapt their words to their faults; they do not mean to lie; but taking no pains to be exact, they give you very false accounts. A great part of their language is proverbial. If anything rocks at all, they say *it rocks like a cradle;* and in this way they go on."

An otherwise honest witness is often mistaken in his testimony for a variety of psychological reasons. For one thing, human sensory organs have physical limitations and the nerves are often inadequate to transmit even simple concrete facts to the mind. It is a practical impossibility to absorb a complicated set of occurrences in a moment. When an accident happens, it is usually over before one knows it has occurred. Afterthought reconstructs it. This has been demonstrated time and again by tests made by psychologists and psychiatrists, as well as in the courtroom.

Daily we encounter newspaper reports such as this one from the New York *Sun:* "New Trial Won by Convicted Man. Witness with Conscience Withdraws Identification. . . . On the stand the witness was positive about the identification, contradicting seventeen persons who agreed that the defendant was home and asleep at the time of the crime."

Or this from the same newspaper: "Check Passer Meets Double. Woman Served Term for the Other's Crimes.

# LOOK AT THE LAW

Identified by the Victims. Pardoned When Frauds Continued While She Was in Jail."

Prof. Edwin M. Borchard, in his book *Convicting the Innocent*, gives sixty-five such cases which he concludes are to be ascribed primarily to mistaken identification or perjury. He says, "How valueless are these identifications by the victim of a crime is indicated by the fact that . . . in only two cases can the resemblance be called striking."

The average witness also suffers from failings of memory due to lapse of time between the date of the occurrence and the time of his testimony. How the law can expect a witness to remember facts for the three, four and five years it sometimes takes to reach a case for trial is properly beyond lay comprehension. And not only the main basic facts, but details. How far were you from the cars when they collided? Whom did you see first? What was he doing? Whom did you see next? What was he doing? How far were you from each one? How far was one from the other? How fast was each traveling? How fast were you traveling? How many seconds elapsed before the collision? How far had he traveled during the intervening period? How far had you traveled? Did you keep your eyes on him during all that time? Where was his fender when he struck? Your rear left mudguard? Etc., etc.

Obviously, any witness who testifies in such detail immediately after an accident is pretending to powers of observation no ordinary man possesses. And a witness who can testify to such minutiae after four or five years is either a phenomenon or a phenomenal liar. Such a witness is not entitled to belief. Yet lawyer after lawyer, day after day, thunders denunciations of witnesses who confess an inability to answer such questions.

In the Hines trial, Hines' counsel had spent hours of his cross-examination in showing that prosecution witnesses

# LOOK AT THE LAW

were incorrect in their recollection of time, that they had given varying answers in fixing months, days and even hours, and that they had varied in testifying to the details of the same conversations. Defense counsel was unsparing in his denunciation of these witnesses, intimating and charging before the jury that the variances in their recollections of the specific time of specific occurrences and of the language used indicated that they were testifying falsely.

However, one of the witnesses called by the prosecution was Max D. Steuer, long recognized as one of America's leading trial lawyers, an astute cross-examiner so noted for his extraordinary memory that legend charged him with having taken notes only during one or two of the many trials he had conducted. Whereupon, the following amusing reflection upon lawyers on and off the stand occurred:

The prosecutor asked if Mr. Steuer had had a specific conversation with the defendant.

"A. I did.

"Q. Can you mention the month in which that conversation took place?

"A. No, I cannot.

"Q. Mr. Steuer, you have the most famous memory of the New York Bar, haven't you?

"The Court: I don't believe there has ever been a competitive test to determine that.

"A. I haven't heard any evidence that the best memory of the New York Bar could tell whether a conversation took place in 1933 or not.

"Q. Well, you can't tell us whether it was in 1932 or in 1933?

"A. I cannot. I wish that I could.

"Q. Can you tell us it was near the end of 1932 or early in 1933?

"A. There is nothing that I recall that occurred in rela-

# LOOK AT THE LAW

tion to the conversation, Mr. Dewey, that would help me to fix the time as being either in 1933 or 1932. But may I suggest to you that Mr. Gelb suggested that he had a memorandum of the date, and I know nothing to the contrary.

"Q. You have given us your best recollection, have you?

"A. I haven't any recollection. That is my trouble."

While testifying to the conversation with the defendant, the witness testified that the defendant said, "I am not interested." Thereupon the prosecutor who had taken a statement from the witness previously in which those words did not occur, asked:

"Did you ever say that Hines said 'I am not interested' before? You didn't say that?

"The Witness: No. I doubt whether I was ever asked, but it wouldn't make any difference whether I said it before or not. You must understand, Mr. Dewey, I don't want this jury to believe, I don't want his Honor nor you to believe or anybody else to believe, that I am trying to pretend that I remember the words that I used or the words that Mr. Hines used, or the words that anybody else used if it was in 1933 or 1932. I am trying to tell the jury just that which I now reconstruct from those things that I positively remember, and that is all that I possibly can do; but in no sense did I pretend to give the jury the impression or the judge or Mr. Dewey or anyone else that I now recall the words that were used by anybody to me or by me to anybody else at that time. I am giving you my present reconstructed recollection of what took place at that time."

There is, of course, an obvious distinction between the honest witness who cannot remember details and the dishonest one who "does not remember" matters which may reveal the dishonest details of a manufactured story. The ready witness is often the more dishonest one.

# LOOK AT THE LAW

The recollection of even an honest witness is bound to be colored by thought or reflection. Wishful thinking is not confined to children. Most witnesses ultimately come to say what they want to believe. Timid witnesses hesitate to stand on their own recollections but they yield to the recollections of others, who may recall or may merely simulate recollection in order to induce the honest witness to conform.

A witness who, after a hold-up, positively identified the defendant, recanted after the defendant had been convicted and sent to prison. In an affidavit which was submitted praying a new trial for the defendant, the witness said that when first confronted with the defendant he had thought he was the man, that after having been told that three other witnesses had also identified him, he had felt certain of the identification, but that it was only after having had an opportunity to reflect that his first uncertainty had again manifested itself.

An honest witness is sometimes driven into a lie and then fears to draw back. One rapid question after another—then, "Did he get half way across the street before he was struck?" "Yes," answers the witness hastily. The answer should have been "No." But having committed himself the witness feels he must not discredit himself, and finds it necessary to build lie upon lie to save himself from original confession.

Ofttimes, the truth seems not wholly plausible and the witness tries to gild it. If a man driving an automobile at an excessive speed is involved in an accident through no fault of his own, assuming that the excessive speed did not cause the accident, would any one expect him to take the stand and admit he was driving too fast? This tendency of even honest witnesses to color the truth is the reason for a number of stock questions on cross-examination that often trip an otherwise honest witness.

# LOOK AT THE LAW

"Did you talk this over with anyone before you came here?" is an almost invariable question. In nine cases out of ten the witness says, "Yes, sir." "With whom?" asks the lawyer. "With the lawyer," answers the witness. In the tenth case, the witness who has otherwise testified honestly and whose story the cross-examiner has been unable to shake, will reason thus: If I say yes, the jury'll think I'm telling a faked story, that I was put up to it by the lawyer. So he answers, "No."

This is the godsent opportunity for the opposing lawyer.

"Didn't you talk to the plaintiff before you took the stand?"

The witness hesitates. "No, sir."

"Or to his lawyer?"

Again the witness hesitates. "No, sir."

The witness is lying, knows it and shows it.

"Or to anyone else?" "No, sir."

"Can you tell us, please, how you came to be subpoenaed?"

The witness hesitates.

"Can you tell us, please, how plaintiff knew you would or could testify for him?"

The witness is destroyed with the jury, which knows that no lawyer puts a witness on the stand without going over his testimony with him.

Another such favorite question is: "Did you receive a subpoena to come here?" If the witness says "No," as is frequently the truth, the jury may think he is friendly, or so the witness reasons. As a result he says "Yes."

"Let us see it, please," asks the cross-examiner. The witness fumbles, pretends to search for it and with a sheepish look on his face, cannot find it.

"Did you get anything besides a paper?"

"No, sir," says the witness.

# LOOK AT THE LAW

"What, you didn't get a witness fee? Don't you know you need not come without a witness fee? Didn't you really come here voluntarily to help the plaintiff out?" follow in rapid succession, leaving the witness bewildered and unnecessarily shaken.

Even assuming that a witness would tell a straightforward story if he were given the opportunity, the fact is that he is not given an opportunity. He may not tell his story in his own way; he must tell it as the law instructs. He frequently is directed to answer questions with "yes" or "no," even though the question is a counterpart of "Who was King Henry the Eighth?" "Do you still buy stolen goods?" He may not say, "I made an agreement with him"; he may repeat only what he told the other person and what the latter told him. Though he cannot recall a conversation he may not give its effect; he must guess at what one must have said to the other and testify to substance in words as though they were really spoken. He may not ordinarily say, "He looked ashamed," or "guilty," or "sorry" in the courtroom though neither judge nor jury would deny him the right to talk thus if he were telling them his story in the courtroom corridor. He may be interrupted and badgered by lawyers, judge and jurors; he may be rebuked, ridiculed and insulted, told to speak up or to lower his voice, as though he were a child, until in resentment and confusion he seeks to adhere to the rules rather than to the truth.

As one witness put it: "There's no place for the honest witness in the courts; they don't want them and they won't believe them. An experienced witness is like a salesman; he gives the customers what they want; if he hasn't got it, he makes it up for them."

Invariably, a garrulous witness is admonished by the judge and counsel not to volunteer anything. Such a witness sometimes holds back important facts simply because he has

# LOOK AT THE LAW

been instructed to answer only the questions he is asked.

A railroad flagman, an obviously honest witness, testified forcibly and at great length that he had waved his lantern frantically to warn an automobile driver who just after dark had run on the crossing and had been struck by the train. The plaintiff had denied that he had seen the flagman's signal; the flagman swore that he had repeatedly waved his lantern. At the end of a fruitless and tiresome cross-examination that got him nowhere, the plaintiff's lawyer suddenly asked in desperation and for no good reason:

"How long before you saw the plaintiff's car did you light your lantern?"

To his surprise and to the defendant's attorney's consternation, the flagman hesitantly answered:

"I didn't light it at all."

"Why didn't you say so before?" asked the lawyer.

"I wasn't asked and I was told not to say anything unless I was asked," answered the flagman.

The rules of examination and cross-examination are made for and by the lawyers, to give them an advantage over the witness and to permit them to appear smart and the witness stupid. The art of cross-examination, which is so fascinatingly explained and illustrated in the books that lawyers write about themselves, largely consists in finding a witness who is dishonest and stupid. If he is dishonest and smart, the average cross-examination will ordinarily produce little result but a repetition of his direct testimony.

If the witness is merely stupid and is trying to tell a truthful story, the lawyer may destroy him by confusing him, but the lawyer is running a long chance of appearing too smart at the witness's expense and thereby discrediting himself with the jury.

The frank trial lawyer will admit that he looks best when he is most fortunate; that the experienced witness is a tough

# LOOK AT THE LAW

nut to crack and that an inexperienced, stupid or reckless witness is a godsend to the average lawyer.

The favorite lawyer-Lincoln story is told of Lincoln's cross-examination of a witness who testified he saw Armstrong, whom Lincoln was defending on a charge of murder, strike the fatal blow with a sling shot or a similar weapon.

Lincoln, pressing him closely, forced him to locate the hour of the assault as about eleven at night, and then demanded that he inform the jury how he managed to see so clearly at that time of night.

"By the moonlight," answered the witness promptly.

"Well, was there light enough to see everything that happened?" persisted the examiner.

The witness responded that the moon was about in the same place that the sun would be at ten o'clock in the morning and was almost full, and the moment the words were out of his mouth, the cross-examiner confronted him with an almanac showing that the moon afforded practically no light at eleven o'clock and had absolutely set at seven minutes after midnight.

Obviously, though the cross-examiner was skillful, he was able to be effective only because the witness was lying and was, in addition, none too clever.

But another time, a more cautious witness checked with the almanac in advance and thereby turned the tables on the famous lawyer, Rufus Choate.

The witness, Barton, chief mate of a clipper ship, had testified: "The night was dark and rainy."

Suddenly Choate asked him: "Was there a moon that night?"

"Yes, sir."

"Ah, yes! a moon . . ."

"Yes, a full moon."

# LOOK AT THE LAW

"Did you see it?"

"No, sir."

"Then how do you know there was a moon?"

"The 'Nautical Almanac' said so, and I will believe that sooner than any lawyer in the world."

### 2.

Deep down in his heart the average witness believes that his job is to out-trick the other side and that he is put on the witness stand not to tell the truth, but to help win the case. He undertakes to do so even if he has to lie in the process.

In these assumptions, the witness is not wholly incorrect. A trial is a contest akin to the old "trial by battel" except that it is played under rules which substitute for physical force the intellectual skill and agility of lawyers and witnesses. As in days of old, each contestant is still permitted to select his champion, but now instead of a burly butcher, he picks a wily lawyer. These champions still use the methods of "battel," they advance and retreat, they use force and bluster, they employ concealment and surprise. Fundamentally the purpose is the same—to win, by hook or by crook, by stealth or by wealth.

A trial proceeds as though it were a mere game. The object of the game is to ascertain who has most successfully complied with the rules. He is thereupon declared the winner. Each contestant is allowed a lawyer and witnesses. The umpires are the judge and the jury. The judge announces the rules, the jury (or sometimes the judge) decides the identity of the winner, presumably according to the rules. Each side claims to be telling the truth and wants the jury to find that what its witnesses say is the truth. Each witness tells what he claims is the truth, though his story is usually

# LOOK AT THE LAW

directly at variance with what a witness on the other side says is the truth. None of the witnesses may tell all he knows, nor may he tell it in his own way to the best advantage. The lawyer on his side tries to suggest by his questions what the witness should say; the lawyer on the other side tries to make him say something else. Each lawyer tries to induce the jury to disregard everything the other lawyer or his witnesses say.

The judge's task is to keep the lawyers from completely bamboozling the jury. The litigants, their witnesses and their lawyers are each trying to win regardless of the rules, whereas the judge is trying to enforce the rules and to help the jury see the case as he sees it. But in many jurisdictions in this country, the judge must not do this openly; he is supposed to stick to the rule end of the business. So he has to convey his impressions of the testimony to the jury by shrugs of the shoulder, lifted eyebrows, facial expressions of incredulity and other nuances that do not appear in the stenographer's record. Otherwise, the higher court will set aside the jury's verdict, as a Federal Court did recently, holding that the defendant's constitutional rights were violated, since, because of the judge's comments, the judicial lantern "ceases to be such and becomes a beacon of light, so dazzling that there is little, if any, opportunity for the jury to follow any road except that shown by this guiding light."

The jurors must decide the case on the witnesses' testimony. They may not go outside the record to convince themselves of the truth. So where a defendant in a Maine criminal case offered an alibi that depended upon how quickly an automobile could be driven from Auburn to Casco, the judge declared a mistrial when a juror, during the noon recess, jumped in his own automobile and tried to see how long it would take.

# LOOK AT THE LAW

The lawyer on each side tries to get the jury angry or disgusted with the other side for reasons which may or may not have anything to do with the case. He tries to fool the jury by appealing to its passions or its prejudices, its emotions, its bias, its weaknesses; in fact, everything but its reason.

From the very opening of a trial each lawyer is busily engaged in this task. How well he does it determines how effective a trial lawyer he is. When he is selecting the jury, he questions the prospective jurors at length that he may discover the men who may be prejudiced against his client's case and those who may be prejudiced against the other side. The first he excuses; the latter he welcomes.

Lawyers want jurors who will take the particular bait they have to offer. They seek a susceptible middle-aged jury when their female client has shapely legs she can cross on the witness stand. A woman recently tried in the criminal courts of New York City evidently obtained a disagreement of the jury by such means, for upon her second trial the District Attorney had a rail erected in front of the witness chair that confined the jury's view to her less stimulating features. She was convicted.

A female defendant's clothes, her demeanor, the way she wears her hair, even her rouge pot and lipstick undergo her lawyer's censorship before she is permitted to enter the courtroom. The widow and infant children of the murdered man are given front row seats. The undergarments of a kidnaped and murdered child are placed tenderly before the jury, reminiscent of Mark Anthony:

> "You all do know this mantle....
> Look, in this place ran Cassius' dagger through."

Gilbert and Sullivan's usher strips bare and rattles the

# LOOK AT THE LAW

legal bones of passion and prejudice in *Trial by Jury*, where Edwin is being sued by Angelina for breach of promise, by the following solo:

> Now Jurymen, hear my advice —
> All kinds of vulgar prejudice
>    I pray you set aside;
> With stern judicial frame of mind
> From bias free of every kind
>    This trial must be tried.
>
> Oh, listen to the plaintiff's case:
> Observe the features of her face —
>    The broken-hearted bride.
> Condole with her distress of mind:
> From bias free of every kind
>    This trial must be tried!
>
> And when amid the plaintiff's shrieks,
> The ruffianly defendant speaks —
>    Upon the other side;
> What *he* may say you needn't mind —
> From bias free of every kind,
>    This trial must be tried!

The lawyer's usual avenues of approach to the jury's emotions are through the implications and suggestions in his questions to the witnesses, the answers he elicits, and in his summation. If he can ask an irrelevant question and get an irrelevant answer before the jury, he feels he has accomplished something. Even if an objection keeps the answer out, the lawyer feels that the insinuation in his question may have gotten across to the jury.

The favorite channel for lawyer-seduction of the jury is through the summation. Here the lawyer plays upon the jurors' passions and prejudices.

From the ancient Grecian orators to our modern Choates and Darrows, juries have been victimized by gifted orators and jury-swayers. Some advocates swear by the ancient forensic school. Ignoring facts, they orate in the grand manner about "desolate homes, lonely children, weeping widows and heartbroken mothers." Others affect a quiet, confidential attitude and, flattering the jury, appear to reason with them. One school indulges in false sentiment; another in false reasoning. Some lawyers affect kindness; others abuse their opponents, following the Baconian injunction to "Slander boldly; something always sticks." None of this is new but every age has its successful proponents of a system, who come to be known as great jury lawyers.

Thus, when Antony, defending the Roman Aquilius, found himself unable to disprove the charge, he gained acquittal for his client by unloosing his robes and showing the jurors the scars he had suffered in his country's service.

And when Thomas M. Marshall, noted Pennsylvania lawyer, represented a youth charged with murder, he regaled the jury with a recital of his own happy home life, his joy at finding his sons when he reached home in the evening—and obtained an acquittal by begging the jury to let "this boy go home to his mother tonight."

The ancient Athenian advocates employed language of the most insulting kind and berated their opponents with disgraceful epithets. The modern counterpart, prosecuting a fellow lawyer charged with a violation of the banking laws in connection with a closed bank, referred to bankers stealing "depositors' money"; pleaded with the jury to "give a little attention to the poverty of depositors who are mulcted by these people"; characterized the defendant as a "pilot fish" that guided "sharks that scour the financial seas"; referred to the defendant's character witnesses as "a veritable parade of the wooden soldiers," as "Bar Association pundits," and to the defendant as "the bloodhound that has tracked down the little shysters, the little ambulance chaser,

# LOOK AT THE LAW

the pot-house politician." The defendant's conviction was set aside upon this as well as upon other grounds.

Even racial and geographic prejudices are invoked in efforts to sway the jury's collective mind. In the Scottsboro trials of a number of Negroes charged with raping white girls of admitted unchastity, the Circuit-Solicitor of Morgan County in summation implored the jury, "Show them—show them that Alabama justice cannot be bought and sold with Jew money from New York." Another member of the prosecution added: "If you acquit this Negro, put a garland of roses around his neck. Give him a supper and send him in to New York City. There let Dr. Harry Fosdick dress him up in a high hat, morning coat, gray striped trousers and spats. This is not framed prosecution. It is a framed defense." The defendants were convicted though the testimony offered by the State was full of contradictions and weaknesses.

Probably the high point of brazen frankness in recognizing the prevalence of jury-swaying by recourse to the jurors' emotions occurred in the course of a hearing to determine the sanity of one Reilly, a criminal lawyer in New York who had achieved some measure of public notice by appearing as chief counsel in the defense of Hauptmann, the Lindbergh kidnaper. Newspapers (March 23, 1938) reported thus the words of the Deputy Attorney General to show that Reilly had found himself incompetent adequately to represent his clients:

"There was the case of a Brooklyn boy killer, whose hopes of escaping the electric chair reposed in Reilly. 'Reilly was in honor bound to deliver in the boy's behalf a summation two hours long, which would reduce that Brooklyn jury to a tearful pulp and inspire a possible not guilty verdict on purely emotional grounds. You gave the lad only eighteen minutes of your oratory. Didn't you?' accused the Deputy Attorney General."

# LOOK AT THE LAW

With such examples as these constantly brought before him by newspaper, magazine and motion picture, the witness is bound to feel that if the lawyer can deceive the court and jury, that if a trial is not a quest for truth and justice but a game played by rules, in which he is a pawn, there is no reason why he should not undertake to contribute his share of the deception to win the case. The consequence is that perjury is rampant and liars flourish in our courts. As on the fictitious Road to Mandalay, in the courtroom there "ain't no ten commandments."

The contemptuous attitude of witnesses toward their perjuries was shown in the Hines case, where the following testimony was recorded:

Mr. Stryker: Yes or no, have you had a regard for an oath up to the time you were called by the District Attorney in this case?

Mr. Davis: No, I committed perjury.

Mr. Stryker: Have you had any regard for an oath, putting your hand on the Bible and swearing to tell the truth? Have you ever had any regard for that before you testified in this case? . . .

Mr. Davis: No, I had had no regard. I have committed perjury at various times. . . .

Mr. Stryker: All right. You committed perjury before the New York County Grand Jury?

Mr. Davis: Oh, yes. Yes, I did, sir.

Mr. Stryker: Then you committed perjury before the Referee in your disbarment proceedings?

Mr. Davis: Yes, I did.

Mr. Stryker: Then you also committed perjury before the Commissioner of Accounts?

Mr. Davis: Yes, sir.

# LOOK AT THE LAW

Mr. Stryker: Then the only two times you have ever gotten on the witness stand and taken an oath to tell the truth, you have knowingly lied under oath, is that right?

Mr. Weinberg: That is right.

Mr. Stryker: There is no doubt about it that you told me that you would commit perjury to get $24,000, didn't you?

Mr. Weinberg: I said I did.

Mr. Stryker: You did, didn't you?

Mr. Weinberg: Yes.

Under our present system, perjury is viewed as an ineradicable evil—and it probably is. Like Jupiter who laughs at lovers' lies, we applaud the successes of legal liars. Perjury has come to be accepted as one of the counters inevitably found in the legal game of the courtroom. It took over twenty years to free Mooney, although the perjury that convicted him was proven beyond doubt.

There is little protection against perjury. We are all too tolerant of it. We not only view it as an ineradicable evil but we come to expect it. In criminal and in divorce cases, everybody expects lying. A man who is fighting for his life or his liberty is not expected to sacrifice either one for an undue sense of honor respecting a mere oath. A defendant in a divorce suit is never expected to confess fault; a co-respondent is considered a cad if he fails to lie like a gentleman in defense of his paramour's honor. In such case, the lesser legal crime of perjury yields to the greater demands of the so-called moral code.

But beyond that, the amusement with which perjury is publicly viewed is illustrated in an article by Westbrook Pegler concerning the life sentence of Mrs. Mae Hall for perjury. "At present," says Pegler, "she is free on bail and nobody seems disturbed about her case—least of all Mrs. Hall, because she will not have to serve the term. They are very informal about such things in Florida."

# LOOK AT THE LAW

It appears that Mrs. Hall had testified at the first trial of four men accused of murder that two of them had admitted the killing. In her second trial she repudiated her testimony and said the sheriff had made her lie. The authorities had her indicted and convicted her for perjury but Pegler says "it should be remembered that Mrs. Hall stands in no danger of going away for long, if at all."

In a recent case in Kings County, New York, a woman witness represented herself to be another person. When her perjury was disclosed and her motive sought, she said "I thought the whole thing was a joke; I didn't mean any harm."

The prevalence of perjury is strongly reinforced by the fact that when it suits their purposes, even prosecutors use admitted perjurers and ask juries to be tolerant of their past perjuries while believing their present ones. A striking example of this occurred in the Hines case, when the District Attorney himself told the jury, in his opening, that he was relying on self-confessed perjurers whom he did not wholly believe himself. The two principal witnesses he offered, Davis and Weinberg, did not belie his statement, as their testimony shows.

Judges, too, are not blind to the prevalence of perjury. The need for some way of curbing it was emphasized by Judge Peter M. Daly of Queens, New York. Judge Daly said many persons felt that "an oath has no binding effect" and "many who do not hesitate to swear falsely are convinced that if they are caught, no punishment will be meted out to them." He said court officials estimated that "fifty per cent of all the evidence received on behalf of the defense in criminal cases is perjured."

Perjury is restricted to neither creed nor sex. Hon. Joseph N. Ullman, Baltimore judge, in an article on perjury in the courts, wrote that some of the most shameless lying

# LOOK AT THE LAW

he ever listened to was done by rival groups of religious trustees in a contest over the control of a church property.

Women witnesses often make consummate perjurers. They are accustomed to concealing things from their menfolk. They have a disarming air of candor. They cannot be pressed or bullied without exciting the jury's indignation, and they testify as they please. According to Josephus, Moses is supposed to have said, "Let the testimony of women not be received on account of the levity and audacity of their sex."

The law is also overtolerant of perjury; its rules make prosecution difficult because, contrary to common assumption, failure to tell the truth is not always perjury.

Lying is merely one element of the crime. To commit perjury in most jurisdictions, one must not only lie deliberately but the lie must be told in the course of a judicial or other legal proceeding and the matter lied about must be something of consequence in the proceeding. One may frequently be guilty of false swearing without being guilty of perjury.

For example, a lawyer wanted to show that a witness had come to court under compulsion, by virtue of a subpoena and not voluntarily.

"Were you subpoenaed to come here today?" he asked.

"No," said the witness.

He was indicted for perjury but escaped conviction upon the plea that he had not been subpoenaed for "today" but for the day before and that he had merely been instructed to return the following day.

Another witness was asked if he knew that part of his tobacco had been left in a barn that had burned down. He replied, "No." When the insurance company proved beyond any doubt that he did know it and sought to charge him with perjury he countered by saying that he had been

# LOOK AT THE LAW

asked if he knew that part of his tobacco had been left in the barn and that he did not know it because the tobacco left in the barn was not his but his wife's.

In another case, "You drive a wagon?" asked the cross-examining lawyer of the defendant's employee.

"No," said the witness.

"Weren't you driving the wagon when this plaintiff was knocked down and run over?"

"No, sir."

"I ask that the witness be remanded for perjury," said the attorney to the judge. "He testified on direct examination that he was the driver."

"Mr. Witness," said the Judge, "are you undertaking to change your testimony?"

"No, your Honor."

"How do you explain your testimony?" asked the Judge.

"He asked me if I drove the wagon. I did not. I drove the horse," answered the witness.

Herodotus tells a story of a defendant who, sued for the return of money which had been left with him for safekeeping, concealed it in the hollow of a walking stick which he put in the hands of the plaintiff. He then swore that although he had received the money he had returned it. As it turned out the walking stick broke accidentally and his half-truth turned out to be the truth.

The lie, if a lie, must be a material lie in order to make the witness guilty of perjury.

A defendant was charged with being the father of a bastard child and liable for its support. In the course of the proceeding the defendant swore he was a bachelor. It turned out that he was a married man. He was found guilty on the bastardy charge and then indicted for perjury for denying he was married. The court held that he was a liar, but not a perjurer, since it was immaterial in the bastardy proceeding

# LOOK AT THE LAW

whether he was married or single, so long as it was conceded that he was not married to the mother of the child.

This sophistry and the sophistry needed to overcome it was illustrated in the Earl Carroll bathtub case. During the prohibition period, the newspapers carried the story of a hilarious and unprecedented party that was given by Earl Carroll, a noted theatrical producer. The newspapers reported that during the early morning, a bathtub had been brought to the center of the stage and the theatrical producer stood by the bathtub while a Miss Hawley came from the wings, dressed in a chemise; that the producer held a cloak in front of her while she slipped from the chemise and got into the bathtub, whereupon the producer announced, "The line forms to the right. Come up, gentlemen." About fifteen or twenty men lined up at the side of the bathtub and, as they passed by, took glasses and filled them with champagne from the tub.

The Federal District Attorney commenced an investigation and subpoenaed the theatrical producer. He testified that, at the suggestion of the property man in his theater, the bathtub had been placed on the stage as a convenient receptacle in which to cool ginger ale, and that the ginger ale had been drawn off by the guests by a spigot inserted in the drain of the bathtub. He swore that the ginger ale was the only beverage put into the bathtub and denied that anyone had bathed in the bathtub. He said that the newspaper stories were untrue, that nobody had been in the bathtub. He was indicted for perjury and was convicted.

The producer appealed, saying that the Grand Jury was merely making an investigation to determine whether or not intoxicating liquors had been furnished at the party and the law thereby violated; that it was immaterial whether or not a nude woman had bathed in the bathtub. The court ruled that anyone who had stepped into the bathtub would

# LOOK AT THE LAW

be a good witness as to whether it contained champagne, as the government claimed, or ginger ale, as the producer claimed; and that consequently, when the defendant denied that a nude woman had bathed in the beverage, he was concealing from the jury the fact that there was an available witness to testify whether the bathtub contained champagne or ginger ale. Consequently, his testimony was held material and the conviction affirmed.

Another barrier to conviction is the rule that it is not enough to prove that a witness charged with perjury made two conflicting statements, but the prosecution, in addition, must prove one of them to be true, and the other false.

In a case in South Carolina in 1922, a defendant accused of perjury openly admitted swearing to two contradictory statements but his conviction was reversed because the prosecution had failed to prove which of the two contradictory statements was false.

Dorothy Dunbar Bromley, columnist, illustrates this legal anomaly by the following story.

"Miss Edith St. Clair, an actress, a number of years ago sued Mr. Abraham Erlanger, the former theatrical producer, for having failed to fulfill the terms of a contract under which he agreed to pay her, 'for services unspecified,' $25,000 in ten yearly installments. She was able to convince the judge and jury of the authenticity of her claim and accordingly won a judgment in the Supreme Court of New York, which ordered Mr. Erlanger to make the yearly payments.

"Subsequently, however, she appeared at the office of Mr. Erlanger's attorney and for some unknown reason confessed that she had lied about the contract, and that her attorney, Mr. Max D. Steuer, had put her up to the story. Her statement was reduced to an affidavit, and the judgment which she had obtained was accordingly set aside. As a

# LOOK AT THE LAW

result of Miss St. Clair's revelations, disbarment proceedings were instituted against Mr. Steuer. But when she was called as a witness she once again recanted and said that she had told the truth the first time and that Mr. Steuer had not been responsible for her claim against Mr. Erlanger. The charge against Mr. Steuer was accordingly dismissed, and the State's next move was to try Miss St. Clair for perjury. But the prosecution suffered from the disadvantage of not being able to prove at which time she had sworn falsely, and so the jury failed to convict."

In a case in Queens County, New York, the holder of a pistol permit was indicted for making false statements in his application for a permit. The notary who had witnessed his affidavit was called to the stand and testified he was unable to recall having administered an oath to the defendant, although his (the notary's) signature, attesting that the defendant had signed and sworn to the affidavit, appeared thereon. (Since a single notary may attest thousands of affidavits in the course of a year and usually for persons they have never met before and never meet again, it is a practical impossibility for a notary to remember administering an oath to a particular person, to say nothing of recalling a particular affidavit.) The Court refused to permit the notary to testify to his general practice of administering an oath.

The consequence was that, under New York precedents, the trial judge felt compelled to direct an acquittal, to which the New York *World-Telegram* remarked editorially:

"There seems a big loophole for perjurers in judicial interpretation that requires . . . sworn testimony of the notary . . . when notarizing something that itself bears the words 'Subscribed and sworn to.'

"It may be sound law. But it seems lacking in sound sense." Incidentally, the higher Court disagreed with the lower Court.

## LOOK AT THE LAW

Ordinarily a trial for perjury simply offers opportunity for more perjury. We have mentioned heretofore the Luckman murder trial where one Louis Luckman testified he did not know a former Assistant District Attorney named Kleinman. Kleinman testified to the same effect. The prosecutor had both indicted for perjury. They were tried separately. Witnesses were produced who testified both ways. In Kleinman's trial the jury believed the witnesses who substantiated the Kleinman-Luckman story and acquitted him; but in Luckman's trial they disbelieved the Kleinman-Luckman witnesses and convicted him although the Appellate Court reversed the verdict of the jury.

Lawyers themselves are frequently responsible for the perjury in the courts. They are the key to the crime and its cure, for witnesses ordinarily cannot lie unless their stories dovetail with those of other witnesses. A client may come to a lawyer with a prepared story and prepared witnesses. But the average client is not astute enough to prepare a fabricated case that will fool the average astute lawyer. Aside from thieves who conspire to have fake accidents and make up their stories accordingly, a lawyer must ordinarily take a hand in concocting a false story. For this reason, even experienced conspirators usually include a lawyer in their number.

It usually requires a lawyer to "coach" witnesses, and clients come to a lawyer expecting such preparation. One client refused to pay his lawyer and when sued complained to the judge that his lawyer had been derelict in his duty; that he had not coached him in what he was to say as well as the other lawyer had coached his opponent and that therefore he had lost his case.

One counsel advised his prospective client that no action would lie unless the witness did. The client took the hint.

# LOOK AT THE LAW

Another litigant conducting his own case was told by the judge to get a lawyer. He said he needed no lawyer since he intended to tell the truth.

There is, of course, a vast difference between going over a witness' testimony with him before he takes the stand and telling him what to say. Every well-ordered trial must be prepared. A lawyer is negligent who fails to talk with each of his witnesses in advance of the trial. But requiring a witness to recall the facts and going over his testimony, pruning it, telling him what to stress and what is immaterial, warning him against pitfalls, telling him how to say what he has to say, is far different from telling him what to say or what to forget. It is because these differences are sometimes so slight that the lawyer's responsibility is so grave. It is an easy matter to suggest a simple change to even an honest witness, a fact which may appear to be of little significance to him but which may lead to an unjustified result. It is not difficult to lead a witness, by repetition, to believe in the truth of something that has been suggested to him. It is even possible to induce witnesses knowingly to lie, with the assurance that the other side's witnesses are going to lie, that all witnesses lie, that the judge and jury expect them to lie, and that the victory goes to the better liar.

A story illustrates the lawyer's contribution to perjury in the courts and the slight shades of difference between lawyers' guile and witnesses' lies. A plaintiff sought to recover damages for breach of a contract of employment. As the jury was being selected, the defendant's lawyer told the plaintiff's lawyer that he had a writing signed by the plaintiff whereby he had released the defendant of all claims. Defendant's counsel thus sought to induce plaintiff's counsel to recommend that his client take a small amount in settlement. However, plaintiff's counsel was not moved to settle; instead he told his client, a foreigner, that if he were

# LOOK AT THE LAW

shown a paper signed by him to say that he had not read it; that he could not read.

The trial proceeded. On cross-examination, defendant's counsel showed plaintiff a number of checks endorsed by him under the printed notation, "In full of all claims." Pursuant to instructions, plaintiff denied he had read before he endorsed, saying he could not read. However, the next day, asked how he came to see a certain person, he referred to a letter and pointed out in the letter a statement which bore him out. Needless to say, defendant won; not because he was right, but because his counsel's lie induced plaintiff's counsel to advise his own client to lie.

### 3.

There is no human system impervious to human chicanery. As in the days of old the consequences, however artificial, of trial by ordeal were manipulated by the use of cold iron, painted red, or by the use of other artificial preparations, so today perjury and dishonest practices in the courts tend to make a lie of justice.

While perfection cannot be achieved, the amount of lying in our courts can be reduced. If we are to retain the oath, it should be administered "in a manner calculated to impress" the witness with its solemnity and dignity. It should be supplemented by a liberalization and enforcement of the laws against perjury so that the witness who does not fear an irate God may have some respect for a persistent prosecuting attorney. Perjury should be summarily punishable by the trial judge as is contempt, with some restriction to enable review by a jury or an appellate court.

As to expert witnesses, a uniform act has been prepared after thorough consideration by a special Committee of the National Conference of Commissioners on Uniform State

# LOOK AT THE LAW

Statutes which restricts testimony from experts to those approved by the court or agreed upon by the parties, limits their compensation, does away with the futile and incomprehensible hypothetical question and otherwise regulates the practice so as to avoid the hokum and fraud that now characterizes expert testimony.

In New York, as a result of a legislative investigation which revealed that improperly qualified medical experts were acting in workmen's compensation cases, doctors and lawyers have been cooperating to create a panel of medical experts to be approved by the courts on the basis of lists certified by accredited examining boards representative of the various medical societies, so that the courts may have adequately qualified experts available and may seek to confine expert testimony to the men so certified. To their credit be it said that this action resulted from suggestions made by the judiciary and the medical profession (and it emphasizes the possibilities of scientific treatment, by cooperation with other professions, of particular legal problems).

Legal procedure should also be altered to permit honest witnesses to be honest. A witness should be permitted to state his conclusion "with respect to ordinary matters subject to explanation ... in a natural and non-technical manner," as the New York Commission of the Administration of Justice recommended as far back as 1934. The vestiges of technical rules that prevented interested persons from testifying to the facts should be lifted, technical rules of relevance and competency of evidence that prevent witnesses from giving the facts to the jury should be discarded. The academic attitude that bars from the scene of the dispute a jury desiring to verify testimony should be liberalized. Treating jurors like morons in restricting the testimony of witnesses should not be tolerated. Lawyer tricks and devices should be exposed by the judge, who should be permitted to comment and discuss the evidence openly with a jury as freely as are English judges. Some or all of these reforms, with less bullying and intimidation of witnesses by lawyers and a more active part in the adduction of facts from the witnesses by judges, would aid the honest witness in testifying honestly and help disarm the dishonest one who testifies shrewdly.

Less formality and greater flexibility, less technicality and more liberality in the courtroom would help make the truth plausible and lies ineffectual. A trial would then seem less like a game, and truth more its end.

If judges, too, would refrain from acting like players in a contest and make determined efforts to obtain the truth, lawyers would be less successful in confusing witnesses and fooling jurors. If the bench were less tolerant of legal trickery in the courtroom, lawyers would be reluctant to indulge in such conduct not only because it would be unsuccessful but because it would be thought improper. Generally, lawyers do what they do only because they justify what they are doing; most of them will not consciously do anything wrong. So long as the law tolerates bad practices, they will continue them. Once the bench becomes as intolerant of them as is lay opinion, they will discontinue them voluntarily.

There will, of course, always be dishonest witnesses. A small percentage does no harm; the law is equipped to deal with them (even pending perfection of a scientific lie detector) by the old methods of examination and cross-examination. It is only when the courts are submitted to a deluge of perjury and when such a state of affairs is endured that the supports of legal institutions are weakened and the structure endangered.

# CHAPTER XII

## *Remedy:*
## THE IMPORTANCE OF IT

ONCE the hollowness of our pretensions to civic virtue and to legal efficiency has been revealed, the man in the street, conscious of his own responsibilities, becomes defensive. "What of it?" he asks. "No system can be perfect. No system ever has been."

The obvious reply to this is that if the past proves anything, it demonstrates that the surest road to the downfall of government is that of public ignorance, public corruption and public apathy. Our democracy as a means of government has proven its value as an instrument making for human happiness. It is still in an experimental stage, and is suffering attack from within and without. It cannot survive without active public support and active public defense. And law is the very core of democracy.

Man can let natural laws operate by and of themselves and live and die by them. He can live by the wild foods that nature sows and die when they fail. Or he may seek himself to sow the crops he needs, he may store for lean years and thereby seek to prolong his existence and to minimize the risk of periodic deprivation and starvation. Once he has undertaken to do this, there is little limit to the call upon him. He must cultivate and irrigate, he must study his soil and rotate his crops.

Once he becomes part of a civilized community, he must find markets in which to dispose of his surplus so he may satisfy his other needs. In short, once man seeks to interfere with natural processes, the effort becomes endless.

So with the law. Once man seeks, by positive rules, to

# LOOK AT THE LAW

level natural defects, to neutralize biologic excesses, to equalize natural inequalities, his need for more rules becomes pressing. The result is a maze of law.

While, as we have seen, "an elaborate and technical system of law is, in many respects, an evil," "we are," as Cicero said, "in bondage to the law in order that we may be free." But an excess of regulatory law endangers a democratic system which rests upon freedom of initiative, individual enterprise and expression, a minimum of government and a diffusion of power, without recognition of caste or class. The antithesis — excessive regulation and restriction by law; concentration of power in one man, as in Germany or Italy, in one group or caste, as in Russia or Japan, or even in a majority — marks dictatorship.

An excess of imperative law tolls a danger to democracy, and those groups — social, economic, political, racial or religious — which wield the diffused power resident in the majority or in strong minorities in a democracy, must not cause such overregulation by abuse of power. They must exercise self-restraint, curb abuses, check and regulate social and economic inequalities, else they compel an excess of regulatory legislation which endangers our American democratic system.

By the same token, the law must express the free and informed will of the majority, and rest upon the free and informed consent of the minority, else we lend aid to those who would destroy our democratic system.

The consent by which a people is ruled may come from the cowed submission of the subjugated, the passive acquiescence of the unenlightened and ignorant, the acceptance of the deluded, or the free and knowing consent of the enlightened. Only the last is the hallmark of true democracy.

The reign of the barbarian requires no moral law. It needs observance only of the barbaric rules of customary law,

# LOOK AT THE LAW

which rests almost wholly on natural physical bases. Dictates of morality, ethics and decency play no part in primitive rule. It flourishes under the emblem of the thonged hammer and the spiked club.

Privileged minorities kept medieval serfs in subjection through fear and ignorance. Voracious and paunchy priests and nobles supplied myths and fallacies for the unquestioning and force for the doubting; soporifics for the one and tortures for the other. This was government which rested upon the passive acquiescence of the superstitious and subdued.

This form of hierarchy finds its modern counterparts. In these modern pretenses of civilized government the forms of law that, slowly enough in the progress from savagery to civilization, took on moral, social and ethical shadings, are swept aside. The executioner's lash in the concentration camp supplants the bailiff's mace in the courtroom. Existing laws which have grown naturally as a product of social life and human development are stripped of moral values and are artificially reconformed to the natural physical skeletons which served the savage. Temples and books are burned, their devotees scourged and thrown to the carnivora like Christians in ancient Roman amphitheaters.

These, however, are but interludes in the steady march from brutishness to Bethlehem. Unfortunately, a millenium is more readily phrased than obtained. On the way from a Louis XIV or a Kaiser to a free democracy, a nation must encounter its Alexanders, its Attilas, its Napoleons, its Mussolinis and its Hitlers.

The period of labor of democracy is so great in comparison with a mere lifetime that to the crawling human ants it seems like forever. From a Czar to self-government, a people must run a series of little tyrannical ambitions which differ only in form from the original abuse. Ulti-

## LOOK AT THE LAW

mately, light penetrates darkness and drives ignorance out of the furthermost corners. The cowed and dull mass begins to awaken. It becomes conscious of its strength and of its opportunities. It pierces the motives of its false leaders. It disavows them and throws off its shackles and seeks self-expression. Force alone will not suffice to keep power. The governed must not resist; even passive resistance will, in the end, defeat the power of force. In the long run, power must rest upon the acquiescence of the governed.

When knowledge comes, the masses seek self-government. They renounce the rule of the guillotine and the tumbril, the knout and the saber. They have had too much of these. The oppressed resort to expressions and compacts of amity. They call to their aid the martyred and oppressed prophets and idealists of former days; they adopt their moral teachings as instruments of government. They enunciate the sovereignty of the people and principles of justice and seek to administer them through the forms of just law.

From this point on, if the revolt has been truly successful, the next voice to be heard is that of the people. The submission or acquiescence of the conquered has become the free and enlightened consent of the governed — the ideal of free and good government, expressed by Lincoln in the phrase "government of the people, by the people and for the people."

The moral law that thus finds its way into the positive law is the purge that rids government of its bile. "Just laws and true policy are like spirit and sinews; the one moves with the other." Just law and tyranny are antitheses; when the first becomes dominant, the latter must give way. Injustice cannot resist a system of just law and its due administration. Despotism rests on falsehood and force; true democratic government on light and amity. An autocracy may inflict an arbitrary will upon the people and they will have no recourse but to force of arms; a philosophic anarchism will make a fetish of no law and, prating of pacifism, invite disagreement and conflict. A democracy, however, is founded upon an underlying agreement to submit to arbitration to ascertain the will of the majority. A negation of all law may suffice for anarchy; a denial of the binding force of the popular will may govern autocracy; but only recourse to covenant, to just law, will support a democracy. The very pulse of a democratic government is resort to law for the settlement of every dispute. The public forum and the ballot box are the touchstones of the entire system.

Once a true democracy is attained, or while, through the channel of a democracy in form, a true democracy is attainable, a people must be jealous of their liberties and their privileges. They must preserve what they have, at all hazards, and make whatever temporary sacrifices may be necessary to continue to make progress towards the ultimate ideal.

These are self-evident truths. Their practice rests, however, upon an understanding that, as democracy and just law are related as are Siamese twins, the one must go where and as the other goes. If a democracy is not a true expression of self-government, it is because the basic law is ineffectual or its administration ineffective.

"The administration of justice is a bulwark of democracy," said President Roosevelt recently, "and its efficiency must be constantly enhanced. More than ever before the people are conscious of these needs."

Though a democracy rests upon the rule of the majority, its rule may not be unrestrained. A majority must respect the rights of the minority and welcome its lawful dissent. The majority represents no permanency of class or condition. It is a variable and constantly shifting mass, a continually changing combination of different and diffuse groups and elements. The minority is likewise ephemeral and composed of constituents who are one day a part of the majority and another day part of the dissenters. Each plays the game; the outs are kept quiescent, though discontented from time to time, by the hope of regaining control or by the knowledge that the blessings of the system, however evil, are preferable to a rule of force. The will of the majority is endurable so long as it comes through the agreed-upon and accepted media and so long as it stays within proper limits of recognition of the rights of the minority.

As a matter of technical constitutional law, two-thirds of the States could repeal every article of our Federal Constitution with the sole exception of the provision for two Senators for each State. As a matter of democratic government, the repeal by however large a majority of the Bill of Rights in the Federal Constitution would be a tyrannical abuse of power. There are inherent human rights which preexist constitutional pacts and merely find repetition and recognition in such instruments.

Recognition of the privileges of the minority must include recognition of its right to advocate change, to oppose in lawful manner the existing order, to clamor for the adoption of ideals and contradictions. The majority must not leave liberalism to radicals. A static democracy may readily become a despotism; the majority must be responsive to valid contentions by the minority. The minority displays initiative while a majority in power tends to grow smug. Individual and minority initiative must be encouraged.

"One mind in the right," said Mr. Justice Holmes, "whether in statesmanship, science, morals, or what-not, may raise all other minds to its own point of view."

Nor may a minority substitute its will for that of the majority, whether by deception or by force. In this country our political system has enabled financial interests to

# LOOK AT THE LAW

control the legislative voices of the people so that the law that comes from bought-and-paid-for so-called representatives of the majority has been the voice of the financial minority. We face present efforts of domination of our legislative channels by labor and other heretofore underprivileged minorities.

Corrupting the administration of laws which evidence the will of the majority, or stifling the voice of the majority after it has been enabled to give its will utterance, can be as effective as attacking the law at its source. The weapons of destruction are primarily money or votes. The results are unfairness and injustice, dissatisfaction and unrest.

There need not be exact justice to support a democracy, but there must be an organized, united and constant effort to obtain as near exact justice as human institutions will permit. The law need not be certain and definite, but it may not be so uncertain and doubtful as to confirm suspicion of its ineffectiveness. The law may lag, but it must find a proper tempo that will keep it immediately behind progressive opinion and scientific progress. The law may be inefficient, but it must promote liberty, equality and the forms and substance of justice; else democracy, notoriously inefficient, cannot compete with autocracy, which offers at least a temporary material efficiency.

Recurrent abuses of the law in individual cases may ultimately destroy a system that depends upon law. Viewed narrowly and objectively, pain and tragedy, misfortune and hurt to a single individual is an unimportant thing in the life of a nation. But the effect is cumulative. Individual injustice breeds disillusion and disrespect for the law. Individuals lose faith in its efficacy and in its ability to solve their problems and alleviate their hurts. The sum total of injury to the individual becomes injustice to a nation, and the masses

## LOOK AT THE LAW

grow restless and call for a new deal. This is inevitable where a minority is in control, perhaps through a fancied intellectual superiority. In such case, the awakening masses seek to match their brawn against the alleged brains of its governors, once the forces of law have proved their impotency. Particularly is this so where the idols that have been worshiped have not only revealed their all-too-human composition, as in the past Harding-Coolidge-Hoover era, but have become arrogant or careless enough to have called for a raising of hands, as in the Presidential election of 1936. In such case, the consequence may be the bloody fall of a nation, and perhaps, where that nation is the keystone and reliance of a democratic system, of a culture and civilization.

Over a known period of five or six thousand years, legal systems have waxed and waned, difficulties have appeared constantly in the administration of justice, judges and lawyers have tinkered with the existing forms, with more or less varying results. Nations and civilizations have risen and fallen for a diversity of reasons. Never has it been possible to maintain a democracy without an efficient system of administering justice. Conversely, a corrupt or inefficient system of justice has prefaced a downfall of the system of government which failed in its administration.

The first standard of oppression, the surest road back to barbarism, is denunciation and evasion of a legal system that requires equal law and equal treatment for all, with its accompaniments of free and open administration of the laws, in public courts and with uncontrolled and independent legal representatives.

"Duce Decides to End Courts, Curb Lawyers. . . . Attorneys to Be State Employees. . . . Pleas for Clients Barred" is the New York *World-Telegram* heading to an Associated Press dispatch of November 13, 1936. Or, "Nazi

# LOOK AT THE LAW

Germany imprisons lawyers who make pleas for their clients which are found distasteful to the heads of the State." Or, "Soviet Russia tries plotters — evidence given in camera." Or, "Nazi judge denounces priests' attitude toward marriage."

Such newspaper headlines confront us daily. They evidence a decaying legal system which nurtures tyranny. While these are contemporaneous events and we lack perspective for ripened judgment, we have the past as guide. These are no innovations. They are reversions—reversions to a past we know only too well, a past which is hurtling all about us and which threatens to overwhelm us.

Our own crises surround us. We could not appreciate the meaning of the 1914-1929 era until we were dropped into the chasm of 1932. Only then, on our backs, could we look up and see towering above us the peaks of our follies, our greeds, our shortsightednesses. Now, from the moral ledges we have regained through years of breathless climbing, we can look down upon the valley of despair from which we are emerging.

For over a third of a century a voracious minority had succeeded in preserving the forms of democracy as a cloak for the rapacious and apparently benevolent autocracy ruled by hard-fisted steel, oil and railroad chieftains. They spread gilded wings behind which a privileged class fastened its hold upon the natural resources of the country and became overlords of its people. With the wealth thus obtained, they bought and maintained the power and prestige of their political overseers who, cracking political whips, enabled them to mold the laws that increased their hold and control of the processes of government.

This privileged minority had, for years, determined the destinies of the majority, through direct bribery or by purchase and ownership of the means of propaganda, by con-

## LOOK AT THE LAW

trol of the law and of its administrators. They had succeeded not only in having laws passed by which they perpetuated their diversion of the instruments of government to their own ends, but they had succeeded in so packing the judiciary that a statute which said one thing was construed by judges to mean another. Where occasion required, they baited their hooks and put out gaily feathered lures. Where labor unions were demanded, they offered company unions; where labor laws were made an issue, they let the legislators pass them and had the judges destroy them. They raised the wages of labor and then took away the excess by increasing prices of food and shelter. They urged thrift and then took the savings of the thrifty by selling them gilded stock certificates. They preached a new day and catapulted the majority into a long black night.

They were the modern counterparts of the "monopolies and spoilers of the people" in the time of Charles I, of whom Lord Colepepper said, at the opening of the Long Parliament: "These, like the frogs of Egypt, have gotten possession of our dwellings and we scarce have a room free from them. They sup in our cup. They dip in our dish. They sit by our fire. They have marked us and sealed us from head to foot. These are the leeches that have sucked the Commonwealth so hard that it is almost become hectical." And for their excesses, they prostituted the law and the lawyers—the lawyers who shaped their practices and molded the law to their purposes.

The years from 1932 to 1940 have witnessed a series of efforts to rid the law of the property-dogma excrescences which five decades of riotous industrialism have visited upon our social system, and to conform the law to the compact, based on, and exemplified by, the tenets of Locke, Rousseau, Jefferson and Lincoln, under which free citizens intended to live and act together. The basic agreement of

# LOOK AT THE LAW

democracy had not been altered during the preceding fifty years but the law had been distorted, in violation of its spirit, to conform with the dictates of the controlling minority. The last decade has seen an effort to restore the law as the expression of the majority will, so that it might cure long-standing social and economic ills.

The situation has not been and is not now without its dangers. There is an undoubted majority in this country which favors a democratic capitalistic system and which is content to reap moderate sustenance from it. This majority wants to work for what it receives and is willing that the fruits of its labor shall approximate the effort it is willing to expend. It wants the opportunity to want much, within reasonable limits, and to seek it fairly; it recognizes the rights of others to be content with less and to strive proportionately to their wants. It demands, however, the right to share equally in the gifts of God and nature, and denies the rights of others to monopolize these things which belong to all or unduly to exploit the majority when they seek to share therein. At the same time, it is unwilling to support in idleness a minority of employables. Within these restrictions, the majority want fair and just rules of law, fairly and equally applied, and they want no more. They want centralized government only so far as it is needful to accomplish these ends; for the rest, they consider local government self-government.

At the same time, we have strong and powerful selfish minorities. To the right we find the old crowd of lawless marauders, the Tories of the Revolution, the Copperheads of the Civil War, industrialists of today, Fascists of tomorrow, employing money and influence, propaganda and deception, to serve their selfish and undemocratic ends.

To the left we find exploiters of the poor, the oppressed, the unemployables, the mental and physical defectives.

# LOOK AT THE LAW

Actuated by vanity or by personal ambition, we find philosophic anarchists, Communists and Bolshevists. They would lead the have-nots into lawlessness and ruthlessness, to serve the ends of their vanities and their greed for power. They employ the weapons of intimidation and force; they preach the dogmas of hatred and class distinction. They, too, deny the law and seek to intimidate our law makers and law administrators.

In between, we find an unorganized and somewhat inarticulate majority, preaching moderation and peace, decrying strife and lawlessness, seeking to find lawful means of satisfying the proper desires of both sides, and of those of the minority on either side who lawfully advocate their just and proper claims in good faith.

Our internal struggles—and these there must always be in a democracy—are fostered and accentuated by the struggle between clashing ideologies in other countries. Even when means of communication were restricted and belated, the democratic struggle in one country sowed the seed of discord in others. Now, with distances obliterated, the spread of anti-democratic movements is conversely sped. And such natural effects are intensified by ruthless and subtle, subsidized and organized penetration from other lands, designed to create, foster and increase internal conflict by convincing the credulous and underwriting the venal.

Today these dangers are great, indeed. As we have pointed out, the minorities can succeed in subverting the will of the majority only by setting at naught just law. Bribery from the right, intimidation from the left—each has this common means and purpose. Let either succeed and our liberties fail. If the law and its forces are not strong enough to hold the balance of power between the forces of arrogance on the one side and the exploiters of the oppressed on the other, physical conflict, revolution

# LOOK AT THE LAW

and bloodshed must result. Deny the law, ignore it, and there is no recourse other than to adopt the methods of the tyrannies which have supplanted what we once thought were impregnable political institutions abroad. But let the law rise superior to the machinations of both, and the rule of the majority, the backbone of democracy, prevails.

The law dominates, or the sword rules. That is the choice, and examples are upon our doorstep. Weaken the law, temper its honesty of administration, and the tramp of marching feet grows louder. Strengthen it, make its application just and curative, and visions of marching hosts grow dim.

There is in this country no real oppression, only a periodic temporary damming of the free forces of democracy by a greedy and shortsighted few. It needs an intelligent resort to legal remedies, a cleansing of our legal system, to drive the contending forces to the ballot box where, with the aid of the sane majority, they can reconcile their differences.

The requisite is just law, fair law, strong law. Law cannot be a mere word; it cannot be a mere rite. It must be practical, thorough, just and honest in its application. It must be intelligent and diligent. It cannot be dogma. It cannot be ritual. It must reflect the compact which we Americans have made and by which we seek to live. It cannot cloak stupidities and abuses, misunderstanding and dullness, with large words and trite phrases. The time for that is gone. The situation is too crucial for trifling or for triflers.

# CHAPTER XIII

*Remedy:*

## HOW TO GO ABOUT IT

*1.*

THE deficiencies of the law are recognized. The need for cure is appreciated. There is constant clamor for law reform. Judges render lip service from the bench; governors and district attorneys call for new and more laws to suppress crime; lawyers gather in bar association conventions; grand jurors file presentments and chambers of commerce, Rotary and Kiwanis clubs hold meetings and adopt resolutions. The average citizen who must periodically hold his head in personal anguish is continually being assured that something is being done or is about to be done about his personal and public woes. But nothing effectual results. The effort is usually insincere, or, at best, half-hearted.

Conventional effort will no longer suffice. Lip service and pretense will no longer fool the people. The old fetishes have gone. No longer can the serf be satisfied by a dunghill and a promise of a gilded world-to-come. No ikon will take the place of bread; holy water in a colored beaker will no longer pass for wine. Science has opened new vistas and has forged bonds that span oceans. The printing press and the radio are like a modern Samson, and the Delilah-like wiles of modern finance and religion will not serve to lull them till their new-found strength is curbed.

We must face realities and prepare to meet them.

But who is going to face the facts and effect a result for us? Is it the lawyer or the legislator? Shall we look to the professor or to the politician? Can we depend on the jurist?

# LOOK AT THE LAW

The past gives us ample testimony. The present stands ready as a witness. Not only can we not depend upon the lawyer and the judge to remedy the defects and abuses of the law, but we may anticipate that any real progress along these lines will meet with their active opposition.

This is not because lawyers and judges are bad citizens. On the contrary, there is less crime and more honesty, less conscious selfishness and more public service and cooperation to be found in their ranks than in most callings.

Lawyers have often fought the fight for legal and judicial reform. Back in the seventies, David Dudley Field led and won the fight in New York State for simplification of legal procedure. Jeremy Bentham led the English crusades that ended so successfully about the same time.

Examination of the annual reports of bar associations, of judicial councils and of law revision committees will reveal recognition of the need for change and suggestions for unadopted remedies running back a decade. The torch lately dropped from the tired hands of Oliver Wendell Holmes and Benjamin N. Cardozo is being carried on by Louis D. Brandeis, Harlan Fiske Stone, Hugo Black, Roscoe Pound, John H. Wigmore, Felix Frankfurter, William O. Douglas, Jerome N. Frank, and a host of others, all lawyer-trained. When all the suggestions for reform are collated, it will be found that lawyers are in the van as advocates of reform.

That being so, one is led to ask why the task cannot be carried to fruition by lawyers and judges. The answer is that the lawyer-reformers are in the minority and that time has proved their execution imperfect and ineffectual.

It is not to be thought that lawyers and judges generally do not try to be social-minded and forward-looking. Or that they are not well-intentioned. But the present-day practicing lawyer who represents the majority of lawyers, by training and heritage, abhors change. He has fixed con-

# LOOK AT THE LAW

cepts. He is a fundamentalist. He conceives the law as something which has grown, consistently and intelligently, with our civilization, out of years of experience. It is not, therefore, in his opinion, something to be lightly rejected or modified.

The average lawyer does not readily appreciate how haphazardly the law has developed; to what extent it is out of tune with the progress of scientific thought and physical development. He does not readily realize that the law has been static while science has been marching onward. He has too little consciousness of the law's defects; he considers its abuses as inevitable, while he magnifies imagined consequences of change as evils supplanting virtues. Instinctively he resents criticism and rejects interference as tending to impede his means of livelihood and to undermine the prestige of his profession. When individually he becomes conscious of abuse, he fears to criticize it, for bar associations and judges have disciplinary powers; he needs the favors of judges and politicians if he is to win cases and obtain advancement. He does not appreciate the value of lay approval nor the danger of lay impatience.

The lawyer needs to make a living and he fears any change that may affect his ability to do so. Though lay agencies may give better service at less cost than he can, he fights their encroachments upon what he considers his exclusive precincts. He weighs reform by its effect on his profits.

Particularly is this so with the big and powerful lawyer. He is sheltered and shielded from the vicissitudes that make men seek change. Lifelong protection and comfort has taken its toll of him. And this well-meaning gentleman controls his fellow lawyers. He designates the heads of the various bar associations, who, in turn, designate those who man the various committees which determine the course and attitude

# LOOK AT THE LAW

of the association. Obviously, the whole can be no more than the sum of its parts. Ten tortoises acting in unison will move no faster than the slowest of the ten; similarly, the conservative gentlemen in the background curb the progress of their more enlightened brethren.

The average lawyer cannot be expected to initiate or support reform. He is too busy trying to make a living out of what he finds at hand.

Henry W. Taft, prominent New York lawyer, put the case charitably enough for lawyers when he said: "While we are all for reform, we are mildly for reform; we don't put any beef behind it, we don't put any power behind it. Nobody is in danger of being run over by it if he gets in the way."

Besides, there is always a minority of lawyers who are ready to sabotage any new proposal. For example, the American Law Institute announces the preparation of a new Code of Evidence designed to rid the law of evidence of an accumulation of parasitical growth. Immediately, a legal commentator comments:

"The layman might suggest a statute something like this: 'All the rules of evidence which prohibit the reception of relevant evidence are hereby abolished.'

"That is what any scientist would do. That is what any honest investigator seeking the truth would normally do. Perhaps so. But the scientist and the hypothetical, honest investigator may and does work under conditions quite different from those under which a court is compelled to function. Any such proposal ignores the adversary theory of litigation."

Nor may we expect our legislators to help much. They are usually lawyers first and legislators afterwards. They frequently are criminal lawyers and zealously guard the technical loopholes in the law by which they make their

# LOOK AT THE LAW

living. They have neither time, capacity, independence nor inclination to do this essential job, except in the superficial and political way in which the legislatures operate.

Most judges are too busy with their judicial business to do much about anything else. Many of them prefer to keep their jobs, and oppose any change that may eliminate litigation or otherwise endanger their sinecures. Like successful lawyers, they know what they have and fear what may result from a new order of things. The law's delays make the judge's job more secure; the more congestion in the calendars, the more judges are needed; the more judges, the less inclination to do anything that may reduce their number.

Finally, when the need for change steps upon political toes, neither lawyers, legislators nor judges can be expected to take a stand for it, for their alliances with the political organization are too close and their dependence upon it too great.

The shortcomings of lawyers and judges in the past, as illustrated in these pages, have weaned public confidence from them. The public has turned to government for protection from the reactionary law and lawyers. Administrative agencies and public law are supplanting judges, lawyers and private law agencies. Lay agencies are successfully and more efficiently encroaching upon what was once the exclusive professional precincts of the lawyer; conciliation, compensation, insurance supplant litigation; businessmen substitute their own processes and negotiation for those of the lawyers and judges.

This process is speeded by prevailing mores, and to these things lawyers and judges have contributed, affirmatively and by their inaction.

Secretary of Commerce Hopkins said in a recent speech:

"I do not think any one outside of the government can realize how much freer government can operate in its relations with

# LOOK AT THE LAW

business — such as the utilities — now that both seem to be rid of the incubus of that self-styled big-city constitutional lawyer. I am convinced most of our difficulties in this field originated with some fancy lawyers who advised their clients not to work things out with the government, on the theory that these lawyers would be able to defeat the government in the courts, so that no working out of the things would ever be necessary. It gives me no little satisfaction to note that the net results of all these constitutional struggles have been to prove that the most unconstitutional thing in the United States was the constitutional lawyer."

Though lawyers are becoming change-conscious and Judge (formerly Dean) Clark says that his "private opinion of the lawyers has gone up immeasurably," their consciousness has not been accompanied by sufficient effort to initiate or promote reform.

All this might be said to be the lawyer's business. If he wants to ruin his profession, well and good, one may say; that is his affair. But the fact is that the lawyer has succeeded not only in discrediting himself, but, in the process, he has discredited our system of government. That, the layman cannot and must not permit the lawyer to do. Instead, the layman must take matters in his own hands and prepare to do the job the lawyer has shown himself unfit to do.

Besides, the law, its formulation and administration, are no longer the exclusive property of the lawyer. Once the lawyers, as once the priests, were the educated class that could look upon these matters as its exclusive prerogative. Today, the scope of the law and its keeping extends into the neighboring realms of science.

Lawyers cannot deal with crime; legislators cannot adopt adequate criminal laws; judges cannot administer fair punishments for criminals, without the intervention of the physician and the psychiatrist. Utilities cannot be regulated without the fact findings and conclusions of econo-

# LOOK AT THE LAW

mists and engineers. Social legislation must be the creation of the experience and reason of the social worker. The lawyers have become mere artisans, chauffeurs and pilots who guide the creations of the scientist, mouthpieces who argue the pros and cons, the meanings and applications of the statutes men of science conceive. The task has grown beyond the lawyer, who has remained static in the face of changing conditions and who today finds himself unequipped to move forward with the man of progress who needs new instruments of government for changing concepts of life and human relations.

Up to this point, there is certainly nothing new about the foregoing. If there is any element of novelty, it must be found in the suggestion that reform of the law and of the lawyers cannot come from within, that it can and will come, as it has in England, only through popular appeal and understanding. The law has been surrounded with fetishes and fallacies that have served to make it mysterious to the layman; and these must be brushed aside if there is to be a popular understanding of the subject. The layman must get on the job and do it himself, for no one who profits by the system will change it to what he thinks is his own detriment.

But some cautions are needed. While the layman may approach the subject critically, he must do so with a measure of tolerance which will come with a real understanding. He cannot accomplish what little may be possible unless he arms and conditions himself for personal combat.

If the layman approaches the law as something sacred, if he permits lawyers and judges to say, "You know nothing and can learn nothing about it, leave this to us," then the quest for betterment is fruitless. If, on the other hand, he carelessly assumes that all the precautions and technicalities in the law are useless, his remedy may be more dangerous than the disease. But if he analyzes our legal system and

# LOOK AT THE LAW

thereby seeks to learn its faults, he can advocate and insist upon their correction. The first requirement is to know something about the law itself—what it is; then to obtain a notion of how it works, and, principally, where and why it does not; and finally, to determine just what, if anything, can be done about it.

As we have shown, there are reasons for many of our abuses that do not lie with lawyers. In truth, if lawyers did not claim credit for so much they would be blamed for much less. If lawyers did not claim that the law was a science; if they said, as they should, that it cannot be made scientific, they would not be blamed when it aimed straight and hit crooked. Pointing out that law is not justice in the moral and ethical sense would seem to preface a denunciation that lawyers lead the poor and unsuspecting law astray for their own private benefit and amusement. Yet when we seek to pin down the law and find out just what it is, we find that it is nothing but the fleeting and momentary breath of the seething, changing mass of humanity underneath; that it is intangible; that it moves only as the volcanic mass beneath it moves; that no one—lawyers, judges, philosophers, professors or anyone short of gods—can do aught but attempt to influence and translate the almost incoherent voice into ephemeral words. Here is where the lawyer is a charlatan, claiming to be a lion-tamer when in truth there is no lion; holding himself out to be a Delphic oracle, as a medium communing with spirits, when there are no spirits. If we could get the lawyer to admit that the forces he pretends to control are beyond his harnessing, that the layman who chides him for his failure is the very steed he seeks to ride, then the problem will be simplified. The horse and rider can seek to run and ride in unison and the credit for success and the blame for failure can be equally assessed.

There is no cure in scratching a case of hives; and, to

# LOOK AT THE LAW

many minds, the analogy between lawyers and hives is not entirely inept. When the technicalities of the law enable the lawyer to make a fee by freeing the guilty criminal, there is no point in scratching at the lawyer. The thing to do is to recognize the perversion of justice as a symptom and to find the cause, be it the age-old custom of praising the evasive and tricky lawyer, the predominance of criminal lawyers in our legislatures, or the tie-in between politics and crime and the ability of the criminal to provide funds for lobbying, if not bribery, in our legislatures.

## 2.

In a democratic system, the layman who complains that the law doesn't work is the man who makes the law and the man who breaks it.

When a child suffers from an insufficient diet or a too rigid curriculum, he has a right to complain, for his law is what his mother and his teacher say it is. When the boss says, "Do this or you'll be fired," you have a right to feel aggrieved about a system that permits rules to be made and enforced without your assent.

But if mother and the teacher say: "You just take care of yourself," or the boss says: "Elect your own delegates and make your own rules," then you can't take them to task when you who make the rules break them or when the rules your representative makes fail to work.

Nor does it suffice for you to claim that you have had no real say in the making of the rules—that your representatives sell you out. The rules are none the less yours. When Louis XIV in a by-gone day said curtly: "L'etat, c'est moi," he was taking too much for granted, as events of a few years later demonstrated. And when a modern community suffers a latter-day New Jersey imitator to parrot: "Me, I'm the

# LOOK AT THE LAW

law," it is merely permitting a superficial adolescent gesture that temporarily fails to reckon with the facts.

Mayor La Guardia has demonstrated in former boss-ridden New York City that the seat of the law resides where the ultimate power is to be found, and the fact that the power isn't constantly exercised, because of interludes of laziness, stupidity or corruption, is no sign that there has been any shift of control. Nor is the failure of the people to remedy the situation during these interludes any indication that they are not remediable.

The layman himself makes the law. But, unfortunately, he does not make it for himself. He makes it for "the other fellow." Though he advocates a law and will vote for its adoption, he won't support it: he won't hesitate to break it down himself—when it serves his purposes to do so.

The man who crosses the street cusses the taxi driver who almost runs him down while trying to beat the red light, and yells, "There ought to be a law." Yet he is the same person who threatens to "get" the cop who gives him a ticket for passing a light when he himself is driving.

The layman talks big and acts small. He preaches the virtues and practices the vices. He advocates a standard of morality in law to which he refuses to subscribe in life. He calls for laws prohibiting prostitution and gambling, and then patronizes brothels and race tracks. He applauds the jailing of Al Capone for income tax frauds, when he slips a bribe to an internal revenue agent to approve his own tax return. He tolerates laws against the sale of contraceptives, while he himself uses them. He preaches morality, yet refuses to support reform administrations that will not wink at immorality. He urges public improvements, and then decries the taxes needed to pay for them.

The layman's contempt for the legal system is boundless. He is incensed at stupid or fixed verdicts of juries,

# LOOK AT THE LAW

yet he evades jury service. He clamors about the delays of the law, yet he instructs his lawyers to interpose technical and dilatory defenses to avoid his own days of legal reckoning. He criticizes the vices of lawyers, yet he hires the slickest one he can find to enable him to avoid his own commitments.

The layman hypocritically tolerates—if, indeed, he does not demand—a political system that caters to his weaknesses and vices. He abhors the link between politics and crime that enables him to get a traffic ticket killed and a labor violation notice fixed. He is contemptuous of the politician from whom he buys special privileges, tariff favors, public service grants and subsidies, and corporate and banking franchises and indulgences. He castigates the legislator whom he corrupts with promises of money or votes or threat of opposition or reprisals. He anathematizes the judge who yields to the importunities of the political intermediary he hires. Generally, he rails against politics and politicians while he makes campaign contributions to both the opposing parties, and plays golf on election day when the machine is electing its candidates.

Commenting on the selection of a jury in the criminal prosecution of Hines, the New York *Evening Post* said:

"Indeed, it seemed that an unusual number of the blue ribbon talesmen, specially selected as citizens of probity and dependability, numbered political leaders among their acquaintances, and selection of a jury seemed likely to be a long process."

The layman waxes wroth over the depredations of racketeers while he supports them by paying money to labor spies, buying off labor union officials and bribing his customers' purchasing agents. Indeed, it is the layman who is himself the racketeer.

Thomas E. Dewey, District Attorney of New York County, thus defined the racketeer:

## LOOK AT THE LAW

"Rarely is a racketeer," he said, "the man who would burglarize your home or pick your pocket. He is usually a quiet, well-dressed citizen ... who ... may and does live in the very best hotels and apartment houses, often with his wife and family. He is on excellent terms with some political leaders. He may and usually does operate one or more ostensibly legitimate night clubs, manufacturing firms or other businesses. He may sit next to you at dinner and your children play with his in Central Park or in private schools."

The racketeer is not necessarily the movie hoodlum who compels legitimate businessmen to pay protection money or who otherwise levies on legitimate enterprises by illegitimate means. He more often operates a business that breaks no written law. In this class are to be found the installment furniture dealer who oversells the poverty-stricken householder so that he will be sure to default on his installment payments and thereby enable the dealer to seize the furniture, recondition and resell it; the usurious lender who encourages his victim to borrow more than he can possibly repay so that he may garnishee his wages or take his automobile or home in an overprofitable repayment of his debt; the stock salesman who switches the prudent saver or investor from his savings bank account or his conservative securities into mining stocks or unsound real estate or utility bonds; the jewelry auctioneer who misleads his buyers by the use of puffers; the merchant who employs fire and removal sales; and similar "come-on" advertising devices.

But these, it will be said, are only a small minority of the laymen who criticize the law they evade. True. But what of the many others who cannot be classed as racketeers? What of the businessman who "takes care" of the buyer's purchasing agent? What of the employer who "sees" the union delegate so his men won't strike or make just demands? What of the manufacturer who fixes the inspector so he won't report a labor, sanitary or building violation? Or of the taxpayer who has someone intercede with the revenue collector? What of the big businessman who puts habit-forming or other harmful ingredients into the patent medicine he sells, who puts artificial ingredients, for color or taste, in the food-stuffs he puts up, who makes false claims for his cosmetics?

These are not the criminals for whom we make the penal laws. On the contrary, they are the laymen who elect the legislators who make our laws; they are the laymen who criticize the laws when they are ineffectual to prevent the abuses they themselves create.

### 3.

The layman must approach these problems realistically. Recognizing his own measure of fault, he must distinguish between the faults and virtues of his opponents.

In combatting the lawyer, the layman must not give the lawyer the choice of weapons. He must not attempt to penetrate the lawyer's Mephisthelean circle of words, phrases and definitions by resort to words, for if the laymen takes to logomachy he will find himself undone.

Only honesty and realism will penetrate the guile and lay bare the falsities of the opposition. Though his armament be no greater than the shepherd David's, the layman must not be tempted to exchange his slings of plain speaking for the verbosities, polemics and terminologies of the opposition. That is all-important. Let him but use "jural" or "juristic" and he is well on the way to the camp of the enemy, his pennants in abject surrender. "The law has outgrown its primitive stage of formalism when the precise word was the sovereign talisman," said an enlightened judge. But that was wishful thinking. In the law, words are the

# LOOK AT THE LAW

camouflage used to conceal the expectant batteries ready to deluge the layman with phrases and definitions that will overwhelm his quest for truth and light.

If the layman knows that the law is not a science, he is not going to be compelled to worry about understanding the "science of jurisprudence." If he starts with the premise that the law is not a "constant norm" about which all life revolves, then he is not going to be concerned with legal fundamentalism or absolutism, or other legal isms.

Consequently, in seeking to inform the layman of the problems he must solve, there is no point in approaching them from the pseudo-scientific point of view the lawman uses. The shelves of law libraries are thick with expositions of the sources of the law, its growth and development, analyses of its past and forecasts of its future. These studies have been made by and for lawyers. Unfortunately, they accomplish little but to add to the total of refinement and distinctions which are the bases of our wealth of legal and judicial confusions. They are not designed for and never reach the general public, which couldn't understand them if it tried. Some of them are, in truth, too erudite and mystifying for lawyers who lack the classical education of the old school.

Another reason for the futility of these tomes is the fact that they are usually written by and for worshipers of the law, devotees of the word, whose attacks upon it, infrequent at best, are made with feather dusters. Usually, these writers sing paeans of praise of the quibbles and technicalities of the law, and seek to justify and perpetuate them. Their effort is rather to explain than to reform. These law writers take a most philosophical view of the public injuries; they make no pretense of probing the wounds; they prescribe salves where incision is needed and use face powders to cover festers which can be cured only by purges.

# LOOK AT THE LAW

We need plain speaking and plain writing for plain men of common understanding. We must brush aside the veils of confusion with which lawyers and judges have surrounded their practices.

The groundwork laid by Jeremy Bentham might have been wasted had there not been a Dickens to put it in form attractive to the layman. Volumes of legal periodicals containing articles on the injustice of imprisonment for debt would have been futile to excite the sympathy created by one Micawber. Write scientific treatises on the system of driving piles into the ground and not one man in a million will ever hear the author's name; but one excavation at Main and River Streets will awaken the midday interest of the town's busiest men in the science of pile-driving. An abstraction means nothing to the average man; he must be hurt or benefited before he can be attracted. Entertainment may help to do the trick; the most effective law reformer of our day may possibly prove to be A. P. Herbert, contemporary English humorist.

To approach the problem of legal reform the layman must also look to his forces. He must lead, but once he blows his pipe, this Pied Piper will find his ranks swelled with hundreds, yea, thousands of lawyers. Young lawyers with nothing but ideals; old lawyers with nothing but ideals, and old and young lawyers alike who know the law for what it is, for what it should be, and who realize its importance to the community as well as to themselves. Lawyers and judges of the type who, armed with truth and knowledge, have stood in the front ranks of every forward-looking movement in the progress of the work will join this movement. Laymen form anti-cancer and anti-tuberculosis societies and hire technicians to wage wars against these diseases. In like manner, laymen can unite and get any added technical help they need to wage war against legal reactionaries.

# LOOK AT THE LAW

Public support will not be lacking. The mutterings and rumblings of dissatisfaction have found liberal and coherent voices in our colleges and in the columns of our newspapers. Daily columns contributed by enlightened thinkers are syndicated throughout the country, and a host of unnamed editorial writers have been making the ground ready for concerted attack. As the drive for a Supreme Court amendment brought many really technical and little understood questions into the open, so a layman's drive against useless and unnecessary legalisms will throw light upon more technical and less understood legal questions. In consequence, the forces of the attackers will far outnumber the occupants of the fortified heights to be taken.

Our judges and lawyers, our bar associations, and particularly our politicians, must be made to feel the lash of public opinion; with public opinion ascertained, legislation and judicial action is bound to follow. Even the United States Supreme Court follows the election returns, according to Mr. Dooley (and according to recent Supreme Court opinions), and their representatives will quickly follow public opinion if only the will of the people can be aroused and expressed.

Our lawyers, our judges and our legal system require a bath of realism. They must be washed as free as possible of political contacts and contracts. At the same time, our citizenry must realize that it is they who are the State and it is they who want to remain the State; that when they are corrupt, it is the State which is corrupt. Wherever their personal inclinations may lead them, they cannot follow their venal ones unless they are willing ultimately to forego the liberties and privileges which a democracy has afforded and which will, with their cooperation and the grace of whatever higher power there may be, continue to afford them.

# CHAPTER XIV

## *Remedy:*
## WHAT TO DO ABOUT IT

THROUGHOUT the ages we have been told and are still being told what to do about the law. It is not difficult really to discern faults and prescribe remedies. But the prescription is for the doctor, while the cure is for the patient. The doctor knows the futility of matching knowledge against human nature. The diabetic breaks his diet, the nervous man worries, the smoker smokes and the drinker drinks, rationalization overcomes advice till death does them part. The doctor feels his task well done if he has prolonged life or lessened pain. The civic counselor must also be content with scant satisfaction.

For cure or alleviation of the basic ills of man and his systems one must go to the laboratory wherein man was conceived. Perhaps the scientist can devise an insulin that will lessen man's craving for power, his selfishness and his greed. Perhaps the biologist can influence the species so that the desire to propagate may not be lessened, while the instinct to hoard for the protection of one's young may be moderated. Perhaps he can temper cupidity, while leaving the initiative that produces progress unchecked.

Or it may be that the economist may soften the rigors of life so that man need not work for selfish purposes while the exponent of some other science keeps him working for the general welfare. How these things may be accomplished, whether truth will serve to satisfy babes or whether the parables of religion are still essential, is beyond the scope of this work, which must rest on the premise that man is basically vile and the law is the expression of his better self.

# LOOK AT THE LAW

There is little doubt that crime can be decreased by economic laws that lessen poverty; by medical and psychiatric applications that check disease, mental and physical; by enactments that promote education and enlighten ignorance. These are tasks for the governors, and it may be said to the credit of many of those now in office that the need has been recognized and effort made to satisfy it.

The evils of our political system are merely expressive of human failings and the subsidiary traits they engender. They thrive in a morass of ignorance, need and carelessness, fertilized by the deliberate rapacities of the more sophisticated. The same intelligent planning that satisfies economic need will largely undermine the crooked political structure which rests mainly on a foundation of patronage, a need for jobs. Let work be supplied by an intelligently planned economic system and the political system that yields jobs for votes will require radical readjustment. Abolish poverty and a district leader will not be able to build political dividends of gratitude by distributing coal and wood to the needy and Thanksgiving baskets to the hungry. With a system of public parks, the political excursion for children to the picnic grounds up the river no longer becomes a means of buying votes. Destroy the political appointment of judges, and the racketeer will no longer contribute money for court favors. And so on.

The primary job is to rouse public opinion. And it has been aroused. The next task is to obtain leadership. And we have leadership. Now we must follow through.

We have separately discussed specific defects and suggested remedies in previous chapters. It remains but to consider here whether and to what extent they coordinate and coalesce.

As we have said so often, the law is little else than the temporary command of our rulers. In a democracy, the rul-

# LOOK AT THE LAW

ers are, or should be, the majority. Assuming that the majority truly made the law, it would necessarily mirror their defects, their selfishness and greed, their vanities, their hypocrisies, their emotionalisms. It would necessarily suffer from the defects of any human institution, the rigidity of rule, the uncertainty of human intervention, the hypocrisies and the technicalities bred by the need of rule. From all these, as we have seen, the law suffers.

But a democratic system of government has graver faults. Rule by the majority is only an academic hope. It is usurped by minorities actuated by human impulses. Whether these minorities be well-meaning pressure groups or selfish moneyed interests, or whether they be benign or greedy political factions acting as agents or as principals, the result is basically the same. The majority is led or swayed by propaganda, vicious or honest, open or secret. It is either urged to action or induced to be quiescent. In any event, the opinions and the desires of the controlling minority become the basis of the law.

Sometimes, under the rule of an intelligent minority, the cause of the law is furthered; at other times, and usually, the law is molded, by prejudice and self-interest. In any case, the tie between the opinions and the rule of the majority is weakened.

Beyond the body of the law itself, the difficulties are increased by administration. Uncertain, yielding, defective, the law requires super-human administration that it may work efficiently. But this it is denied, because of the human forces of stupidity, lust and greed, the need and desire for profit, that maltreat the law itself and divert its effectiveness. Here politics and selfishness play large parts in preventing the selection of the most competent administrators and in impeaching the efforts of those they permit to be selected.

# LOOK AT THE LAW

It must be evident that the abuses from which the law suffers are interrelated; that they must be viewed as a whole; that treatment of general underlying causes will remedy apparently dissociated effects.

We can reduce the bulk and weight of our law and as we slenderize it we can concurrently eliminate some, if not many, of its uncertainties, remembering, however, the danger of simplicity beggaring precision. Let each State segregate its public, private and local statutes, and then collect, codify, repeal, revise, authenticate, arrange, authorize, index and publish the public laws. With that base, let future statutes, drafted by a bill-drafting bureau, be similarly codified and added to existing law by a bureau of experts and let their work be approved and adopted at the succeeding session of the legislature.

Let the legislature's work be done in cooperation with judicial agencies, with a Judicial Council, with a Law Revision Commission, with its own and other fact-finding bodies, with executive boards and agencies. Let it be coordinated with the work of legislatures in other States through the National Conference of Commissioners on Uniform State Laws.

Let the rule and law-making power exercised by executive agencies and sub-legislative and quasi-judicial bodies be drawn to central sources and some measure of uniformity be assured by collection and collaboration.

Let us make a profession of law-making. Why should legislators not be required to qualify by examination and experience before they may be nominated and elected? Why should they not be compensated so that they may give all their time to their duties? Why should we not give legislators longer terms so that they need not devote the first half of their terms to recuperating from one campaign and the second half to preparing for the next one?

# LOOK AT THE LAW

Parallel attack on our judge-made law and judicial law administration can readily be made effective.

The irreplaceable Justice Cardozo said that of the cases which came before his court, a majority could only be decided one way, and no statement of reason was even needed. Of another large percentage, the law was a settled quantity; the only question was as to the application. The remainder, a far smaller percentage, involved determination of the law and in only these cases could a legal opinion be justified. An intelligent and realistic judge, Joseph N. Ulman, estimated that 88 per cent of judicial opinions could be readily dispensed with, without loss.

The judge-made law should not be left to private companies to collate and digest. That work should be systematically, continuously and officially done by an agency sufficiently equipped to perform the task and possessing the necessary judicial and legislative authority to collect and declare the law.

It may be that with the experience and effort already made by the American Law Institute (which was organized "to promote the clarification and simplification of the law and its better adaptation to social needs, to secure the better administration of justice, and to encourage and carry on scholarly and scientific legal work"), that organization, with public support, could extend its effort to organize the law into a cohesive body and determine methods for correcting defects in the law.

More States should adopt the New York system, which, following Justice Cardozo's suggestion for a Ministry of Justice to keep the substantive law in repair, created a Law Revision Commission and a Judicial Council. Other States lack the Law Revision Commission but have Judicial Councils, and since 1930 there has been a National Conference of Judicial Councils.

# LOOK AT THE LAW

Under the guidance of judicial councils, ample rule-making powers should be entrusted to the courts and fully exercised to make legal administration businesslike and efficient, even to the point of being elastic and informal. These and kindred matters to improve the functioning of the courts are within the scope of the tasks which have been allotted to Judicial Councils. Their activities should gain greater support, so that courts may be unified, their efforts co-ordinated and their administration put upon an efficient basis.

The administration of our courts should be less technical and more liberal, less forward and more efficient, less rule-conforming and more justice-producing. Lawyers and judges should be more concerned in getting at the truth than in observing formalism in the hearing of controversies. An informal talk with counsel and parties before trial by a judge will settle most controversies and limit the subsequent trial, where the parties are intransigent, to a fraction of the expense and delay which formality produces. Sensible, liberal and informal procedure in the selection of jurors, and intelligent rules of evidence, will yield results more consonant with justice than at present, and again, with less expense and delay. Dispensing with formality and technicality will lessen error and eliminate useless appeals and, where appeals occur, will cut down the delay and expense which now attend them.

Remedy does not lie in derogation of the courts, in abuse of lawyers and judges, in setting up ponderous administrative bodies to absorb the work of the courts. Human experience proves that, in the long run, greater faith can be laid in our judges than in lay or other forms of legal administration. Administrative bodies more readily prove corrupt, faithless and inefficient than do our courts. Lawyers are more reliable and faithful, by and large, than laymen. The

## LOOK AT THE LAW

lawyer's faith and pride in his profession is basically justified; the community's respect for its judges is largely warranted. Nothing is gained by exalting the layman or berating the lawman, but much will be accomplished by educating the layman to higher standards while keeping the lawyer from accepting for himself the standards of the layman.

Whatever is done to supplement the work of the judge through administrative agencies, the way must be left open for the courts and lawyers to protect minorities when lay bodies do not.

No administrative body that acts as prosecutor, jury and judge (and this is the procedure under which various of our administrative agencies now function) will ever command the confidence of a democracy-loving people. The present increase of administrative bodies is due to public chafing at the technical restraints about the judicial system and impatience with the difficulty of discarding them. Improvement of the judicial system and willingness of our courts to execute efficiently the tasks properly theirs will find the people ready to turn those tasks back to them. The administrative agency has its proper function; if our courts function properly, the spheres of the courts and of administrative agencies will find and keep their respective peripheries.

Similarly, if litigation is conducted in the courts upon a more flexible and less formal basis, litigants in nontechnical matters will not be driven from the judges to arbitrators. Arbitration has its proper field; in technical matters it is essential, but it should not be burdened with the business of the courts because of unnecessary expense and delay.

There is none of this which has not previously been known. Lawyers under the leadership of Roscoe Pound, Lloyd K. Garrison and John H. Wigmore, to mention only three, have made similar and more studied suggestions in

# LOOK AT THE LAW

particular fields. The fruits of these investigations lie ready at hand.

The Section of Judicial Administration of the American Bar Association has made enlightened and helpful suggestions concerning Judicial Administration, Pre-Trial Procedure, Trial Practice, Trial by Jury including Selection of Jurors, Law of Evidence, Appellate Practice and Administrative Agencies and Tribunals which, if followed, would do much to obviate many of the deficiencies in administration discussed in the foregoing pages. They would provide an excellent beginning for a thorough purge of our adjective law so as to make it more analogous to practical business methods and less similar to Hindu mysticism.

The American Law Institute has just announced the preparation of a Modern Code of Evidence by Professor Edmund H. Morgan of Harvard Law School and Dean John H. Wigmore. It is announced that this Code will not be "a restatement of existing law, but the proposal of a set of rules representing what the profession thinks ought to be the law."

However, little can be done without intelligent and independent judges. Even though we step up, as we should, the qualifications of our lawyers, we must go beyond that in selecting our judges. A judge should, of course, be lawyer-trained, but even that is insufficient. Up to 1936, according to Martin, seventeen State legislatures required judges to be "learned in the law," and seventeen courts were construing the phrase to mean merely that they should be admitted to the bar. Forty-one States required additional professional experience and only three States had a character requirement. And many States permitted laymen to be judges.

A judge ought to be "learned in the law" and proficient in its administration. There ought to be agreement, as a

## LOOK AT THE LAW

result of research, upon the qualifications a judge should have. Such capacity will be found to be something more than legal training or a number of years' experience at the bar. Years ago, Sir Matthew Hale laid down the qualifications of a good judge, and they would serve today to indicate that requirements of character, temperament, learning and experience, far beyond the needs of the ordinary advocate or scrivener, should be the basis for judicial selection.

Today judges need, even more than the lawyers, a broader knowledge than mere acquaintance with legal precedents and statutes brings. They must test their judicial reactions, they must view the subjects of their judicial surveys by recourse to economic, social and other scientific fields. From the lower court judge who seeks to deal justly with a minor offender, to the highest court judge who wrestles with a constitutional question, all must know something of the natural and the physical sciences; the whys and wherefores of the concepts they enunciate and the rules by which they enforce them.

Lawyers should have such basic education and training. Beyond that, let the bench be a special career, with postgraduate education and training. Colleges do not indiscriminately tender law-teaching posts to lawyers. Let designation for the bench be equally selective. Make the requirements such that they cannot be acquired by nights spent in the political clubhouse. Let salary and tenure in office be conducive to independence, while restriction on extrajudicial and, particularly, on political activities, adds dignity to the office. Let there be qualification by examination and investigation by a governmental or bar association body composed of lawyers. Let there be a system of promotion based on service and merit. Let there be a supervisory body charged with keeping records of fitness, service and effi-

# LOOK AT THE LAW

ciency. Let there be easier removal or demotion by the higher judges or the appointing authority, moved by proper yet restrained complaint.

Mayor La Guardia, of New York City, has sought to show the way in this, as in many other important governmental channels, by making tentative and temporary bench appointments for training and experimental purposes, and by introducing and practicing a system of judicial promotion in the minor courts under his control. The New York Judicial Council has recommended a constitutional amendment for removal of judges by the higher Court in addition to the existing method of impeachment by the Senate.

Where selection is by election, let there be a method of nomination, by the governor or by an impartial governmental commission, by lawyers or by bar associations, that will obviate the present political convention or primary method of nomination. Political emblems and designations on the ballot should be eliminated. Renomination should be assured, even by appointment where the system of election prevails, when a judge's record has been satisfactory.

Subjudicial appointments should be made from panels of lawyers who have qualified by fitness and experience for the tasks assigned to them, as receivers, trustees, masters, and the like. They should be paid at standard rates from which there should be no deviation. A record of their service should likewise be kept so that the fit may be retained, the unfit eliminated.

Judicial administrative personnel should be civil-service chosen and under the direct control and supervision of, and wholly accountable to, the judges.

There should be training courses established for court clerks and attendants; legal training and admission to the bar should be required for the higher clerical offices. The rate of pay should be fixed so that these offices may not be-

# LOOK AT THE LAW

come attractive political plums for political leaders. The positions would be attractive by virtue of the opportunities they would offer for advancement to judicial posts, and ultimately the administrative field would be the proving ground for the judicial personnel itself.

A comprehensive system of keeping administrative statistics, full and complete and available to the judicial council and other law enforcement agencies would prove invaluable in keeping administrative and judicial personnel fit and eager for advancement.

But even good judges can do nothing without the aid of lawyers, who hold the keys to the solution of many of our legal problems.

Let lawyers subscribe to their code at whatever cost to their personal fortunes. They must keep these obligations paramount and they must subordinate the selfish interests of their clients to it. They may not permit their desires for wealth or self-aggrandizement to tempt them to violate the code, for when they do, they stultify their profession and jeopardize the cause of democratic government.

Though lawyers must be of the people, they may not share their faults. Their morals must be superior to those of the layman. They cannot be mere craftsmen or tradesmen. History teaches that when the bar is virile and manly, the cause of popular government flourishes; that a decadent bar means a decadent nation. The advocates of ancient imperial Rome refused to martyr themselves in the hopeless cause of liberty even as today the legal practitioners of Germany and Italy are unheard while their judges serve the despotic demands of tyrannical governments.

When the lawyer works for money alone he necessarily violates his obligations to the State. He puts himself first and the State last. We must restore to lawyers a sense of their importance and obligation to government. We must take their support from underneath the crookedness of business structure and political government. Without it, neither can stand; with it, our industrial and political structures are endangered.

Higher standards of legal and scholastic training, higher admission requirements for admission to law schools and to the bar would do much to inculcate in lawyers a greater ability to serve their proper purposes, to discourage litigation rather than to promote it, to attack sharp practices rather than to fashion them, provided the profit motive can be subordinated. That is the paramount requirement.

Restricting lawyers to avoid overcrowding would tend to lessen the temptation to indulge in sharp practices to make money. Restricting and governing fees and charges might lessen the temptations offered by rich amoral clients. But these are panaceas that beg the heart of the problem, that deny the concept of lawyers as officers of the State, in number and equipment adequate to serve all the people.

Certainly only thus will the poor and the middle class of moderate means be served with preventive legal aid and furnished with adequate legal protection. As we have pointed out, poverty and justice are incompatible under our present system; and assigned counsel, public defenders, specialized small claims, wage, domestic relations, conciliation and compensation courts, legal aid societies and clinics, desertion and social service bureaus, are mere expedients. Socialized legal aid groups, akin to those more familiar in the medical field, are needed and have been suggested by writers on this subject, including Professors Llewellyn and Bradway and Reginald Heber Smith. While these measures, to the extent that they are practicable, will aid the layman, they will not solve other problems which the unrestricted and unregulated fee-seeking lawyer creates.

The problem of regulation of the lawyer has led to the

# LOOK AT THE LAW

suggestion that bar associations should not be private but public associations; that each community should have an incorporated association of which every lawyer should be required to be an active member in order to practice his profession in that community; that each bar association should be an integral part of an incorporated Statewide organization and each State association a unit in a nationwide organization. Each of the smallest of these units would be democratic in its nature and practices; the educational requirements for admittance to practice would be of such nature that there would be no need for social distinctions between lawyers even in large cities.

Bar associations, under the present system, have been forces for good as well as evil. When they come to be controlled by the big lawyer, as ultimately they do, they tend to be reactionary. It is only after a severe attack, such as that which was made against the American Bar Association, that long-established bar associations attempt to become factors for real reform. Periodically this causes younger men to organize new associations (as in the case of the National Lawyers Guild), and these, at the outset at least, are enthusiastic and intense in their search for change.

The American Judiciary Society is engaged in promoting the efficient administration of justice and has been fostering a movement for an integrated bar in each of our States. It is furthering campaigns to make the local bar association a community force in the rendition of public service, in the election of non-political judges and prosecutors, and the like.

Local bar associations have numerous committees studying various phases of these problems.

At the heart of the entire structure is found the question of how to deal with the lawyer, how to make him a true officer of the court, how to induce him to employ his tal-

# LOOK AT THE LAW

ents for right and justice, how to keep him from prostituting them for personal gain. We must bend the lawyer to the service of the State, while leaving to him the independence and initiative he must be free to exercise in defense and protection of the oppressed and the unpopular. It may be that the integrated bar system offers a solution; we may have to go further and subsidize a portion of the bar for socialized and public service to those who cannot pay for needed aid and advice.

Within the narrow margins of this work, we can only indicate the problems and hint at their remedy. For further study and solution, there is material galore, ready and waiting. But impetus is needed. Obstructions raised by selfish political and economic forces which preach foreboding results while disregarding present abuses must be leveled. For this, the initiative and vigor, the clarity and simplicity of a practical business approach is needed.

The general scope of this work justifies only superficial treatment, a mere indication that conditions are not hopeless, or reform impossible. Remedies have been forged and welded, but we need a stimulated body of citizens to apply them. To that fond hope we dedicate this effort.